Spatial Regulation
in New York City

Routledge Advances in Geography

1. The Other Global City
Edited by Shail Mayaram

2. Branding Cities
Cosmopolitanism, Parochialism, and Social Change
Edited by Stephanie Hemelryk Donald, Eleonore Kofman and Catherine Kevin

3. Transforming Urban Waterfronts
Fixity and Flow
Edited by Gene Desfor, Jennefer Laidley, Dirk Schubert and Quentin Stevens

4. Spatial Regulation in New York City
From Urban Renewal to Zero Tolerance
Themis Chronopoulos

Spatial Regulation in New York City

From Urban Renewal to Zero Tolerance

Themis Chronopoulos

Routledge
Taylor & Francis Group
New York   London

First published 2011
by Routledge
711 Third Avenue, New York, NY 10017

Simultaneously published in the UK
by Routledge
2 Park Square, Milton Park, Abingdon, Oxon OX14 4RN

Routledge is an imprint of the Taylor & Francis Group, an informa business

First issued in paperback 2013

© 2011 Taylor & Francis

The right of Themis Chronopoulos to be identified as author of this work has been asserted in accordance with sections 77 and 78 of the Copyright, Designs and Patents Act 1988.

Typeset in Sabon by IBT Global.

All rights reserved. No part of this book may be reprinted or reproduced or utilised in any form or by any electronic, mechanical, or other means, now known or hereafter invented, including photocopying and recording, or in any information storage or retrieval system, without permission in writing from the publishers.

Trademark Notice: Product or corporate names may be trademarks or registered trademarks, and are used only for identification and explanation without intent to infringe.

Library of Congress Cataloging-in-Publication Data
Chronopoulos, Themis.
 Spatial regulation in New York City : from urban renewal to zero tolerance / by Themis Chronopoulos.
  p. cm. — (Routledge advances in geography ; 4)
 Includes bibliographical references and index.
 1. Urban renewal—New York (State)—New York. 2. Urban renewal—Social aspects—New York (State)—New York. 3. New York (N.Y.)—Social conditions—20th century. 4. Law enforcement--New York (State)—New York. 5. Crime prevention—New York (State)—New York. 6. New York (N.Y.)—History—20th century. I. Title.
 HT177.N5C47 2011
 307.7609747'109045—dc22
           2010042311

ISBN13: 978-0-415-85079-7 (pbk)
ISBN13: 978-0-415-89158-5 (hbk)
ISBN13: 978-0-203-81908-1 (ebk)

Contents

List of Figures		vii
Acknowledgments		ix
	Introduction	1
1	The Betrayal of the Liberal Assumptions of Urban Renewal	5
2	The Failure of Urban Renewal as a Spatial Ordering Apparatus	33
3	Times Square: New York's Most Disorderly Place	58
4	Neoliberalism, Neoconservatism, and Spatial Regulation	78
5	Graffiti as a Manifestation of Social Disorder	91
6	The Declining Appearance of Order, 1978–1993	118
7	The Radicalization of Spatial Regulation, 1994–2001	147
	Epilogue: The Legacy of Displacement and Exclusion	181
Notes		185
Selected Bibliography		217
About the Author		225
Index		227

Figures

1.1	Map of Morningside Heights and its immediate surroundings.	10
1.2	Map of spatial fortification around Morningside Heights.	15
1.3	The General Grant Houses and Morningside Gardens.	16
1.4	Columbia University faculty housing.	17
1.5	Columbia University faculty housing facing West 125th Street.	18
1.6	Urban renewal areas in the Upper West Side.	22
2.1	The Bernard M. Baruch Houses in the Lower East Side.	34
2.2	Cruciform towers of the Baruch Houses.	36
2.3	Part of the Manhattanville area that Columbia University eyed for expansion in the 1960s.	52
5.1	Graffiti piece in the southern Bronx.	92
5.2	Mural of Notorious B.I.G. in the Bronx after his untimely death.	93
5.3	Graffiti on an anchorage of Williamsburg Bridge.	97
5.4	Graffiti mural in the Bronx.	102
5.5	Mural located in the Lower East Side depicting Mike Tyson after his infamous boxing match with Evander Holyfield.	107
5.6	Graffiti piece in Queens.	116
6.1	One of numerous Puerto Rican pieces in the Lower East Side.	129

6.2	Memorial mural depicting Tupac Shakur in the Lower East Side.	137
7.1	Mural criticizing Giuliani's spatial policies in Williamsburg, Brooklyn.	149
7.2	Memorial mural of Amadou Diallo in Soundview, Bronx.	164
7.3	The electrocution of free speech in Williamsburg, Brooklyn.	178

Acknowledgments

In the course of writing this book, I have accumulated numerous professional and personal debts. I am deeply grateful to Mari Jo Buhle, Bob Lee, and Susan Smulyan of the Department of American Civilization at Brown University for supervising my doctoral dissertation, from which this book originated. I am indebted to the faculty members of the Department of History at the State University of New York, Stony Brook, where I have been a faculty member for the last few years. In particular, I would like to thank Chris Sellers, Ned Landsman, Nancy Tomes, Michael Barnhart, Larry Frohman, Kathleen Wilson, Donna Rilling, Bill Miller, April Masten, Gary Marker, Iona Man-Cheong, Eric Beverley, Gene Lebovics, and Young-Sun Hong for their encouragement and comments. I also thank Jean Wood, Susan Grumet, Gabriela Garreffa, Nina Froes, Jorge Manuel Reboredo, James Morone, Anne Galvin, Peter Derrick, Alexis Stern, Mike Murphy, Lisa Scrocco, Rebbecca Brown, Patrick Keilch, Ray Guins, César Edgardo Soto Cepeda, Robert Harvey, Briann Greenfield, Krin Gabbard, David Goodman, Adam Charboneau, Fred Moehn, Michael Cisco, and Ira Livingston for their help and generosity. Finally, I would like to thank Max Novick, my editor at Routledge, for making this book a reality.

This book would not be possible without the considerable assistance of librarians, archivists, and staff members of numerous research institutions and archives in New York City. My thanks goes out to the staff members the Municipal Archives of the City of New York, the Columbia University Archives and Columbiana Library, the Columbia University Rare Book and Manuscript Library, the Columbia University Oral History Research Office, the Schomburg Center for Research in Black Culture, the New York Public Library, The Bronx County Historical Society, the interlibrary loan staff at Brown University and SUNY Stony Brook, and the New York University library. This research has also been assisted with grants from the Gilder Lehrman Institute of American History, the Fine Arts, Humanities, and Social Sciences Research and Interdisciplinary Initiative Fund at SUNY, Stony Brook, and the United University Professions at SUNY, Stony Brook.

Introduction

In 1982, James Q. Wilson and George L. Kelling advanced the "broken windows" theory, which laid the groundwork for a reinterpretation of the decline of U.S. cities in the postwar period. Instead of focusing on economic restructuring, deindustrialization, suburbanization, and shrinking government budgets as indicators of urban decline, Wilson and Kelling argued that the behavior of "disorderly" people in urban space affected the desirability of cities in profound ways and that urban centers had become undesirable because city officials had not adequately dealt with this problem. They described "disorderly" people as "not violent people, nor necessarily criminals, but disreputable or obstreperous or unpredictable people: panhandlers, drunks, addicts, rowdy teenagers, prostitutes, loiterers, and the mentally disturbed." Ultimately, Wilson and Kelling contended that if tolerated, social disorder could easily mutate to serious crime and that the authorities had the responsibility of tackling minor incivilities with the same rigor that they fought dangerous crime. The "broken windows" theory elevated order-maintenance into one of the most important functions of city governance.[1]

The public policy version of the "broken windows" theory, which became known as order-maintenance policing, was practiced by Mayor Rudolph Giuliani in New York City between 1994 and 2001. Employing the term "broken windows" policing and supplementing it with terms such as "quality-of-life policing" and "zero tolerance," Giuliani and his police commissioners employed strategies of aggressive policing to transform New York into an orderly city. Police officers targeted low-income "disorderly" populations who were mostly people of color and displaced them from high-profile public spaces. Since the considerably enlarged police force that the Giuliani Administration inherited also reduced serious crime, "zero tolerance" was accepted as a way to improve urban fortunes. Proponents of the "broken windows" theory were vindicated as successful urban policy experts. New York City, which had precipitously declined in the postwar period and become unlivable according to many observers, became popular once again among middle- and upper-class people. The city that even in its darkest days remained an epicenter of finance and culture had made a resounding comeback in terms of mainstream investment, real estate, and quality of life.[2]

This book complicates this narrative of urban recovery by providing a historical perspective on the relationship of city governance and urban disorder in New York City since 1945. The assumption that the city government of New York began to consider urban disorder as an important variable in the 1990s is inaccurate. The ordering of urban space has always been a preoccupation of city administrations in New York City and this preoccupation intensified in the postwar period because of anxieties about the direction of the city. However, different governments pursued different policies, which corresponded to period-specific trends of spatial ordering and dominant political ideologies. Liberalism, which was the dominant political ideology in New York City up until at least the 1960s, emphasized physical solutions to urban disorder, which were based on the production of orderly individuals and communities through interventions in the built environment. Liberals believed that the elimination of urban slums and their replacement with decent housing based on modernist architecture would make the people living in them orderly, healthy, and productive. This way of ordering urban space in New York City was discredited in the 1960s as the city continued to decline, crime steadily increased, and the new modernist housing developments were as disorderly as the ones they replaced. After the fiscal crisis of 1975, neoliberalism and neoconservatism became the dominant ideologies of governance in New York City and their prescriptions of ordering space prevailed. New York became a neoliberal city with the city government promoting mainstream economic development while cutting budgets and services to low-income populations. Neoliberals believed in the ability of the free market to order individuals and their activities. However, neoliberals were overwhelmed with the effects of human displacement visible in public space because of the contraction of government, the disappearance of manufacturing jobs, and the reduction of housing for the poor. Homelessness and poverty rose to levels never seen before. Left without an efficient spatial ordering strategy, neoliberals embraced neoconservative prescriptions such as the "broken windows" theory and order-maintenance policing. Instead of seeking to produce orderly individuals like the liberals, neoliberals and neoconservatives sought to banish "disorderly" ones.

The city's changing urban fortunes were exemplified in October of 2002, when former mayor Giuliani announced that his consulting firm, the Giuliani Group, had agreed to help Mexico City's police officials design a zero-tolerance model of spatial regulation. Mexico City had been considered one of the most disorderly cities in the Americas with low-income people having overtaken its central parts. Giuliani was invited to Mexico City by Mayor Andrés Manuel López Obrador, whose government had joined forces with a group of powerful businessmen. The businessmen, who wanted to eliminate crime and disorder from the downtown area of their city so that they could pursue lucrative investment strategies, paid the $4.3 million fee for Giuliani's consulting firm. Although Giuliani's involvement in Mexico City was criticized by criminologists and journalists in the United States and Mexico and had no real effect in reducing crime or disorder, what went unnoticed was the fact that a former New York City mayor was invited to consult the authorities of another world city. Such an invitation would have been unusual in 1992, 1982, 1972, or 1962. Indeed, the last time that leaders of other world cities widely considered a New York City official to have been implementing successful urban solutions was in the 1950s; that official was not a mayor but master planner Robert Moses. During this period, Moses was involved in urban renewal.[3]

On the surface, urban renewal and zero tolerance appear to be two unrelated public policy processes. Urban renewal refers to a method of urban redevelopment under which urban areas perceived as slums were bulldozed and replaced with sizable modernist projects. Zero tolerance refers to a type of aggressive policing under which the authorities target individuals who commit minor infractions in public space. Although urban renewal has been viewed as a way to physically rebuild cities and zero tolerance has been viewed as a way to reduce crime, both of them also seek to make urban space more orderly by attacking urban disorder.

This book provides a history of spatial regulation in postwar New York by utilizing the concept of urban disorder, which is comprised of two subconcepts, physical disorder and social disorder. Physical disorder encompasses the decayed condition of buildings, streets, lots, and sidewalks. Social disorder concerns the congregation and activities of "undesirable" people. In effect, physical disorder is based on the disrepair of the built environment whereas social disorder is based on the misbehavior of ordinary people in public spaces. The combination of physical and social disorder, which in this book is referred as urban disorder, generates an urban space that appears disorderly, undesirable, dangerous, unsanitary, blighted, and in decline. After World War II, urban disorder became a way to explain the decline of cities in the United States. Though employed by Erving Goffman, Lyn Lofland, John Sampson, and others, the concepts of physical and social disorder were appropriated and popularized by proponents of the "broken windows" theory, which argued that visible signs of urban disorder are unacceptable because they make neighborhoods unsuitable for the middle classes and invite serious criminals.[4]

Social and physical disorder are politically loaded concepts based on perceptions that encompass the activities of low-income and racialized populations as well as their neighborhoods. For urban elites and public officials, the employment of these concepts (and related terms) is useful because it is impossible to reduce all the activities of "disorderly" populations under the category of crime and categorize the physical condition of all "disorderly" neighborhoods as slums. These uses of "disorder" seek to improve and enable real estate fortunes, mainstream consumption patterns, status-oriented city life, and capitalist development. They also seek to criminalize routine activities taking place in public space under the pretext that they are a gateway to serious crime.

This narrative questions how urban elites, public officials, and business interests sought to eradicate physical and social disorder in postwar New York. The eradication of physical disorder became equated with the rebuilding of a declining New York that was suffering from urban blight. The eradication of social disorder became equated with making New York attractive to white middle-class populations by eliminating the "nuisances" generated by low-income people. Both of these patterns of urban disorder elimination acquired qualities that defined what types of environment and behavior were synonymous with middle-class respectability and the good life. Physical environments and social behaviors that did not conform to these standards suffered. This is because in a sizable and diverse city such as New York, it is not possible to effectively reduce perceptions of urban disorder without violating civil and human rights. The effective regulation of urban disorder requires a strong and determined municipal government that is willing to displace certain groups of people from their neighborhoods or public space by employing all kinds of legally questionable methods, including the use of brutal force. Without coercion, the efficiency of fighting urban disorder is compromised.

Strategies to eliminate urban disorder in post-1945 New York fell into two general patterns. The first pattern, physical solutions, sought to employ architectural and urban planning strategies so that the physical landscape of "disorderly" areas would be eliminated and the people living in them displaced. In postwar New York this pattern was exemplified by urban renewal. The second pattern, social solutions, sought to disable the "disorderly" behavior of people in public space through aggressive policing, increased penalties for minor offenses, and exclusionary zoning. In the 1990s, this pattern was exemplified by order-maintenance or zero-tolerance policing. In general, the first pattern has sought a radical rearrangement of space so that the blighted built environments and the people living in them would disappear, whereas the second pattern has targeted the disorderly people themselves or the places where they gather for shopping and entertainment.

1 The Betrayal of the Liberal Assumptions of Urban Renewal

> The sociologist Herbert Gans has called my attention to the importance of tuberculosis and the alleged or real threat of it in the slum-clearing and "model tenement" movements of the late nineteenth and early twentieth centuries, the feeling being that slum housing "bred" tuberculosis. The shift from tuberculosis to cancer in planning and housing rhetoric had taken place by the 1950s. "Blight" (a virtual synonym for slum) is seen as a cancer that spreads insidiously, and the use of the term "invasion" to describe when the nonwhite and poor move into a middle-class neighborhood is as such a metaphor borrowed from culture as from the military: the two discourses overlap.[1]
>
> —Susan Sontag

In the 1890s, while writing about the problem of the slum, Jacob Riis articulated the mutual existence of physical and social disorder in New York City. Riis realized that the slum was not simply a problem of inadequate housing, but one of social structure that included both tenements and people. In that sense, effective housing reform had to consist of a complete reconstruction of the neighborhood environment so that the way that people lived their lives could change. Riis admitted that this task of changing people would be difficult because adults had already been fashioned both by the hardships of the slum and the influence of the old country. But, at the least, physical and social reform could influence the children of the immigrants who seemed the most likely segment of the destitute population to embrace and realize middle-class American values. The professional affiliations that crystallized during the Progressive Era with the aim of bettering the conditions for the poor branched off into the two main trajectories that Riis had articulated: urban planners and architects focused on the physical dimension while social workers, educators, and law enforcement officials focused on the social dimension.[2]

Although the attempt to eliminate slums, provide decent housing, and reform the poor by remaking their environment is rooted in the Progressive Era, meaningful housing reform did not take place before the New Deal, and even then it was compromised. At the turn of the century, reformers, under the leadership of Lawrence Veiller, believed that slums degraded the customs, manners, and health of their residents and promoted building codes over other approaches of housing reform.

However, Progressive Era efforts to restrict, regulate, and improve tenements in New York City had limited results because landlords opposed them, city agencies lacked the capacity to enforce codes, and capitalists were reluctant to build decent housing for the poor. In the 1930s, housing reformers sought solutions that went beyond the enforcement of building code violations. Ideas about how to resolve the New York housing problem came from Europe. Between 1919 and 1933, about six million homes were built in European cities such as London, Frankfurt, Paris, and Vienna, and about half of them were constructed by public agencies. Housing reformers in New York City were astounded to observe that in Great Britain, which was experiencing a profound economic decline, millions of apartments were being built in former slum districts. During the Great Depression, public policy makers in the United States embraced the European model of public housing as the best way to clear slums, build decent low-income housing, and create construction jobs. In 1937, U.S. Congress passed the United States Housing Act, which established a federal public housing authority to assist local public housing agencies building public housing; conservative politicians were able to limit this act by placing income ceilings on the people eligible for public housing and requiring that one slum unit be demolished for each public housing unit built. After a promising start, this public housing program languished because anti–New Deal politicians elected to the U.S. Congress refused to fund it, and World War II set different funding priorities.[3]

In the 1940s, the idea of slum clearance was embraced by business groups that opposed public housing. As central sections of cities further declined due to disinvestment, real estate interests, landlords, businesspeople, and city officials feared that commercial districts would be engulfed by slums and fail. Business advocacy groups lobbied U.S. Congress for slum clearance legislation without the public housing component, which they detested. Elected representatives and senators found themselves in a political deadlock over the issue, with liberals wanting a comprehensive housing bill that included a generous public housing portion and conservatives opposing it. In the end, these political groups compromised and passed the Housing Act of 1949.[4]

Though it represented the most important legislative achievement of President Harry Truman's Fair Deal, the Housing Act of 1949 was a compromise between liberals and conservatives, who warred over redevelopment strategies for many years. Though the act professed to provide a decent home for every American family, it actually offered heavy subsidies to local governments so that they could replace urban slums with private or public developments. Though the act revived low-cost public housing programs that had stalled after 1938, it placed too many restrictions on them, allowing only poor people to move into cheaply made structures. According to this act, blighted areas did not have to

The Betrayal of the Liberal Assumptions of Urban Renewal 7

be replaced by public housing, while public housing could not be built without the destruction of slums. Whatever the case, most bulldozed slums were replaced with modernist housing projects, of which few were public.[5]

In New York City, Robert Moses possessed the technical expertise, political connections, and power to carry out the legally complicated and socially questionable aspects of the Housing Act of 1949. He argued that this act was nothing more than a slum clearance bill, and in the 1950s he embarked on an effort to clear and rebuild substantial swaths of land in the city and redistribute populations according to race and class. After the passage of the Housing Act of 1954, which appended that of 1949, this method of urban redevelopment became commonly known as "urban renewal." Moses understood the imperatives of urban renewal and was able to coordinate them. Urban renewal required an efficient and strong municipal government that could mobilize substantial resources to thwart opponents. Since the rapid, complete, and inexpensive displacement of existing residents of areas designated as slums by authorities was required, the city government needed the capacity to remove resisting residents, meet court challenges, and compromise political opponents; sometimes it even meant the ability to intimidate people on the way. Moses single-handedly coordinated most of these tasks, though his projects still depended on the cooperation of the city government.[6]

Though urban renewal in postwar New York took place under a liberal Democratic regime, it was eventually weakened by liberals who found it to be implemented in unacceptable and brutal ways. For a while, liberal groups and politicians accepted the misinformation coming from Moses's office, which included unrealistic plans to humanely relocate people displaced by slum clearance. Gradually, there were rifts in the liberal coalition, because Moses had managed to completely hijack urban renewal. Moses's implementation of the program undermined most of its redistributive housing elements while the human displacement caused by slum clearance became difficult to ignore. Moses began to lose power in the late 1950s, after liberal elected officials began to question the rationale of his projects and withdrew support. By then, most of the urban renewal projects to be realized were already being constructed. Many of them had already been completed.[7]

This chapter examines how urban renewal was implemented in various parts of the Upper West Side, which became an area with numerous urban renewal projects, after the passage of the Housing Act of 1949. Columbia University and other prestigious institutions located in the northern tip of the Upper West Side used urban renewal in order to stop the expansion of Black Harlem into their neighborhood and to eliminate areas that they considered to be blighted. In the southern part of the Upper West Side, the city government constructed the Lincoln Center for the Arts, seeking to attract affluent populations, both as residents and as patrons, back to that part of

Manhattan. In other parts of the Upper West Side, smaller projects aimed to achieve similar results. These urban renewal interventions sought to displace "disorderly" populations, remake the way that space was used by residents, eradicate structures that seemed to be blighted, and achieve a more orderly appearance through modernist urban design. The way that urban renewal was implemented in the Upper West Side shows the extent to which business and institutional interests took over the program. Housing for the poor was relegated to an afterthought. Urban renewal was used for neighborhood defense, the displacement of African Americans and Latinos, the destruction of low-income neighborhoods, and the construction of white middle- and upper-class cultural infrastructures and housing.

COLUMBIA UNIVERSITY AND THE GROWING "SLUM" OF HARLEM

Columbia University and other prestigious institutions located in the northern portion of the Upper West Side were among the first powerful interests to use elements of the Housing Act of 1949 to their advantage. In the 1940s, Columbia administrators concurred with businesspeople who found downtown areas endangered by the influx of minority populations. Columbia's neighborhood, Morningside Heights, was in the midst of racial transition. Puerto Ricans were moving in great numbers to the blocks located south of Morningside Heights, while African Americans moved from Harlem into the northern edge of Morningside Heights. In response, the prestigious educational, medical, and religious institutions of Morningside Heights decided to engage in comprehensive neighborhood planning in order to reverse the influx of minorities into the neighborhood.

In fighting the spatial war of Morningside Heights, the institutions, led by Columbia University, relied on perceptions of social and physical disorder based on derogatory narratives of race and class. Morningside powerholders argued that urban disorder was exemplified by the blighted appearance of buildings and by the unacceptable use of public space by low-income African Americans and Puerto Ricans. These narratives about urban disorder were used to justify the public policies promoted by Morningside powerholders allied with government officials. In their quest to eliminate urban disorder, Morningside institutions pursued physical solutions based on modernist city planning and urban design.

Columbia University moved from midtown New York to the plateau of Morningside Heights in 1897. Morningside Heights seemed the ideal location for the university, allowing it to remain in New York City but to escape the congestion and other disturbances of downtown and midtown. By moving to Morningside Heights, the university joined the Cathedral of St. John the Divine and St. Luke's Hospital. Almost immediately after Columbia's move, other institutions became interested in Morningside Heights in order to take advantage of the prestige of the university and the beauty of the neighborhood. These included the Jewish Theological Seminary (1903), Corpus Christi Church (1906), Union Theological Seminary (1910), the Institute of Musical Art (1910) which later merged with the Juilliard School of Music, the International House (1924), Riverside Church (1930), and the Interchurch Center (1958). As early as 1896, Morningside Heights claimed to be the "Acropolis of the new world" because of the concentration of prestigious private educational, medical, and religious institutions. This phrase remained in use throughout the twentieth century.[8]

Morningside Heights urbanized rapidly after the opening of subway service in 1904. During this period, apartment houses gained a general acceptance among New York's middle and upper classes. Indeed, new neighborhoods like Morningside Heights attracted many well-to-do families seeking to live at a safe distance from the poor neighborhoods and the commercial districts of downtown. They desired apartments built with the latest amenities and near a subway line that connected them with the rest of the city. Morningside Heights was so successful as a neighborhood in the fifteen years that followed the opening of the subway that professors, other institutional staff members, and graduate students had difficulty finding affordable housing there. In order to remedy this problem, in 1919, Columbia and Teachers College purchased several buildings to house faculty, staff, and students.[9]

The contentment that Columbia and other institutions felt about their immediate environment evaporated during the 1930s. Since 1906, Black Harlem had expanded in outward concentric circles from 135th Street and Seventh Avenue, and the possibility of further expansion was evident. A number of indicators showed that African Americans might move to Morningside Heights, challenging the white middle-class character of the neighborhood. In retrospect, the middle-class fiber of Morningside Heights began to erode in the 1930s, not because of the presence of African Americans, but because of the Great Depression and the demand for rooming houses. Families, in their effort to meet housing expenses, began to take in boarders as unemployment caused a downward slide in incomes and lifestyles. At the same time, the city government lifted regulations that prevented the operation of single-room occupancies (SROs) in the Upper West Side, predicting that the 1939–1940 World's Fair would generate great demand from visitors seeking more rooms than the city's hotels would be able to provide. The city government did not reinstate these regulations after the World's Fair. People with low incomes—especially those who moved to New York during World War II but became unemployed after demobilization—became a staple of the neighborhood.[10]

In the 1940s, another demographic transition that troubled institutional officials of Morningside Heights commenced. Puerto Ricans, unable to participate in their island's transition from an agricultural to an industrial economy, migrated to the United States and began to settle areas of

10 *Spatial Regulation in New York City*

the Upper West Side, south of Morningside Heights, in massive numbers. Without the means to afford decent housing, Puerto Ricans moved to windowless basements and subdivided apartments. Sometimes an entire family could only afford a room in an apartment shared with other families. In the meantime, many white middle-class residents of the Upper West Side, fearing racial succession and neighborhood deterioration, decided to relocate to suburban locations inside and outside the city. This process threatened the middle-class identity of the southern boundary of Morningside Heights.[11]

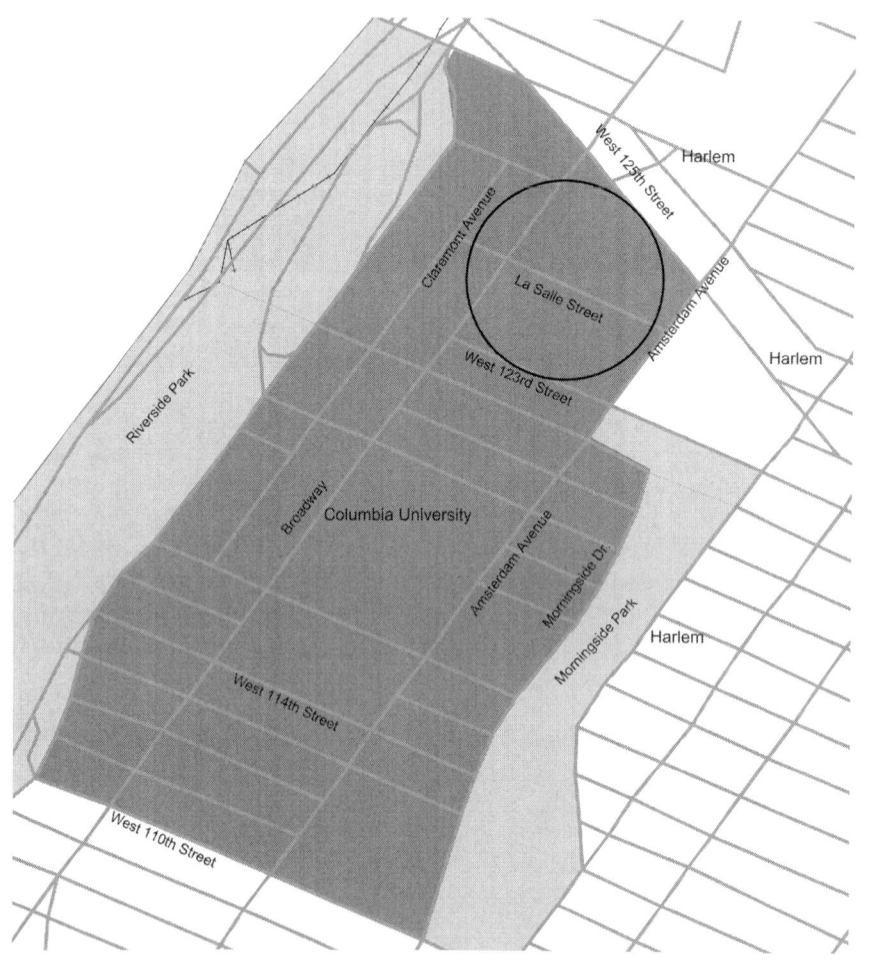

Figure 1.1 Map of Morningside Heights and its immediate surroundings. Morningside Heights, the neighborhood of Columbia University and the other prestigious institutions, is displayed in dark grey. Harlem is located northward and eastward of Morningside Heights. The circle roughly indicates the location of the La Salle Street "slum" as defined by MHI and Columbia officials. (Map designed by Themis Chronopoulos, 2010).

The Betrayal of the Liberal Assumptions of Urban Renewal 11

Bewildered by these socioeconomic changes, in the immediate postwar period, Columbia University administrators worked to find an appropriate course of action. In 1946, newly retired Columbia President Nicholas Murray Butler wrote to the university's Board of Trustees and stated the most obvious solution to Columbia's problems: he urged them to purchase all property between 114th and 122nd streets and between Amsterdam Avenue and Morningside Drive (Figure 1.1) for future expansion and to protect the area from the "greatly feared invasion from Harlem which has been threatened more than once."[12] The trustees knew that the university lacked the funds to purchase this much land but also understood that Morningside Heights could be declining. They asked Columbia economist Ernest M. Fisher, head of the Institute for Land Use, to explore conditions at Morningside Heights and prepare a report. Fisher commissioned a committee of Columbia social scientists, which included sociologist Robert K. Merton and economist Raymond Saulnier, to study the area. The conclusions of the report confirmed Butler's fears:

> To even the casual observer, a process of deterioration is conspicuous in the Morningside Heights Area. This deterioration is manifested in the condition of buildings, in the character of enterprises that are penetrating the area, and in the occupancy of much of the commercial and residential facilities of the area. Unless a program of deliberate planning and action is undertaken within the next few years, it seems likely that the deterioration will have progressed to a point where the area will become largely inappropriate as the location of institutions with religious, educational, and cultural objectives. Such institutions do not exist in isolation. They and their staffs must be served by commercial and residential facilities appropriate to their cultural objectives. It is the deterioration of residential and commercial facilities that threatens the future of these institutions. They face, therefore, the alternatives of taking constructive action to defeat these forces, or abandoning the area, or of attempting what may well be nearly impossible—the maintenance of their usefulness in the midst of a blighted area.[13]

The social scientists who wrote this report argued that Morningside Heights was in the process of becoming a blighted area. They defined blight as the deterioration of the physical condition of buildings, the questionable character of businesses invading the area, and unacceptable trends in residential occupancy. They did not provide any recommendations for action other than a general statement that the forces invading Morningside Heights had to be defeated.

Columbia's administrators and social scientists approached the expansion of Black Harlem toward Morningside Heights in ways that mirrored the racial prejudice of the housing market during the same period. The Federal Housing Administration (FHA), in its *Underwriting Manual,* declared that homogeneous neighborhoods represented better investments and supported the practice of redlining, which denied racially mixed and minority neighborhoods credit. In the 1940s, willful racial mixing violated the code of ethics of the National Association of Real Estate Boards while, with the encouragement of the federal government, realtors required home buyers to sign court-enforceable restrictive covenants that prohibited property owners from renting or selling to racially disharmonious groups. In New York, discrimination in the private housing market became open and widespread. According to a State of New York document, "Whites Only" signs appeared on most buildings located on the fringes of Harlem, including Morningside Heights. In the 1940s, Columbia administrators could not imagine how an elite university could operate in a racially mixed neighborhood at a time when even the federal government considered racial mixing to contribute to the downfall of neighborhoods.[14]

In 1946, the trustees of David Rockefeller's International House, located in the western part of Morningside Heights, invited Wilbur Munnecke, a sociologist, planning consultant, and Vice President of the University of Chicago, to advise them on the future of the neighborhood. At the time, Munnecke had a reputation as someone experienced in dealing with problems created by advancing urban decay. He had previously coordinated attempts by the University of Chicago to restrain the expansion of Chicago's Black Belt into its immediate territory. After touring Morningside Heights and meeting with the trustees of International House, Munnecke concluded that the neighborhood would change for the worse unless the institutions took preventive action. Munnecke argued against old methods of neighborhood protection based on "vertical restrictions, that is, by barring commercial properties, apartment buildings, Negroes, Jews, or any other group or class different from the group or class within the community."[15] Munnecke found zoning restrictions and exclusive covenants to be "wrong in principle" and that they amounted to nothing more than delaying inevitability. Munnecke was proven right. Two years later, the U.S. Supreme Court ruled in *Shelley v. Kraemer* that judicial enforcement of racially restrictive covenants violated the Fourteenth Amendment.[16]

Munnecke recommended a comprehensive spatial plan for Morningside Heights. He made a case for "horizontal restrictions," which were "positive actions" designed to keep and attract desirable neighbors. The positive actions that he called for represented his realization that, unless white middle-class New Yorkers had incentives to live in Morningside Heights, the neighborhood would be dominated by low-income African Americans and Latinos. These incentives included city and state programs in the form of mortgage subsidies and tax incentives for the middle and upper classes. But even Munnecke believed that such positive actions had their limits. Thus, he also recommended a process of wholesale redevelopment that would target the housing of "undesirables" in and around Morningside Heights. Munnecke suggested that the institutions in the area act in concert to renovate Morningside Heights but advised that Columbia should take the lead because of its real estate holdings and sizable endowment. Munnecke's suggestion became a reality in 1947 when various area institutions founded Morningside Heights, Inc. (MHI). David Rockefeller became the President of MHI, and Lawrence M. Orton, a planning commissioner of New York City, became its Executive Director. Rockefeller supplied the new organization with prestige and political connections. Orton provided the practical expertise of an urban planner and the ability to overcome red tape through his position as a city planning commissioner.[17]

After the establishment of MHI, the first concern of its administrators became to stop urban blight from spreading into Morningside Heights from adjacent areas. At the very least this plan required the fortification of the neighborhood's northeastern boundaries, an area where Harlem and Morningside Heights blended into one another. Many Morningside officials believed that structures such as housing developments would eliminate blight on the fringes of Morningside Heights and disrupt the spatial continuity between the interior and the exterior of the neighborhood. These housing developments would function as buffer zones and separate the middle-class respectability of Morningside Heights from the low-income problem of Harlem. Because these buffer zones would include many city blocks, Morningside Heights would no longer border neighborhoods where unwanted people resided. Furthermore, these housing developments would displace "undesirable" residents from the fringes of Morningside Heights, eliminating their presence in the area completely. Morningside powerholders understood that such ambitious boundary fortification would never materialize without governmental assistance. Thus, they lobbied for slum clearance legislation in the late 1940s that would earmark public funds for the demolition of blighted areas and their rebuilding. Lawrence Orton understood the significance of slum clearance and how to practice it in ways favorable to the interests of Morningside institutions. Slum clearance promised the complete elimination of disorder by using public subsidies to transform space.

The most comprehensive redevelopment project proposed by MHI, and sponsored by the city government, involved the clearing of the La Salle Street slum in the northeastern edge of Morningside Heights (Figure 1.1). MHI was mostly interested in using Title I of the Housing Act of 1949 in order to construct a middle-income development called Morningside Gardens in place of approximately three thousand low-rent apartments. MHI administrators agreed with *New York Times* architectural critic Gertrude Samuels, who called the LaSalle Street slum "a human wasteland . . . which connects with Negro Harlem."[18] With the encouragement of Orton and Moses, MHI lobbied to expand the clearance area and to ask the New York City Housing Authority (NYCHA) to build public housing in the area immediately northeast of Morningside Gardens. The NYCHA accepted, and the General Grant Houses became the public housing development.

14   *Spatial Regulation in New York City*

The General Grant Houses fulfilled two goals: they appeased many activists and politicians who opposed the removal of low-income people and their replacement with middle-class ones, and they enlarged the northeastern boundary fortification of Morningside Heights. Gradually, the development ballooned even more. Local and federal government officials encouraged MHI to enlarge its proposal in order to include the sufficiently extensive area required under federal slum clearance guidelines. As a result, MHI proposed the reconstruction of an area that stretched all the way to West 135th Street. Eventually, most of the area between West 123rd Street and West 133rd Street became the site of the low-income General Grant Houses and Manhattanville Houses. The area between West 123rd and La Salle Street, located adjacent to the prestigious institutions, conveniently became the site of middle-income Morningside Gardens (Figure 1.2).[19]

This project walled off Harlem, prevented its expansion into Manhattanville and Morningside Heights, and displaced about 36,000 people who stood in the way of redevelopment and did not conform to the middle-class standards that MHI officials had in mind. A Columbia survey categorized 4% of the people to be displaced as "oriental," 22% as "Spanish speaking," 27% as "Negro," and 47% as "white," which meant that the area was ethnically and racially mixed. In the same survey, half of the respondents expressed satisfaction with their housing, noted that the rates of overcrowding were low by Manhattan standards, and believed that the characterization of the neighborhood as a "human wasteland" had been unjustified. However, MHI administrators and government officials only reported the dissatisfaction that half of the respondents expressed about their housing. Residents facing the bulldozer to make room for Morningside Gardens formed a multiracial coalition with the assistance of the American Labor Party that they named Save Our Homes Committee to campaign specifically against MHI and Columbia. They tried to reverse the decision for slum clearance by petitioning the Board of Estimate, storming the BOE's meetings with hundreds of demonstrators, and winning electoral victories in the local school's parents' association and the Manhattanville Neighborhood Center. They presented statistics showing that they lived in decent housing in a successful racially mixed community and that their incomes were not high enough to allow them to buy into Morningside Gardens. They pointed out that, even if all of the units in the nearby NYCHA buildings were allotted to displaced La Salle residents, they would only be able to house half of the displaced residents. MHI and Moses replied by branding the organization's leader Elizabeth Barker as a Communist and by claiming that the American Labor Party and Communist activists were behind the tenant mobilization. The mass media accepted the arguments of the Morningside institutions and dismissed the Save Our Homes Committee as a fringe left-wing organization. In the cold war climate of the 1950s, this was not unusual. In addition, Robert Moses had an extraordinary ability to convince public officials to support slum clearance even when the projects

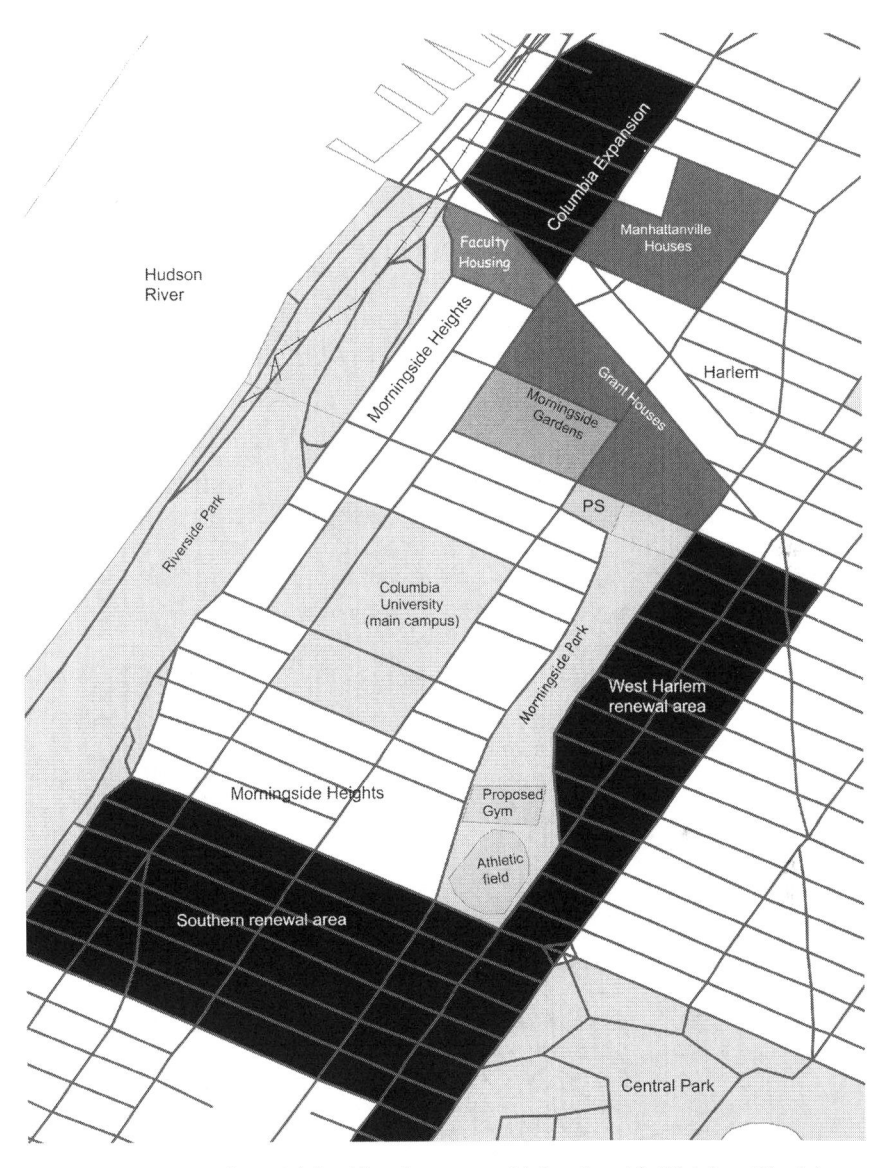

The Betrayal of the Liberal Assumptions of Urban Renewal 15

Figure 1.2 Map of spatial fortification around Morningside Heights. The Morningside Gardens and General Grant Houses were completed in 1957, the Manhattanville Houses in 1961. The faculty housing buildings were completed in 1964 and 1967. The West Harlem renewal area, the southern renewal area, and the Columbia expansion were proposed and planned but not realized. Columbia University is currently expanding in the exact area that it had proposed in the 1960s. (Map designed by Themis Chronopoulos, 2010.)

16 *Spatial Regulation in New York City*

were controversial and would potentially damage their electoral prospects. In the end, the Save Our Homes activists never had a chance. They could only delay the inevitable.[20]

Morningside Gardens and the General Grant Houses began to accept tenants in 1957. They were racially integrated only because MHI did everything to attract white and Asian families into the developments. The Morningside Gardens development was composed of six twenty-one-story towers providing 980 tenant-owned units for middle-income people. The General Grant Houses comprised nine twenty-one- and thirteen-story towers providing 1,940 rental units for low-income people (Figure 1.3). When applications arrived, the project sponsors realized that many middle-class African American families wanted to move to Morningside Gardens. However, MHI officials kept the number of African Americans in Morningside Gardens at 20%, believing that this was an acceptable ratio because of fears that Morningside Gardens would become a Black development. The General Grant Houses more closely reflected the demographic makeup of applicants since they were administered by the NYCHA. Although MHI officials were hoping that half of General Grant Houses residents would be white, it turned out that about 90% of the new tenants were African American. Urban renewal in Morningside Heights was largely considered

Figure 1.3 The General Grant Houses and Morningside Gardens. In the foreground are the General Grant Houses. Morningside Gardens buildings appear in the distance with balconies. No matter how they are viewed, these projects are immense, generating a spatial discontinuity between Morningside Heights and Harlem. (Photograph by Themis Chronopoulos, 2001.)

to be humane because efforts were made to relocate the displaced residents in theory; in practice, the story was more complicated. Moses argued that fewer than half of the original tenants moved to the new developments because most preferred to live somewhere else.[21]

The Morningside Heights boundary fortification did not stop with the construction of Morningside Gardens and the General Grant Houses. In 1964, Columbia University completed a twenty-one-story apartment building accompanied by a four-story parking garage for 355 automobiles at the corner of West 125th Street and Riverside Drive for 180 Columbia faculty. Playgrounds and a landscaped terrace were constructed on top of the garage (Figure 1.4). Three years later, another twenty-six-story tower that housed offices and one hundred faculty apartments was built right next to the previous faculty building, with an enclosed passageway linking the two buildings. Columbia administrators believed that these two buildings, inhabited by middle-income residents, would fortify the northwestern boundary of the neighborhood between Riverside Park and the General Grant Houses. None of the buildings had entrances that faced West 125th Street, which emphasized the idea that Columbia faculty had no interest in interacting with anyone in Manhattanville (Figure 1.5). These projects solidified and completed the fortification of the neighborhood's northern boundaries (Figure 1.2).[22]

Figure 1.4 Columbia University faculty housing. Pedestrian access to Columbia University's faculty housing is through a ramp controlled by security guards. The housing complex has its own common areas above the street level. (Photograph by Themis Chronopoulos, 2001.)

18   *Spatial Regulation in New York City*

Figure 1.5   Columbia University faculty housing facing West 125th Street. There are no entrances facing northward. (Photograph by Themis Chronopoulos, 2001.)

Morningside institutions saw Morningside Park as another boundary troublespot, though not because of the threat of physical blight spreading into the neighborhood. Since 1935, Morningside institutions had routinely advised their affiliates to avoid using the park because of crime. But "undesirables" from west Harlem used the park to gain access to the Heights. In order to minimize access to Morningside Heights from the park and make it more orderly, Columbia tried to reduce the park's size. In 1955, Parks Commissioner Robert Moses authorized Columbia to construct a five-acre fenced-in athletic field and a field house at the southern portion of the park (Figure 1.2). Columbia students would have exclusive use these of these facilities during weekdays from October 31 to May 31. Community children, under the direction of Columbia staff, would have access to these facilities on Saturdays and Sundays all year and every day during the summer. The withdrawal of public park space for semiprivate use had begun. Columbia enclosed this area with an eight-foot-high iron link fence. In 1960, MHI convinced the New York City Parks Department to install gates at each of the entrances of Morningside Park, which closed at dusk each evening. They also recommended placing thorn bushes and barbed wire beside the gates, something that the Parks Department did not do. In addition, MHI hired additional private security guards to patrol Morningside Drive along the park and installed spotlights on its buildings to illuminate the edge of the park. In 1965, after lobbying by MHI, the local government decided to allocate the northwestern corner of Morningside Park for the construction of a public school, even though there had been an alternative site for the school outside public parkland. In 1967, Columbia gained governmental permission to build a gymnasium in the park, which would further reduce the space within the park open to the public. MHI officials believed that this reduction of public park space would make for a more orderly park, while the security measures would make for a more disciplined access to Morningside Heights by Harlem residents. Surprisingly, the City Planning Commission opposed plans to further reduce the size of the park. Using strong language, as early as 1964 the Commission stated that "Morningside Park has already been encroached upon severely," citing the athletic field that Columbia operated. The Commission also argued that the "unfortunate situation" that prevailed in the park was due to poor maintenance and that the park should be rehabilitated rather than eliminated. Commission members were concerned that overcrowding in many parts of the city would tempt the political establishment to start using park land for private uses. Morningside Park represented a prime example of such a possibility.[23]

Morningside institutions also planned to fortify the southern boundary of Morningside Heights (Figure 1.2). In 1948, an MHI-sponsored study showed that about 14.2% of the population in the area between West 108th Street and Cathedral Parkway (West 110th Street) were low-income Puerto Ricans or other Latin Americans. This study also showed that most of these Spanish-speaking people had moved to those blocks during the previous five years and that they used space in a disorderly manner. However, government officials continuously rebuffed MHI proposals to construct public housing in the area bounded by Amsterdam Avenue, West 108th Street, and Cathedral Parkway because they believed that conditions in the neighborhood could not justify slum clearance as defined by federal requirements. With the construction of massive public housing out of the question, MHI decided to apply for demonstration projects under Section 314 of the National Housing Act, which provided public funds to remake small parts of Morningside Heights' southern boundary. Another proposal targeting Morningside Heights' southern boundary made by Columbia, St. Luke's Hospital, and St. John's Cathedral called for a "low-coverage residential development" that would cover the area bounded by West 110th Street, Central Park West, West 108th Street, and Columbus Avenue (Figure 1.2). This project would remove Puerto Ricans from the southern border of Morningside Heights and provide a physical barrier between Morningside Park and Central Park. In effect, this would prevent southern Harlem from expanding between the two parks and into the area directly south of the Heights.

In the words of MHI officials, "with Harlem to the north and increasing non-white occupancy to the south and east, the whole proposed study area is fated to become an extension of Harlem if nothing is done."[24]

In the years that followed, the southern fortification proposal was expanded and amended so that it could include west Harlem and Manhattanville. The new plan would comprehensively displace low-income people from as far east as Eighth Avenue, as far south as West 100th Street, and as far north as 135th Street (Figure 1.2). The southern and eastern (west Harlem) urban renewal projects would create substantial buffer zones between Morningside Heights and areas considered to be disorderly. The northern urban renewal project would provide Columbia with much-needed additional space in its quest to become one of the largest urban universities in the United States. However, community opposition, lack of money, and governmental change of heart derailed this project. These were proposals devised under the principles of urban renewal that prevailed in the 1950s. By the mid-1960s, they were unattainable. Instead, Columbia and MHI concentrated their efforts on areas located inside Morningside Heights.[25]

THE UPPER WEST SIDE SOUTH OF MORNINGSIDE HEIGHTS

In October of 1955, Mayor Robert F. Wagner released a plan to physically rehabilitate the entire Upper West Side. The plan called for about two hundred city blocks from West 59th to West 125th Street to be designated as an urban renewal area. Under the plan, with the exception of a few spots with religious, educational, cultural, and government institutions as well as existing luxury housing, the entire Upper West Side would be demolished and rebuilt. As it turned out, this plan was found to be too ambitious even by agencies and public officials who had championed urban renewal. After meetings with many city departments and close advisers, Wagner realized that there was too much opposition and skepticism over demolishing most of the Upper West Side. He decided to reduce the scope of the project to twenty city blocks and called this new plan a "pilot project." If the pilot succeeded, then the city would consider expanding it to the rest of the Upper West Side.[26]

This was not the first time in the postwar period that someone proposed to do away with a substantial swath of the Upper West Side. In 1946, real estate developer William Zeckendorf proposed that the area bordered by West 34th, West 79th, Broadway, and the Hudson River become an industrial area with an airport. His plan included the building of thirty-five ten-story buildings for industrial purposes, terminals for buses and trucks, commercial and freight railroad lines, and an airport standing above the buildings and streets on a sizable deck. The proposal was completely unrealistic, but it reflected the problems that the West Side of Manhattan was experiencing as a predominantly residential area.[27]

In the postwar period, the Upper West Side was clearly in decline according to mainstream spatial standards. Real estate development in the Upper West Side, which had abruptly ended in the late 1920s, did not reemerge. Many middle- and upper-class families viewed the area with skepticism and preferred to relocate elsewhere. Affluent populations were being replaced by low-income Puerto Ricans, African Americans, whites, and young people. These populations found nothing wrong with conditions in the Upper West Side; however, the city government and the real estate sector considered these populations to be disorderly and in transition. In general, African Americans, Puerto Ricans, and young people were viewed as unsuitable for one of New York's premier locations.

The 1955 proposal by Wagner to place the entire Upper West Side under urban renewal suggested that there were no urban redevelopment projects in that area, when in fact the opposite was true. The city administration under the guidance of Robert Moses had already taken a direct redevelopment approach toward the Upper West Side south of Morningside Heights. It ended up constructing and subsidizing all kinds of low-, middle-, and upper-income housing in areas where urban blight was supposedly taking hold. The most substantial projects constructed south of Morningside Heights were Manhattantown (1951–1960), which cleared the area bound by Amsterdam Avenue, West 100th Street, West 98th Street, and Central Park West in order to build middle-income housing. The Frederick Douglass Houses (1957–1970) cleared the area bound by Manhattan Avenue, Amsterdam Avenue, West 100th Street, and West 104th Street in order to build low-income housing. The Lincoln Center (1955–1976) razed the area between West 59th and West 70th Streets west of Broadway and Columbus Avenues in order to build the Lincoln Center for the Performing Arts, a campus for Fordham University, upper- and middle-income housing, and a headquarters for the Red Cross. The Columbus Circle area (1952–1957) redeveloped the area bound by Columbus Circle, Broadway, Columbus Avenue, and West 58th and West 60th Streets in order to build a Coliseum and middle-income housing. Added to them was the West Side Urban Renewal Area, which was the twenty-block pilot study, from the originally proposed 200-block aborted proposal that included the area bound by West 87th Street, West 98th Street, Amsterdam Avenue, and Central Park West. This area was designated for the rehabilitation of brownstones and the building of new upper-, middle-, and low-income housing (Figure 1.6).

The urban renewal project of Manhattantown set the tone of the proposals and projects that followed. The original urban renewal proposal

22 Spatial Regulation in New York City

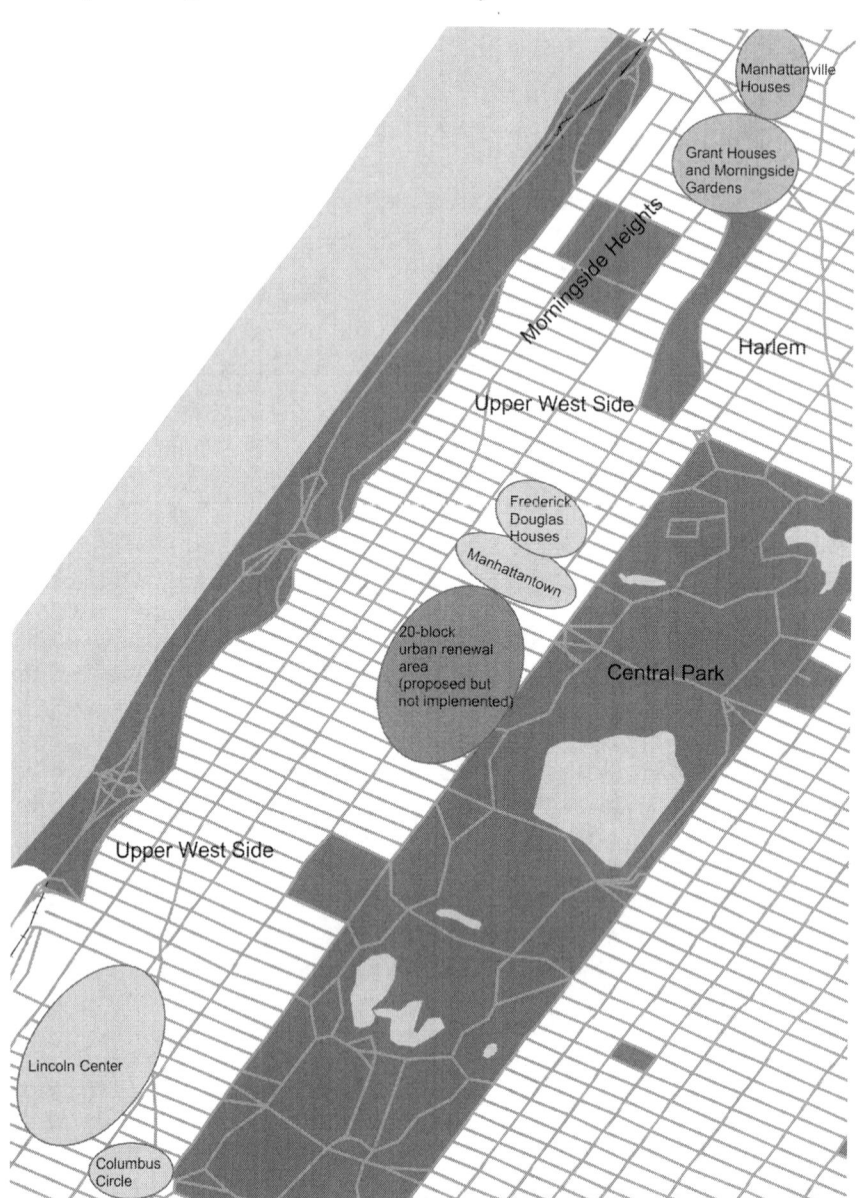

Figure 1.6 Urban renewal areas in the Upper West Side. The boundaries of the projects are not exact. (Map designed by Themis Chronopoulos, 2010.)

for Manhattantown did not make a good case for redevelopment. However, it was accepted by various governmental branches given that during this early period there was almost no scrutiny of the projects that Robert Moses undertook. The proposal described the project as follows:

> Approximately 6 blocks of old, overcrowded and deteriorating tenements and commercial structures will be replaced by modern apartments, off street parking spaces, garage areas, new stores, play areas for children, and grass and trees between in the open spaces between buildings allowing for plenty of light and air. New stores along both sides of Columbus Avenue and the commercial property on Amsterdam Avenue will tend to form a buffer to protect the residential buildings from the noise and dirt of those Avenues. Closing West 98th and West 99th Streets for two blocks on each street eliminates uneconomic street areas and protects the children within the project, also making available more area for landscaping. On the east end of the project we have the natural beautiful boundary of Central Park.[28]

This passage characterized the buildings to be cleared as deteriorating tenements and commercial areas; yet the photographs included in the pamphlet displayed beautiful four- and five-story brownstones and commercial structures that were not any different from other areas not considered slums. To be sure, the photos did not show the inside of these buildings, some of which had been subdivided into SROs, but it was difficult to call the neighborhood a slum. In terms of commercial use, the area included thirty-nine food stores, five drug stores, twelve home furnishing stores, four restaurants, six clothing apparel stores, and six general merchandise stores. It was not so much the character of the stores in the neighborhood that was the problem but the character of their working-class customers. The claim that West 98th and West 99th Streets should be closed and become part of towers with gardens because they were uneconomic was preposterous. The sheer volume of residents and visitors ensured high degrees of business activity for all of these stores.[29]

While the area was overcrowded, what alarmed powerholders even more was the racial makeup of the people living there. The population of the area had increased from 450 residents per net acre of residential use in 1940 to 910 residents per net acre of residential use in 1950. However, this was no reason for clearance of the area; despite overcrowded conditions, the neighborhood seemed to flourish and its overcrowding showed the demand for housing in New York that did not call for transformation into a lower-density development. One statistic that made the greatest impression in the original slum clearance proposal was that of the racial and ethnic makeup of the population; in 1940, 60.3% of the area residents were "native whites," 30.9% "foreign-born whites," and 8.8% "non-whites" while in 1950, 45% were "native whites," 34% "foreign born Spanish speaking people," and 20% "non-whites." These statistics meant that the non-white population, which mostly referred to African Americans, had increased from 8.8% to 20%, and the "foreign-born Spanish-speaking people," which mostly referred to Puerto Ricans, had increased from virtually none to 34%. This made the area majority "non-white." Though low-income whites were also considered to be problematic, the proportion of "non-whites" made the designation of the area as blighted much easier.[30]

Manhattantown was blamed for spreading urban disorder in adjacent Upper West Side neighborhoods because people displaced for the urban renewal project moved only a few blocks over. Walter Fried, a resident of West 94th Street and counsel of the Federal Housing and Home Finance Agency, discovered that conditions in the blocks around Manhattantown declined sharply once clearance in that area commenced. Fried described urban disorder near the Manhattantown clearance site in terms of garbage, overcrowding, houses in disrepair, and the appearance of low-income residents in public space during the summer. He first noticed an increase in the number of garbage cans in front of many of the brownstones, which, he claimed, indicated that a space that had previously been inhabited by a family of five was now occupied by twelve people. Landlords had been subdividing apartments to meet the demand of more people moving in. Fried also noticed buildings seeming "a little seedy, a little run down." In the words of Robert Caro, once the heat of the summer arrived, the changes of the neighborhood became visible:

> Leaning on the windowsills of the brownstones-turned-tenements, sitting on their stoops, crowding the benches on the islands in the middle of Broadway, people, poor people, Negro and Puerto Rican people, people in such numbers that the Broadway benches, long crowded anyway with Jewish grandmothers and grandfathers, were now crowded as never before. It wasn't just the fact that these people didn't have white skin that disturbed the older residents of the West Side; it was that they obviously didn't have money either; it was that so many were obviously drunk or on drugs. And it was that there were so many of them.[31]

Fried realized that the neighborhood was crumbling because of Manhattantown. When he walked nearer to the slum clearance site, conditions worsened. There he began to observe the full impact of urban renewal:

> In little more than a year, the streets immediately adjacent to the development—always poor and predominantly Negro but, previously with well-maintained buildings—had become a slum, a teeming, seething hive of humanity—a place of squalid, run-down, dilapidated tenements so overcrowded that children had to sleep in shifts, of doorways filled with drunks and narcotics addicts and gutters filled with garbage.[32]

The presence of drunks and drug addicts was definitely part of what middle-class people and public officials considered to be part of social disorder. As for the garbage, overcrowding, poverty, appearance in public, and housing deterioration, all of these phenomena were evident in this portion of the Upper West Side.[33]

During the same period, Marya Mannes, who had grown up in the Upper West Side, also lamented changes in the area, though her observations were more hostile to the new populations. Mannes was the daughter of two well-known musicians who founded the distinguished Mannes School of Music. She received a first-class education both at home and in Europe and she belonged to New York's cultural and economic elite. Between 1959 and 1961, she wrote a series of articles about the condition of the Upper West Side that culminated in a book. Mannes wrote:

> "Nice" people still live in these brownstones—many of them refugees from the late 1930's, German and Austrian Jews who are psychiatrists, scholars, musicians, teachers, artisans, unable to afford living elsewhere; together with a number of American professionals, they form islands of decency in a brown sea of squalor. For greater poverty has moved in next to them: Puerto Ricans crowded ten in a room, spilling over the stoops into the streets, forced through no fault of their own to camp indoors as well as out, warming their souls on the television set and blanking out thought with the full volume of radio. And for every mother who keeps her bare room tidy and her children spotless, there are those who shuffle, pregnant, with five children to market; their long hair matted, their high heels worn, gaudy in magenta. And for every clean and cheerful and diligent delivery boy or proficient and pretty manicurist, there are the sullen boys with pomaded ducktails and the tough girls with scornful eyes, hanging around the stoops, chattering roughly. Although the Puerto Ricans are no tougher or rougher, no more sullen or scornful than native New York equivalents here and elsewhere, they have taken over, without will or design but merely by numbers and poverty, those parts of the city doomed by avarice and abandonment to be slums. Their only sin lies in their majority; they outnumber their white neighbors-in-squalor—the perverts, addicts, delinquents, criminals, and failures to infest the city.[34]

Though Mannes in parts of her narrative insisted that Puerto Ricans made the neighborhood disorderly through no fault of their own, she ended up blaming them for it. She juxtaposed "nice people," professionals of a previous generation, with newcomers who were Puerto Rican or Black. Even among the Puerto Ricans she found differences; there were some who tried to do their best under the circumstances, such as the women keeping their rooms clean and their children well groomed; however, they were outnumbered by those who were loud, promiscuous, had too many children, wore gaudy clothing, and did not care about housekeeping or child rearing. Mannes also argued that most of the Upper West Side criminals were Puerto Ricans. In the same article, Mannes continued her litany of complaints about newcomers, which included homosexuals renting apartments previously occupied by "respectable" people, exhibitionists, drunks, and the unemployed. She argued that many Upper West Siders wished that the development of Lincoln Square would "clean up some of the dirt." Mannes was only one of many powerful people complaining about conditions in the Upper West Side and requesting the intervention of the city's political and economic establishments.[35]

Manhattantown proved to be one of the most controversial and corrupt urban renewal undertakings in New York. The first controversy concerned Manhattantown, Inc. becoming a slumlord of the area that it was supposed to redevelop. Although the site was acquired in 1952, under Title I of the Housing Act of 1949, no construction took place for several years. Moses originally predicted that the project would commence in the beginning of 1954; however, this did not happen, and most of the slum clearance area remained intact. In 1954, the U.S. Senate Banking Committee, in its investigations of Federal Housing Administration scandals, discovered that the Manhattantown developers continued to operate the so-called slum area of Manhattantown at a profit by collecting rent without providing any services. Building and fire violations were left unattended. Samuel Caspert, secretary of Manhattantown, Inc., testified that he believed his corporation could continue running the Manhattantown area tenements without addressing existing violations. The second controversy concerned tenant relocation. In his informational brochures, Moses had claimed that displaced Manhattantown tenants would be able to move to the new middle-income development and that others would move either to public housing or to a residence comparable to the housing they lost. However, most people living in the Manhattantown site would never be able to afford the middle-income rents of the new development. In addition, the site sponsors performed a poor job in relocating tenants and Moses used the same public housing vacancies for every urban renewal project that he was involved in. This meant that there were simply not enough public housing apartments for all of the families that were removed. When volunteers of the Women's City Club began to investigate the situation, they discovered that tenants of areas to be cleared were simply removed without any counseling, assistance, or compensation. Most of the existing Manhattantown residents after 1951 were too scared and intimidated by the slum clearance authorities and the developers to do anything about their situations.[36]

In their visits to Manhattantown, the volunteers of the Women's City Club painted a very different picture from that of Moses and conventional city planners. In the introduction of their survey on Manhattantown, a passage about the residents of the area summarizes their predicament:

> Many tenants were reluctant to move. Some had lived in their homes for more than forty years and, although a majority of the dwellings had deteriorated through years of neglect, facilities were still generally

better than those in other areas of the City at comparable rentals. Members of minority groups were greatly troubled, for to them this meant even more intolerable living conditions, more doubling up and more basement and cellar occupancy. Negro and Puerto Rican families especially, who comprised 55% of the families interviewed, considered themselves fortunate to be living where rentals were cheap. Many who had counted on quarters in public housing projects found that they were not eligible for admission. Others who were eligible found their hopes shattered because of a severe cutback in public housing construction. All these and many more problems closed in on the people living on the site of West Park.[37]

Most families were not eligible to move to public housing, and those who were eligible could not move in because of a lack of vacancies. Rents in the area were inexpensive and the housing was not so bad. If forced to move, most residents of Manhattantown would have to relocate to areas with more deteriorated housing and live in the worst parts of a building, such as the basement. These claims challenged Moses's arguments that the people of Manhattantown were being relocated adequately and humanely. The survey also found that the claims that most of the people living in the neighborhood were transients—a quality of people considered to be disorderly—were inaccurate. Only 9% of the people living in the neighborhood were lodgers. There were families that had been in the area for thirty-five, forty years, or even in one case, fifty-four years. The average time spent in the neighborhood was also long: 43% of the families had lived in the same apartment for at least ten years, and 67% of the families for at least five years. The people in the neighborhood knew each other and had established strong social bonds and support networks. For New York standards, this was a stable neighborhood with almost no transients. A majority of the families interviewed also said that they preferred to live in a racially mixed neighborhood. Most families were satisfied with neighborhood facilities, schools, shopping, and transportation. They also argued that schools, shopping, garbage collection, and snow removal were better in nonsegregated neighborhoods such as Manhattantown. Only 9% of the families interviewed wanted to move to the suburbs. Although there were problems with some of the housing, residents took care of their own quarters as much as they could by painting their apartments and making their own repairs. Had property owners provided proper building maintenance, the neighborhood would not have appeared to be in decline.[38]

In 1957, the city government replaced the original developers, and the project was eventually renamed Park West Village. It was completed in 1960 and featured seven towers ranging from seventeen to twenty stories. The buildings were surrounded by gardens, parking lots, and tennis courts. The development was middle income and contained 2,700 apartments. The Aluminum Company of America (ALCOA) was one of the main sponsors of the development. Despite numerous setbacks during the 1950s, Park West Village transformed the neighborhood that it occupied completely since the previous built environment and residents were replaced.[39]

The Columbus Circle urban renewal development was also controversial despite the fact that it did not displace as many families. In 1953, C. Clarence Kaskel, a pawnbroker owning a store in the Columbus Circle area, sued the City of New York for designating the area as a slum and suitable for slum clearance. Kaskel's lawyers argued that the area bounded by Columbus Circle, Broadway, Eighth Avenue, Ninth Avenue, West 58th and West 59th Streets was not "substandard and insanitary," as New York General Municipal Law §72-K required that only slums could be cleared. Kaskel requested that the courts hold a trial that would determine the validity of the conclusion that the Columbus Circle slum clearance area was indeed a slum. The case went all the way up to the Court of Appeals of New York (the state's highest court), where the judges dismissed the appeal by a vote of 5–2. The majority opinion argued that a number of public bodies that included the Triborough Authority, the New York City Planning Commission, and the Board of Estimate of the City of New York determined that the area was a slum and that the court would have to invalidate the decisions of all of these public entities in order make its own determination. Instead, the majority uncritically accepted the notion that the Columbus Circle area was a slum:

> In rounded figures, 20% of the land proposed to be taken is occupied by dwellings all but one of which are more than sixty years old, 7% of the site is covered by hotels and rooming houses, 34% is in parking lots where once there were outmoded buildings, and 39% is occupied by nonresidential structures. Of course, none of the buildings are as noisome or dilapidated as those described in Dickens' novels or Thomas Burke's "Limehouse" stories of the London slums of other days, but there is ample in this record to justify the determination of the city planning commission that a substantial part of the area is "substandard and insanitary" by modern tests, and that the whole 6.32 acres, taken together, may reasonably be considered a single "area" for clearance and redevelopment purposes.[40]

The majority opinion also stated that, since the plaintiff did not claim corruption by city agencies that led the slum clearance decision, the court had no choice but to reject the complaint. The dissent argued that the court unanimously agreed that General Municipal Law §72-K allowed municipal funds to be used to acquire real estate by condemnation, but only for slum clearance and not for any other public purpose. Though the dissent repeatedly characterized the construction of a coliseum in the area as laudable, it questioned the depiction of the area as a slum and argued that what was happening in the Columbus Circle area was not slum clearance:

> It is undisputed that not more than 27.1% of the entire site area is occupied for dwelling purposes of any kind. Thirty-three and eight-tenths per cent of the site area is vacant land devoted to parking lots; even if some of this vacant land was formerly occupied by substandard and insanitary dwellings, there is no need to spend public funds to eliminate them since they have already been eliminated by private capital. Thirty-nine and one-tenth per cent of the site area is occupied by business or commercial buildings which have not been classified as substandard or insanitary by the municipal authorities. It does very well to cite Dickens' novels, or Thomas Burke's "Limehouse" stories of the London slums of other days, but these have nothing to do with condemning the Manufacturers Trust Building in this "slum" area, assessed at $1,500,000, in order to make way for a coliseum—a laudable object, to be sure, but not one whose connection with slum clearance is so clear as to be taken for granted without a trial.[41]

In the case, former chief of planning for the New York City Housing Authority William C. Vladeck testified that only 10% of the tenements in the area could be characterized as "substandard and insanitary" and that only 2% of the entire clearance area could be characterized as a slum. He also reported that it would be a mistake to designate all old law tenements (buildings built before 1901) as substandard since the majority of them were equipped with running water, modern bathroom facilities, adequate ventilation, central heating, and fire-fighting devices and met the requirements of the city's building and fire codes. Vladeck argued that one-third of New York City was composed of such old law tenements.[42]

The Columbus Circle case displayed how Robert Moses could do whatever he wanted in New York when it came to slum clearance projects. The court case showed that Moses was very astute in filing the right papers, addressing all possible legal questions, and getting his proposals through city government bodies. Because much of the area in Columbus Circle was not a slum, acquisition costs were the highest in the nation. The project displaced 243 families and 362 hotel and rooming house residents. In order to meet the residential requirements of Title I, Moses counted the construction area of car parking garages as residential. Once construction began, the project was almost dropped from the federal Title I program because Moses had concealed the office building portion of the project; Mayor Wagner was able to save the project by intervening and convincing the federal government to allow the project to proceed as part of Title I. From the beginning, architectural experts criticized the design of the Columbus Circle Coliseum as pedestrian and ordinary. Once built, Frank Lloyd Wright said that the Coliseum was alright for New York, a city that he disliked, but he hoped that it stayed there. A taxi driver said that "they should have got in an architect to design it for them."[43] Most observers remained bewildered by the design of the Coliseum. Nonetheless, Robert A. M. Stern, Thomas Mellins, and David Fishman, writing decades after the completion of the Coliseum, argued that it represented a "pivotal factor in the rebirth of the Upper West Side, attracting attention to the area as a whole and to the potential of Columbus Circle in particular."[44] In this instance of urban renewal, the number of people displaced was not as high as in the rest of Upper West Side urban renewal sites.

The Lincoln Square urban renewal project is considered to be the crowning achievement of Moses when it comes to Manhattan, in spite of controversy and the fact that it was not completed while Moses was in charge of redevelopment. Conceived and planned by Moses and John D. Rockefeller III, Lincoln Square covered eighteen city blocks and approximately fifty-three acres. Unlike other Upper West Side projects that displaced a high percentage of African Americans and Puerto Ricans—the percentage of nonwhites displaced in Morningside Heights was 65%, in Manhattantown 52%, and in Columbus Circle 54%—in Lincoln Square more than 50% of the displaced people were white working class. After the City Planning Commission declared the area a slum, Moses announced a redevelopment plan that featured the performing arts center, luxury housing, a commercial theater development, a headquarters building for the Red Cross, and a campus for Fordham University. After uproar over the prices of luxury housing, Moses added a middle-income cooperative development, and after disagreements with the federal government, Moses dropped the commercial theater project. In their effort to characterize Lincoln Square as a slum, city officials and other slum clearance proponents used statistics, metaphors, and descriptions influenced by the discourse on physical and social disorder.[45]

The physical disorder of the area was described by Moses's Committee on Slum Clearance. It argued that the great majority of the buildings were old law tenements and that many of them had experienced unsavory conversions from residential use to either businesses or rooming houses. The report found 386 stores located in residential buildings to be deteriorating like the buildings that housed them. It also claimed that the conversion from residential to business use, when combined with the lack of new construction in the area, indicated economic blight. Most of the buildings required major repairs: many of them had heating and plumbing problems, and only a few of the 482 sizable residential structures were worth bringing up to code. Although many of the findings were biased, the report argued that physical decay defined the area. The City Planning Commission concurred with Moses's report, contending that "this area now exercises a blighting and depressing influence on surrounding sections" and that "it is an important factor in the gradual deterioration which has marked Manhattan's Upper West Side, a section

The Betrayal of the Liberal Assumptions of Urban Renewal   31

which by location, accessibility, and amenities is potentially one of the finest in New York City."[46]

Depictions of the social disorder of the area were more startling than those of the physical disorder because they included many value judgments made by people out of tune with New York neighborhoods. City planner Frederick Gutheim, in an article for *Harper's Magazine,* took issue with the diversity of the area:

> Like many "recent" New York slums, the area is a thoroughly mixed one. Though most of the residential buildings are Old Law Tenements built before 1900—and though 96 per cent of them were recently found to be substandard—it is not structural defects that make this a slum. Rather it is the overcongestion, disease, delinquency, crime, and other attendant ills of a cramped and scrambled population. Here are 110 rooming houses, all built before 1902. About a quarter of the nearly 20,000 people living in the area are members of minority groups, mainly Negro and Puerto Rican. The newsstands display *La Prensa* and *El Imparcial* along with the English language press, and *bodegas* are numerous. Heavy trucks pound north and south day and night, on Columbus and Amsterdam Avenues. Crosstown streets are clogged with parked cars. Perhaps the conflicting strands of violence and respectability are succinctly conveyed by the sign on a dry-cleaning shop: "Stain Specialists. Expect Removal of Blood, Ink, Nail Polish, Vomit."[47]

After arguing that the physical defects of the area were not as important as overcrowding and related problems generated by the presence of too many low-income people, Gutheim zeroed on the numbers of minority groups, who did not even constitute the majority of the population. He found diversity to be as disturbing as automobile congestion and Spanish-language newspapers to be as problematic as trucks using the area's major avenues. Russell Bourne, in an article for the *Architectural Forum,* agreed that Lincoln Square was "one of New York City's most traffic-tangled socially polyglot renewal-ready areas."[48] The editors of the *New York Herald Tribune* wrote that the development of the Lincoln Center would bring both the arts and "a whole lost neighborhood . . . back to life."[49]

In the late 1950s, with most substantial urban renewal projects either under way or completed, Moses gave up his position as construction coordinator and the Slum Clearance Committee was disbanded. By that time, the power of Moses was declining because of the controversial elements of his projects, the removal of his allies from scandal-ridden agencies such as the NYCHA, and because Moses himself understood that it would be difficult to continue demolishing neighborhoods. His desire to focus on preparations for the 1962 World's Fair also interfered with his urban renewal projects. Two of Moses's critics, J. Clarence Davies, Jr., and James

Felt, took over as redevelopment officials. Though the new redevelopment officials appeared to be more sensitive than Moses on issues such as the removal of people from urban renewal sites, assumptions that urban disorder was caused by low-income people persisted. In the early 1960s, a plan to redevelop the twenty-block area between West 87th, West 97th, Amsterdam Avenue, and Central Park West, exemplified these assumptions (Figure 1.6). Although the great majority of residents living in this area were low income, the plan called for the construction of 2,800 upper-income apartments, 4,200 middle-income apartments, and only 1,000 low-income apartments. In fact, the plan originally allocated only 400 low-income rent apartments, but it was revised after protests by African American and Puerto Rican groups. Davies, Jr., who was Chairman of the Housing and Redevelopment Board, cautioned that builders of the upper- and middle-income developments had threatened to withdraw from the project if the numbers of low-income apartments increased. Felt, Chairman of the City Planning Commission, concurred with Davies, arguing that it made little sense to build too many low-income apartments in such a desirable area and that the city needed a concentration of upper- and middle-income apartments in order to attract affluent residents there. Most agreed that, if not for such apartments, the city's tax base would further erode because of white flight to the suburbs. As a result, in the early 1960s the plan for this specific twenty-block area and the Upper West Side was that the numerous low-income minority people would be removed, their housing would be altered or destroyed, and private developers would build sizable apartment buildings for white middle- and upper-class people.[50]

What was important in this case was not the urban renewal project, since it was never completed, but the assumptions that guided it. The twenty-block neighborhood in question had become problematic to a great extent in terms of tenancy and urban disorder because other urban renewal projects in the Upper West Side had displaced low-income residents there; one of them was the Manhattantown project. The site was also the home of numerous SROs. The expectation was that upon completion of this project, the Upper West Side would be on its way to rebirth since the rest of the projects that were under way promised the displacement of disorderly people and the removal of substandard buildings. As it turned out, after Moses moved on it became more difficult to complete urban renewal projects in New York. In addition, throughout the nation urban renewal was being discredited as a redevelopment mechanism. Changes in the city administration along with the strengthening of local community boards made the process more arduous in New York. Litigation and a reduction in federal money also played a role.

2 The Failure of Urban Renewal as a Spatial Ordering Apparatus

> We are constantly being told simple-minded lies about order in cities, talked down to in effect, assured that duplication represents order. It is the easiest thing in the world to seize hold of a few forms, give them a regimented regularity, and try to palm this off in the name of order. However, simple regularity and significant systems of functional order are seldom coincident in this world.[1]
>
> —Jane Jacobs

> Designed or planned social order is necessarily schematic; it always ignores essential features of any real, functioning social order. This truth is best illustrated in a work-to-rule strike, which turns on the fact that any production process depends on a host of informal practices and improvisations that could never be codified. By merely following the rules meticulously, the workforce can virtually halt production. In the same fashion, the simplified plans animating rules for, say, a city, a village, or a collective farm were inadequate as a set of instructions for creating a functioning social order. The formal scheme was parasitic on informal processes that, alone, it could not create or maintain. To the degree that the formal scheme made no allowance for these processes or actually suppressed them, it failed both its intended beneficiaries and ultimately its designers as well.[2]
>
> —James Scott

Urban renewal failed on many fronts, though none of these failures was as staggering as its inability to tame disorderly neighborhoods. In New York City, it gradually became obvious that the displacement of targeted "disorderly" people from certain neighborhoods did not solve what was perceived to be a citywide problem. The construction of identical cruciform towers surrounded by gardens (Figure 2.1) did not structure the behavior of low-income people and did not make them conform to middle-class standards. Administrators of Columbia University and other Morningside Heights institutions found that urban renewal and other physical solutions did not even address what they considered to be social disorder. By the late 1960s, the failure of urban renewal as an ordering strategy was almost complete and the way of ordering cities shifted from the physical to the social arena.

Figure 2.1 The Bernard M. Baruch Houses in the Lower East Side. Completed in 1959, the Baruch Houses were the largest NYCHA development in Manhattan. The original development comprised of seventeen towers surrounded by gardens. In 1977, an eighteenth tower was built to house senior citizens (photograph by Themis Chronopoulos, 1997).

This chapter examines the spatial ordering assumptions of urban renewal in theory and practice. In the 1960s, a number of architects and city planners attacked urban renewal as an inhumane method of urban redevelopment that failed to achieve most of its promises. These critiques came from people who felt that proponents of urban renewal did not understand how city neighborhoods worked. Powerholders who had viewed urban renewal as a way to order space and make it conducive to mainstream investment and consumption were also disappointed. As it turned out, the comprehensive remaking of urban space according to modernist city planning was not identical to spatial ordering. By the late 1960s, urban renewal had been discredited and the city government looked for other methods of urban redevelopment.

THE FAILURE OF LE CORBUSIER'S ORDERING ASSUMPTIONS

In 1961, Jane Jacobs in her book *The Death and Life of Great American Cities* advanced the most well-known critique against urban renewal. Jacobs rejected the emphasis on towers with gardens and the infatuation with visual order that had nothing to do with actual order. She singled out

Le Corbusier (1887–1965), the Swiss-born French architect, as the mastermind behind modernist city planning and attacked his theoretical assumptions and their manifestations. In the 1920s, Le Corbusier used conceptions of the garden city in order to advance his idea of the Radiant City; this was an area of twenty-four skyscrapers surrounded by lawns where pedestrians were separated from automobiles and businesses from residences. Jacobs claimed that Le Corbusier's designs based on his theoretical construction of the Radiant City appeared to be orderly when observed from a distance, yet in reality they were superficial and impractical and the type of order that they promised was not based on actual human behavior. By the time that Jacobs was writing her book, modernist city planning had become the new planning orthodoxy around the world and Robert Moses had employed many of its principles in his urban renewal projects.[3]

Le Corbusier did not invent but combined many elements of architectural and planning theory that existed since the Renaissance in order to insist that visual order based on urban design was a major precondition of urban order. Architects have historically assumed a connection between order in architecture and order in society and have aimed to regulate and anticipate social relations through architectural design. Efforts to avoid chaos through the use of architecture were stimulated by the French Revolution. The events of 1789 confirmed the fears of political elites that society was essentially disorderly and unstable and that measures had to be taken so that it would not degenerate into chaos. Experiments that began in prisons following Jeremy Bentham's panopticon were applied to buildings of all kinds of institutions that dealt with potentially dangerous people at the margins of society such as the poor, industrial workers, the young, the insane, and the sick. Thus there was an emphasis on the architectural design of factories, asylums, schools, hospitals, and workhouses so that social disorder could be anticipated, easily controlled, and minimized. Urban planners have also presumed that cities are inherently chaotic and that urban order can be achieved only through meticulous and rational planning that would include the careful arrangement of buildings, streets, and squares. Baron Haussmann's modernization project of Paris in the 1860s, under which overcrowded neighborhoods with narrow streets were torn down and replaced by bourgeois housing and wide boulevards, is a prime example of physical ordering. The older neighborhoods were conducive to revolts because people frequently barricaded the narrow streets for defense purposes during times of upheaval; the new urban design displaced and dispersed many of these rebellious populations while the wide avenues allowed troops to easily march into certain neighborhoods and restore order. This belief in urban design and its taming effects continued to have currency into the twentieth century and Le Corbusier adopted it in his conceptual expositions.[4]

Le Corbusier believed that formal order in city planning was a precondition of efficiency. He advocated that the lessons of standardization and efficiency of Taylorism and Fordism be applied in city planning and building construction. He disliked the disorder that centuries of urban development had created in cities like Paris where overcrowding, vehicular congestion, slums, and an inefficient built environment dominated. Le Corbusier likened Paris with "a vision of Dante's inferno" and proposed that nothing less than its destruction would allow for the achievement of real improvements. In his Plan Voisin, Le Corbusier proposed to bulldoze most of central Paris north of the Seine and replace it with sixty-story cruciform towers arranged in an orthogonal street grid surrounded by open green spaces. In his city plans, he advocated a planned functional segregation so that areas for housing, work, shopping, entertainment, government, and monuments could be all separated. Le Corbusier also wanted to segregate different types of movement for the sake of efficiency; thus, pedestrian traffic would be separated from vehicular traffic and slow-moving vehicles would be required to use different roadways from fast vehicles. Though the great majority of Le Corbusier's planning schemes were never built since they required immense political resolve and financial resources, many of his theoretical doctrines were adopted and applied by planners and architects around the world. He was behind many of the influential manifestos of the Congrés Internationaux d'Architecture Moderne (CIAM). Le Corbusier became known for urban rebuilding in the form of towers surrounded by gardens (Figure 2.2).[5]

Figure 2.2 Cruciform towers of the Baruch Houses. When they were built in 1959, they epitomized the promise of modernist architecture (photograph by Themis Chronopoulos, 1997).

These assumptions of spatial ordering, which are top down and require a powerful government with ample resources to realize them, were embraced by liberals in the United States, who viewed comprehensive urban interventions as a way to provide inexpensive housing for the masses. Liberals favored a strong intervention of the state in society and advocated redistributive politics; urban renewal fulfilled both of these goals since it occurred because of government activism and provided homes to ordinary people. Urban renewal was viewed as a modernization project, and liberals supported such projects as a way of achieving progress and making the government more responsive to the needs of the population. Finally, liberals believed in the production of orderly people and communities through reform; no reform was more important than housing reform. Urban renewal promised to eradicate physical environments that promoted disorder and replace them with environments that structured and reformed the behavior of individuals.[6]

The problem with the implementation of urban renewal in New York City is that it betrayed many of the aspects championed by liberals. While the use of a powerful government with resources was required for the successful completion of projects, most redistributive elements or urban renewal were compromised. Urban renewal emphasized the removal of low-income populations from slums and de-emphasized their humane and adequate relocation to the housing projects replacing the slums. Instead of producing orderly individuals and communities, urban renewal dispersed disorderly populations to other parts of the city, which in turn became disorderly.

In his exposition against "the imperialism of high-modernist, planned social order," James Scott has discussed Le Corbusier's belief that the city plan and its wisdom "sweeps away all social obstacles," which include the voting public, the judiciary, and public officials. Scott shows how Le Corbusier viewed urban design to be a technical solution to urban problems and wanted the plan and the planner to act as dictators. For Le Corbusier, modernist urban design would meet the standards of "discipline, purpose, and order" so that unnecessary physical and human obstacles would no longer interrupt the processes of production and movement. The new planned cities would both aesthetically and functionally represent order in its most austere degree. People in such cities would always know their place whether they worked, stayed at home, consumed, or traveled because urban design would separate all of these activities spatially.[7]

Jane Jacobs rejected Le Corbusier's search for efficiency, geometric austerity, and order and their manifestations in Moses's urban redevelopment projects. She argued that modernist planners did not understand or like cities and that the separation of functions "helped rationalize city rebuilding into the sterile, regimented, empty thing it is." She tried to prove this point by arguing that the leaves of trees falling in the autumn or the interior of an airplane engine appeared to be chaotic to the untrained eye; but for the person who understands these processes, they can be viewed as systems of order. In her own words, "to see complex systems of functional order as order, and not as chaos takes understanding." Jacobs found that the main problem of Le Corbusier and his disciples was that they did not understand city life, and since they concluded that it was chaotic they sought to eliminate it. Jacobs described the idea of towers with gardens as ugly, inhumane, unsafe, and impractical. She glorified the city block with its sidewalks where "intricate minglings of different uses" occurred.[8]

By the time Jacobs was writing her book, the promise of urban order because of modernist urban design had begun to show its limits. Jacobs described an incident in 1958 in the low-income Washington Houses of Manhattan where a resident group placed three Christmas trees with trimmings in various parts of the development. The chief tree was placed in a landscaped central mall and promenade in the middle of the housing project. The two other trees were placed in outer corners where the housing project intersected with the old city and abutted busy streets and avenues. The smaller trees, which were easy to carry in their entirety, were left unharmed and so were their trimmings. The larger, more difficult-to-carry tree was stolen during the first night of its appearance and everything on the tree was also taken. The problem was that the supposedly safe area in the interior of the housing project was shunned by residents because it did not lead anywhere and because it was impractical for congregation purposes. People who wanted to steal the tree could do so without anyone noticing or caring. On the other hand, the smaller trees located near busy streets were much more difficult to steal because of constant pedestrian traffic. Anyone trying to steal the trees or their trimmings on these streets risked observation and intervention by strangers regardless of their residence.[9]

Even before Jacobs began to write against modernist urban design, social reformers had arrived at similar conclusions after surveying public housing developments in East Harlem. Ellen Lurie, who was a volunteer at East Harlem's Union Settlement House, along with other interviewers surveyed residents of the first six buildings of the Washington Houses. To her surprise, Lurie, who had been an avid supporter of public housing, discovered that there were too many problems with the design of these developments. The biggest problem was that the new tenants complained that they felt uprooted from their old neighborhoods and that the new living arrangement of towers with gardens was confusing and monotonous. Lurie's report found that the old neighborhood that was cleared as a slum was functional and that its residents were satisfied. The area was racially diverse and possessed a vibrant commercial and cultural life: "many small cafes, groceries and candy stores could be found along each block; storefronts or tenement basements housed churches, political clubs and poolrooms."[10]

Most of the new residents who moved from another neighborhood expressed their dissatisfaction with the Washington Houses, which ensured

The Failure of Urban Renewal as a Spatial Ordering Apparatus

social isolation because of their anti-urban design. The report about a woman from Manhattantown illustrated this situation:

> Mrs. Becker lived with her husband at Central Park West and 99th Street, on the Manhattantown site. They first moved into that apartment 22 years ago, right after they were married. Childless, she kept on working at a bakery-restaurant around the corner. Now both her apartment and the bakery have been torn down. Although she has lived in Washington Houses for more than a year, she still has her pictures and mirrors on the floor waiting to be hung. The living room looks like she moved in yesterday—or planned to move away tomorrow. She thinks the project is too cold and public a place, her old building was homey and friendly and private. She was terribly frightened once in the elevator when a Puerto Rican man smiled at her. She cried for a long time during the interview; although it was mid-afternoon, she was still in nightclothes, lying on the sofa. She has no friends here, but still goes back to the site to visit her friends in buildings not yet vacated.[11]

The account of Mrs. Becker contained many elements of testimonies that other Washington Houses residents provided. Many of them continued to go back to their old neighborhoods to visit friends and family, attend church services, and shop. For example, Mrs. Minor, who had moved from central Harlem, continued to return to her old neighborhood for many social functions and eventually began to shop in Central Harlem again because she found the supermarket near the Washington Houses to sell food of poor quality. Mrs. Reese continued to attend services in the Salem Methodist Church in Harlem and to send her daughters to Sunday school there after looking for a Methodist church near the Washington Houses and failing to find one. Mr. Payne lamented the absence of theaters with English-language first-run-movies and the lack of decent cafes to take his wife to on Saturday nights. He even claimed that the area surrounding the Washington Houses did not even have a decent luncheonette. Although not all newcomers to Washington Houses disliked the new neighborhood, a great number of them did, and what they missed the most was the secure and socially rich old urban neighborhood. Others complained that with the new living arrangement there were no places in the housing project where they could meet people and make new friends, that there was no sense of pride over the community, and that the new housing was too machinelike and vast to be adopted as their own. Since most of the families selected to live in the housing project had young children, surrounding school facilities and playgrounds became extremely overcrowded. Many of the former single middle-aged residents such as widowers, boarders, transients, aunts, cousins, and uncles were excluded from the project and displaced from the area. While many of these people represented what powerholders considered to be disorderly people, they were essential. Their presence in the streets and in windows made the neighborhood safer. Sometimes they helped neighbors make housing repairs, assisted with babysitting, ran errands, and took care of sick people. In general, they contributed to the neighborhood's well-being.[12]

After researching and observing the changes of East Harlem, Lurie grew critical of urban renewal and modernist urban design. She began to question the new projects that provided cheap rent, fresh air, sunshine, and modern plumbing because they dehumanized everyday existence. She wrote: "now we remembered nostalgically the old Italian band concerts, the colorful street fairs, the rowdy political rallies. With slightly sentimental fuzziness, we longed for the 'cop on the beat who called us all by name', 'the friendly game of stoop ball where everyone knew everyone else', 'the neighborhood grocer' who combined cheap advice with not-so-cheap but always available credit."[13] In the 1960s, voices against the demolition of old but socially rich neighborhoods like Lurie's became louder and began to be taken more seriously. Although there were also other forces working against urban renewal and modernist urban design, these critiques were important.

In 1972, Oscar Newman expanded Jacobs's ideas on the relationship of crime and urban design and placed them into focus. Newman surveyed the incidence of crime in public housing developments in New York City and linked it to their architectural design. One of his original premises was that public housing and its modernist design is not only stigmatized by society, many of its designs also enable crime:

> Society may have contributed to the victimization of project residents by setting off their dwellings, stigmatizing them with ugliness; saying with every status symbol available in the architectural language of culture, that living here is falling short of the human state. However, architecture is not just a matter of style, image, and comfort. Architecture can create encounter and prevent it. Certain kinds of space and spatial layout favor the clandestine activities of criminals. An architect, armed with some understanding of the structure of criminal encounter, can simply avoid providing the space which supports it.[14]

In other words, Newman still believed that urban design could structure the behavior of people; what he rejected was the idea that modernist urban design devised by Le Corbusier and his disciples had the capacity of making people's behavior more orderly. Newman identified a number of physical characteristics that reinforced criminal behavior in low- and middle-income housing projects. He found that most of these projects were sizable and accommodated more than a thousand families. Typically they had apartment towers of more than seven stories each and housed from 150 to 500 families. These sites were superblocks encompassing what used to be four to six city blocks with buildings positioned in a way that defied the former street gridiron. The substantial grounds around the buildings were open to the surrounding streets and were designed as one continuous space that did not belong to any particular building. The lobby of each building faced the interior grounds of the project rather than the street. Finally, each building possessed a number of stairways for evacuation in case of emergency that conformed with building and fire codes; these stairways had their own exits in addition to the main entry. Such housing projects were vulnerable to crime because residents could not adequately survey the nonprivate areas of the development. There were no territorial attributes outside the buildings that they understood because the buildings and their lobbies were disconnected from the street and the surrounding neighborhood and because too many stairways and exits functioned as a way for criminals to move around undetected. Although these physical attributes made these housing projects dangerous, Newman added that there were upper-income projects with similar attributes that had doormen, fences, security guards, and resident superintendents. He found that these expensive additions made the upper-income developments functional.[15]

Jane Jacobs made similar comments in her book in 1961. She argued that many sizable housing developments had begun to surround themselves with fences because security guards were no longer able to control crime. In reality, housing projects differed in their approach. Although almost all of them added some fences in the interior or the exterior of the development, it was still possible to walk into the interior of places like Stuyvesant Town and Morningside Gardens. These developments insisted on using security guards to protect themselves rather than tall fences. Others such as Park West were fenced from the beginning, ensuring that outsiders encountered much more difficulty in entering the developments. This meant that safe middle- and upper-income developments were islands of affluent and safe respectability that were disengaged from the rest of the neighborhood.[16]

In the 1970s, the New York Housing Authority attempted to implement some of Newman's proposals but they proved unsuccessful. At the highrise Bronxdale housing development, Newman subdivided the buildings into clusters in a way that would provide tenant observation of strangers. Each cluster had its own spatial logic with its own playgrounds and sitting areas. Moreover, fences were placed in the interior and exterior of the development. These fences forced residents to take the same path into the center of the superblock before being able to venture into their own apartments. Residents found these fences scary and impractical. Criminals broke the fences and moved about them undetected because tall fences reduced visibility. Eventually, the NYCHA redesigned the fences and introduced lower versions.[17]

According to Nicholas Dagen Bloom, public housing in New York City worked because of a consistency in maintenance and service despite an increase in urban disorder. Though the rise of juvenile delinquency and crime tarnished the image of public housing in New York in the early 1970s, the NYCHA insisted on security innovations, continuous maintenance, and routine service provision to keep life in the housing developments tolerable. This was the main difference between the "failed" public housing projects of Chicago and the "successful" public housing projects of New York. However, by the 1970s many observers who argued that modernist urban design had failed pointed at public housing and disorderly conditions that occurred there.[18]

THE FAILURE OF PHYSICAL SOLUTIONS TO ERADICATE SOCIAL DISORDER IN MORNINGSIDE HEIGHTS

Urban disorder along the boundaries of Morningside Heights was mostly defined in physical terms in need of physical solutions; when it came to the interior of Morningside Heights, the institutions defined urban disorder mainly in social terms that demonized low-income minority groups. The social disorder that institutional employees encountered in Morningside Heights concerned first-hand interactions with people they disliked rather than an abstract fear of slum expansion. It involved a small percentage of "objectionable" people who lived in the neighborhood and who coexisted with middle- and upper-class neighbors rather than a homogeneously "objectionable" community isolated in a chunk of land that could be redeveloped. Social disorder in the absence of slum clearance as a strategy for displacement required other more delicate approaches than wholesale redevelopment. According to Morningside Heights, Inc. (MHI) officials, the problem of social disorder in Morningside Heights arose in the 1930s and 1940s with the proliferation of single-room occupancies (SROs)—single-room housing for low-income people who shared bathroom and kitchen facilities—which allowed poor people to move into the neighborhood. In the 1950s, the problem worsened; a State of New York study showed that while in 1950 whites comprised 88% of the area's population, by 1957, they comprised only 74% and this after the La Salle Street slum had been razed. Furthermore, the study stated that the majority of nonwhites lived in SROs. By that time, about thirty-four SROs operated in Morningside Heights, housing the majority of the neighborhood's Puerto Ricans and African Americans, and more than 4,000 families and individuals. Another twenty-nine SROs located in Manhattan Valley between Cathedral Parkway and West 104th Street interfered with the image that institutional administrators wanted to project. The presence of large numbers of people described by MHI officials and the state as problematic generated an atmosphere of decline and disorder. Although SROs usually housed students, returning veterans, the elderly, and the working poor, their existence was criticized throughout the postwar period.[19]

Morningside Heights' institutional officials drew upon the discourse of disorder so that they could adequately frame the problems that the neighborhood encountered, perceived or otherwise. They spoke of overcrowded

The Failure of Urban Renewal as a Spatial Ordering Apparatus 43

conditions that propagated disease and squalor, street activity that degenerated into crime, and groups that had no place in a respectable community. In 1950, T. L. Hungate, Controller of Teachers College and Chairman of the MHI Subcommittee on Public Safety, reported:

> Some years ago it was possible to walk down Amsterdam or on 120th Street and see an occasional automobile parked on the street, and meet a few people within the course of the block's walk. Today the streets are packed with parked cars, often double parked, and you jostle the crowds on the street. I am told there are apartment houses in which small apartments are as a general rule occupied by two families. I have heard of 14 persons living in a four room apartment—and this is within short walking distance from my office. And with this overcrowding is associated a host of evils—dirt, disease, and lawlessness.[20]

This depiction lamented the loss of exclusivity that Morningside Heights had projected in the past and the shock that disorderly crowds lived so close to such prestigious institutions. Alluding to the cold war climate of the period and the role that Morningside institutions played, Joel Schwartz has written: "Those who devoted themselves to postwar Protestant unity, the international monetary system, and Free World responsibilities chafed at the shabby facilities that Morningside Heights provided their efforts."[21]

Stanley Salmen, Executive Director of MHI and Planner of Columbia University, further outlined the behavioral problems posed by "undesirables" in Morningside Heights. In 1961 he wrote:

> These houses, also, are the houses of many who are drunk on the sidewalks and benches, who play cards on the stoops, who call from sidewalk to fifth floor windows, who clutter the streets with tons of rubbish of all kinds and who congregate in noisy groups until late at night. It is the children of these families who learn to dismantle cars, snatch pocket books, to dominate a street with games which lead to drinking and to gambling among the spectators and participants. They form groups around an older adolescent, giving him an audience and other means to establish a place in the sun in relation to some other leader. Some of these children start to use narcotics by the time they are twelve and start extorting money from other children and stealing by the age of seven.[22]

Salmen resorted to clichés such as gambling, gangs, drug use, environmental pollution, and public drinking because at the time he led Columbia's campaign against SROs located in the neighborhood. In addition, many of the activities he described such as playing cards on stoops or children congregating in the street represented behavior that people who lived in low-income neighborhoods found routine. However, institutional administrators decided that such activities ruined the middle-class character of their neighborhood and that sharing the public space of Morningside Heights was unacceptable. Moreover, one could only imagine the reactions of parents of prospective Columbia students or wealthy alumni visiting Columbia and encountering poor residents at the corner of Broadway and 116th Street, in Riverside Park, or around the Cathedral of St. John the Divine.

A major problem that the "undesirables" embodied was their constant presence in public space, a characteristic that did not conform with middle- and upper-class behavioral patterns. Since they often lived in overcrowded quarters such as single rooms, whenever the weather allowed, Blacks and Latinos spent their time in the streets making the environment disorderly "through stick-ball, group drinking, and gambling with cards."[23] Furthermore, even when the weather did not allow their appearance in public, their presence in the neighborhood could be felt by the number of garbage cans placed in the sidewalk, the number of children overcrowding the area's public schools, and the presence of commercial establishments that catered to them specifically.

In various stages of the postwar era, Morningside institutions followed the prescription of the Progressives, holding that social workers should deal with social disorder by paying particular attention to the children, the most likely segment of the population to achieve middle-class status. As a result, the longest-lasting social program implemented between the late 1940s and the late 1960s targeted boys from Morningside Heights and west Harlem and encouraged their involvement in athletic activities coordinated by Columbia. However, this program had limited effects, and as juvenile crime statistics rose during the 1960s, Columbia administrators realized that they lacked the money and capacity to provide comprehensive social services to their neighbors.[24]

Losing faith in the ability of social workers to remedy social disorder, MHI officials turned to law enforcement. In order to counter the problems that "undesirables" caused in the community, MHI worked closely with the local police precinct to beef up institutional security and establish citizens' patrol units. After requests by MHI for better police protection, in 1956 the local government increased the police force of the 24th Precinct from 172 to 430 officers, many of whom could, at the suggestion of area institutions, enforce the local sanitary code and make the neighborhood appear more orderly. Four years later, the city created Precinct 26 after pressure wielded by Morningside institutions. Although the new precinct ran between West 110th and West 143rd streets, at the time, it was "widely regarded as a private platoon of the institutional complex, sensitive both to its needs and its demands."[25] In December of 1960, the New York Police Department deployed forty men from the citywide Tactical Patrol Force, usually assigned in "major trouble spots in the City," to Morningside Heights to work independently of the police precinct, even though the police force admitted that the area around Columbia lacked a high crime rate. In fact,

The Failure of Urban Renewal as a Spatial Ordering Apparatus   45

throughout this period, Morningside Heights remained one of the four safest neighborhoods in Manhattan. Security guards employed by the various institutions and the Morningside Street Patrol established by MHI in 1961 joined these officers, making the area well policed. In 1964, after complaints by the institutions, the local police precinct announced that some of its officers would patrol the one block of the SRO Bryn Mawr. However, all of these measures made uniformed presence around the Heights too noticeable. As MHI officials eventually admitted, "the constant necessity for police to control this rootless population gives the impression of a police state, which is unattractive to students, faculty and responsible citizens."[26] Even the control of the "undesirables" through law enforcement and security measures posed problems for the image of the community.[27]

Besides the image problem, police action could only regulate objectionable residents, not remove them from the area. By the end of the 1950s, Columbia decided to eliminate poor residents from the neighborhood through a campaign against SROs that would involve the muscle of the local government. The City of New York undertook this campaign in late 1958 when Mayor Wagner inaugurated "crash enforcement" by city inspectors on Morningside Heights SROs. In less than two months, inspectors fined eleven SRO owners for building, code, and occupancy violations for approximately $10,000 in fines. Because of this "crash enforcement," most SROs began to comply with city codes and kept their fines for violations to a minimum, which was not exactly what MHI officials had in mind. The institutions of the area wanted to eliminate SROs, not make them comply with building and sanitary codes.[28]

During the "crash enforcement" campaign, Columbia administrators concluded that full control of the university's surrounding environment required them to buy as many buildings as possible, even if Columbia had no immediate use for them. Until 1934 the university owned only twenty-seven off-campus buildings in the Heights. Between 1934 and 1954 the university bought another twenty-two buildings, which is not necessarily an extreme number for a period of two decades. However, after 1954 acquisitions accelerated rapidly, often for no other reason than to evict people who made the environment disorderly. Between 1955 and 1959 Columbia acquired eighteen new buildings, another fifty-three between 1960 and 1964, and another sixty-two between 1965 and 1968. The continuous purchases of buildings by Columbia resulted in the dislocation of thousands of people from the area. Morningside Heights' institutions worked to eradicate disorder through displacement. Whether MHI used slum clearance in order to fortify the neighborhood's boundaries or Columbia bought up buildings in order to evict "undesirables," the goal had been to displace low-income African Americans and Puerto Ricans from the neighborhood by attacking their housing.[29]

From the very beginning of redevelopment in the area, many people did not simply capitulate to the wishes of Morningside powerholders. Every step along the way, the less affluent neighbors of the institutions resisted. Typically, oppositional actions only delayed the projects that Morningside institutions had in mind, but there were times when protest actions derailed Columbia and MHI projects. After the completion of Morningside Gardens and the General Grant Houses, the spatial battleground shifted from the fringes to the interior of Morningside Heights and involved Columbia University against SRO residents and other apartment building tenants. Lacking the social movement organization that would allow for political mobilizations and encountering extreme hostility from the mass media and the area's institutions, SRO residents used everyday forms of resistance. These actions angered Columbia officials, who increased evictions and became convinced that the removal of SRO residents from the area would reestablish order.

SRO residents refused to cooperate with Columbia employees and were unwilling to move out of their apartments. To retaliate, Columbia workers sealed the dumbwaiters so that garbage had to be carried out in person. If the building had elevators, they were allowed to break down. Columbia also resorted to measures such as withholding heat during the winter and turning it on full blast during the summer. If all of these actions failed, but the eviction paperwork had been completed, Columbia, with the assistance of the authorities, physically removed "undesirables" from the buildings. Even then, SRO tenants would sneak back into their rooms. Columbia employees painted large Xs on the windows of rooms to be vacated and boarded up windows once the tenant had been forced out. A variant of this strategy entailed the plugging of keyholes with wax in the hope that residents would be unable to enter their apartments. Columbia workers also showed up in apartments and threatened residents or used police officers to harass tenants and search their apartments in the hope of finding something illegal. Sometimes, all of these strategies failed. If so, Columbia offered SRO tenants relocation costs. Although by middle-class standards the relocation compensations appeared minuscule, for some low-income SRO residents the idea of receiving $50 or $80 to move to a room eight blocks south proved attractive.[30]

The battle between tenant groups and Columbia intensified in the 1960s. A report written by the SRO Committee of the Morningside Renewal Council (an organization representing about sixty community groups united by their concern over Columbia redevelopment activities) affirmed the complaints of residents who lived in buildings that had been recently bought by the university. According to the report:

> The members of the committee were disturbed by the conditions they found in this Columbia-owned building. Upon our first visit, we found tenants without heat and hot water, without properly functioning elevators, with broken windows and plaster in public and private areas, with unlocked doors . . . with rat and roach infestation, with

improper removal of refuse, and with other conditions hazardous to health and safety.[31]

Although many people who lived in these buildings decided to move, those who decided to stay were brought to court for dubious reasons. For example, the families of Walter Hedges and George Stevenson were brought to court for having children under sixteen in single rooms. The courts dismissed the charges since these families occupied apartments with more than one room. However, the families had to pay legal fees out of their own pockets. The great majority of people taken to court were African Americans. According to Morningsiders United, "it is no coincidence that persons suffering this kind of harassment are Negroes."[32]

As evictions proceeded, west Harlem residents began to join Morningside Heights residents in actions that showed their resentment toward Columbia. In various cases, they attacked Columbia professors and expressed their hatred for "white men." Many of these incidents were not independent muggings; they reflected a growing militancy by African American and Puerto Rican youths who lived near Morningside Heights. In a report on the matter, MHI executive director Edward V. Solomon wrote that "'Five Percenters' who believe that they must "Kill Whitey" and that they, the blood brothers, will not die are alarmingly numerous and are growing in number and militancy. Some 300 are said to live in St. Nicholas Houses, 200 in Grant Houses. Our Stone Gym is a target. Threatening signs have been carved on the doors of the Center."[33] The residents of these housing projects that the 1950s institutional powerholders viewed as pillars of stability had turned into throngs of hostility.[34]

These actions reflected the increasing dissatisfaction of African Americans with conditions in New York City. In the late 1940s and 1950s, state and federal courts struck down discriminatory statutes and the New York state and city governments passed legislation that prohibited racial discrimination in housing and the workplace. However, city and state officials were unable to desegregate schools, improve municipal services in minority neighborhoods, incorporate African Americans and Latinos in New York's housing market, and change the way that the police department dealt with a demographically changing city. In 1964, when Columbia officials began to notice a hostile west Harlem, Black leaders threatened to block the roads leading to the World's Fair in order to attract nationwide attention to the problems that New York's African American population faced. In July of that year, a four-day riot erupted in Harlem after a policeman killed a Black teenager. The riot displayed the growing frustration and political radicalization of Harlem residents during the period.[35]

Gradually, Columbia administrators, exasperated by the inability of their employees to remove "undesirables" from the area quickly enough, adopted a harder line. Columbia fired Bertram Weinert, Director of Neighborhood Services, because he failed to remove tenants in a timely fashion.

According to Columbia Vice President Lawrence Chamberlain, Weinert was fired "because he wasn't doing his job." Chamberlain added that "we want to be fair and humane . . . but we do have to move people out and start demolition inside of our deadlines."[36] Weinert's replacement, Ronald Golden, "placed more emphasis on meeting deadlines."[37] The harder line became reflected by more inflammatory statements made by MHI and Columbia officials with regard to "undesirables." For example, Stanley Salmen, who served as Executive Director of MHI and Columbia's Coordinator of Planning, claimed that the university was "looking for a community where the faculty can talk to people like themselves. We don't want a dirty group."[38] In 1965, in a tumultuous Board of Estimate Meeting, Columbia Provost Jacques Barzun justified the plan of displacing "undesirables" from Morningside Heights and of creating buffer zones in west Harlem by saying that Columbia trained the leaders of tomorrow and that "they must not be subjected to an environment that requires the perpetual qui vive of a paratrooper in enemy country."[39] Barzun added that Morningside Heights had been besieged by "transient, foot-loose or unhappily disturbed people."[40] All of these statements and actions represented public relations disasters and angered nearby Harlem residents, who began to consider Columbia an enemy of their community.

In the early 1960s, while acts of resistance abounded in Morningside Heights, political mobilizations began to reemerge. In 1962, James Farmer, National Director of the Congress of Racial Equality (CORE), accused Columbia of systematically excluding Blacks from its newly acquired housing in a demonstration against the University of Chicago, thus giving the issue nationwide attention. In 1963, tenant groups began to picket the house of Columbia's president, Grayson Kirk. Eventually, community groups also picketed Columbia's campus at large in order to publicize their claims. In 1964, demonstrators staged anti-Columbia neighborhood rallies at Riverside Church and elsewhere, while graffiti with messages that attacked Columbia began to appear in appropriated buildings. After 1964, protest actions became a frequent occurrence.[41]

The continuous uproar over Columbia evictions attracted the attention of elected political leaders, mainstream political organizations, and public commissions, though all proved unable to reverse the process. In 1961, the New York State Commission Against Discrimination began to investigate charges that Columbia was targeting the Puerto Rican and African American populations of the area. In 1964, the district leader of the Mahattanville Reform Democratic Club charged that "it hardly seems a coincidence that while most of the residents of Morningside Heights are not Negro or of Puerto Rican descent, most of the buildings that Columbia has recently vacated or demolished have contained a preponderance of these minority groups."[42] In 1965, the New York City Commission on Human Rights sent a letter to Columbia calling on the school to abandon its "reliance on tenant removal as a solution to social problems incidental to its expansion."[43]

During the same year, Manhattan Borough President Constance B. Motley became outraged when she found out that despite a Board of Estimate resolution that limited Morningside Heights institutional expansion only to projects already announced, Columbia had just evicted another 350 tenants from four SROs that had not been included previously in any expansion plans. Columbia employees continued to evict people from their homes and take advantage of the ambivalence with which the local and the state government regarded SRO residents. Columbia's Office of Neighborhood Services removed about 7,500 people from their homes in Morningside Heights during the 1960s. Most of these people had to move because of their race and class.[44]

The plans of MHI and Columbia to expand their redevelopment activities into Harlem and the previous removals of African Americans from Morningside Heights brought the university and the African American community onto a collision course. Area residents founded the West Harlem Community Organization in order to collectively face their predicament. The Columbia chapter of CORE began to organize tenants in the area bounded by West 104th Street, West 108th Street, and Central Park in order to effectively respond to the renovation planned for their neighborhood. After the inflammatory remarks made by Barzun at the Board of Estimate meeting, a group of Harlem residents invaded his office and sought a public apology. Barzun apologized and claimed that he wanted to work with the West Harlem Community Organization. However, the damage to the relationship between Columbia and its neighbors could not be undone.[45]

The issue that caused a continuous campaign against Columbia by the Harlem community and by Columbia students and faculty was the construction of a quasisegregated gymnasium in Morningside Park (Figure 1.2). Under the agreement with the State of New York, Columbia would lease the air rights of 2.12 acres of Morningside Park for a nominal fee in order to raise a sizable gymnasium for the university and the community of Harlem. Columbia's eight-floor gymnasium would rest on top of a two-story structure built by the university for children of the community. Although the two gymnasiums, one for the community and one for the university, would be located in the same building, there would be no access from one to the other, and each would have a different entrance. Columbia's entrance would be at the top of the park, while Harlem's entrance would be at the other side of the building at the bottom of the park. This meant that Columbia students, faculty, and administration would never encounter the residents from Harlem in the gymnasium since the two sites would be completely separate. Moreover, the community portion of the gymnasium would be available only to youngsters who would be supervised by Columbia staff. The 1965 election of John V. Lindsay as mayor encouraged African Americans from Harlem as well as Columbia students to oppose the construction of the gymnasium in Morningside Heights. His

Parks Commissioner, Thomas P. F. Hoving, announced that he was upset by Columbia's plans and also urged the community to oppose them. Hoving added that by giving two floors out of ten to Harlem residents, Columbia claimed to be donating 20% of the new gymnasium to the community. However, the cliff on the park slanted sharply, making the two bottom floors the smallest in the building, amounting to 12% of the total space. Hoving's statements illustrated the potential alliance between a member of the elite and ordinary people. It proved enough to mobilize Harlem residents and their elected representatives, mainly Basil Patterson, Percy Sutton, and Charles Rangel, who also began to speak out against the park and Columbia's designs for spatial takeover.[46]

Unlike some Harlem politicians who believed that the project could not be stopped and tried only to obtain additional space for community use, neighborhood organizations continued to oppose Columbia's plans. Dwight C. Smith, chair of the Morningside Renewal Council, embarked on a letter-writing campaign that asked the mayor, the Manhattan borough president, and various other politicians to reconsider the agreement they had made with Columbia. Smith also sent letters to local newspapers, trying to make the council's opposition as public as possible. Community organizations from Morningside Heights and west Harlem held numerous meetings to plan oppositional strategies. Between 1966 and 1968, a large number of people became involved in a social movement that opposed not only the construction of a Columbia gym in Morningside Park but also any other spatial plan of Columbia.[47]

After two years of popular opposition, Columbia went ahead and began construction in 1968. That spring, Columbia students who were angered and disappointed with their administration on a number of issues, including the gymnasium affair, began to occupy campus buildings. The conflict that ensued with the police, who on at least two occasions used excessive force inside the campus and chased bystanders such as administrators up and down Broadway, generated a chaotic atmosphere. African American students occupied Hamilton Hall with various demands, including a general opposition to the construction of the gym in Morningside Park. Continuous marches of Harlem residents to the campus, led by radical leaders such as H. Rap Brown and Stokely Carmichael, clashes between SDS students and the police, and publicity of these events made the situation untenable and forced administrators to end the spring semester early.[48]

Having lost confidence in his leadership and with the fear that popular contention would escalate in the fall, in August of 1968, Grayson Kirk, (the president of Columbia since 1951 and architect of Columbia's spatial wars in upper Manhattan), announced his early retirement. The trustees of the university named Andrew Cordier, Dean of the School of International Affairs and a former Under Secretary in the United Nations, as interim president because of his reputation as a conciliator. Cordier took his role seriously and worked toward a reconciliation of the university with

The Failure of Urban Renewal as a Spatial Ordering Apparatus 51

the community as well as a reconciliation of the warring functions inside Columbia with a firm hand uncharacteristic of an interim president. The embattled trustees sided with Cordier since political mobilizations and hit-and-run tactics against the university continued from both Columbia students and residents of Harlem until 1970.[49]

The greatest dilemma faced by the Cordier Administration had to do with Columbia's future spatial strategies. Although Columbia had fortified the boundaries of Morningside Heights and displaced most of the minority residents from the neighborhood, its dream to expand into Manhattanville and create buffer zones beyond the area's boundaries had been largely unrealized. Cordier had to decide what to do with the elements of the already planned *Morningside General Neighborhood Renewal Plan*, which rendered Columbia a major developer of the area north of 125th Street (Figure 1.2). The area immediately north of Morningside Heights and west of Broadway that Columbia eyed for expansion and renewal was one of the oldest heavy industrial and commercial areas in Northern Manhattan. It had various names such as Manhattanville West, Piers Area, or West Harlem Market. Exclusive of streets, the area occupied a bit more than nineteen acres and was known for a meat market located there. In the late 1960s, the 111 active firms in the area employed about 5,395 people—half of them were white while the other half were African American and Puerto Rican. The renewal plan called for the construction of substantial high-rise housing, office space, research laboratories, a marina, parking facilities, and open recreational spaces. The plan suggested that the area would be shared with noninstitutional users and residents and it focused on the creation of a middle-class commercial, institutional, and recreational space (Figure 2.3). The *Morningside General Renewal Plan* reserved very little space for low-income people. Harlem organizations such as the Architects' Renewal Committee in Harlem, Inc., as well as national organizations such as the Urban League criticized the plan because it bypassed community consultation altogether and was insensitive to the needs of Central Harlem residents. In the end, Cordier, understanding the potential opposition to this plan and realizing that Columbia did not have the funds to actually contribute to this project, abandoned the proposal. Columbia's cancellation of the Manhattanville expansion coincided with the decline of urban renewal. It was not only controversy and lack of funds but the disappearance of Robert Moses from urban renewal projects and an overall skepticism toward modernist urban design and its effects that halted the plan. Moreover, Columbia's plan required substantial land takeover under the principles of eminent domain. Conflict with community organizations in Harlem and Manhattanville would potentially be more acrimonious than the discord that had ensued over Morningside Park.[50]

The Cordier Administration also reconsidered the construction of the gymnasium at Morningside Park. Because community and student opposition continued, in February of 1969 Cordier decided to withdraw from

Figure 2.3 Part of the Manhattanville area that Columbia University eyed for expansion in the 1960s. This expansion plan has recently been revived (photograph by Themis Chronopoulos, 2006).

the project in a manner that would save face for the university. He sent a poll to two hundred community and political leaders in Harlem that asked whether the university should proceed with the building of the gymnasium. As expected, the poll produced overwhelmingly negative results. Cordier recommended to the trustees that construction of the gymnasium should be abandoned in deference to Harlem objections. The trustees voted to terminate the project and to restore the portion of the park where excavation had taken place. In another conciliatory move, in November 1968, Columbia hired renowned architect I. M. Pei as its first master planner in more than seventy years and asked him to come up with a growth plan that would no longer displace the university's neighbors. Pei completed his study in 1969 and argued that Columbia could satisfy its spatial needs without going beyond the university's boundaries. His proposal called for an underground gymnasium and other facilities below South Field and for two high-rises at the eastern and western ends of the South Field. According to Pei, by building above and below ground, Columbia would no longer need to engage in spatial takeover.[51]

By the time that William G. McGill became its tenth president in 1970, Columbia had withdrawn from most of its controversial spatial endeavors because of the mounting pressure from oppositional groups in the area against the university through political mobilizations and everyday forms of resistance. Columbia emerged from this conflict injured in public opinion and in its relations with the surrounding communities. Still, one would think that because Columbia transformed Morningside Heights into a middle-class neighborhood, the university would have been able to control its immediate environment after 1968. That was not the case. Throughout the quarter century that followed World War II, Columbia University led efforts to stem the decline of Morningside Heights by removing elements that made its space disorderly. Columbia and MHI administrators believed that if the redevelopment efforts succeeded, Morningside Heights would once again become one of the most desirable neighborhoods in New York City because of the cultural capital that Columbia and the rest of the institutions of the area offered. However, the results of these efforts were mixed at best.

Columbia, in its quest to "improve" Morningside Heights, relied on two types of displacement: first, targeting "undesirables" who lived in Morningside Heights and second, focusing on "undesirables" who used the space of Morningside Heights but lived elsewhere. Columbia administrators generally believed that the first type of displacement was their priority, since unwanted people who lived in Morningside Heights not only used its space but also had a certain right to do so. Furthermore, unlike poor people who lived elsewhere, Morningsiders sent their children to the area's schools, made the buildings in which they lived fall into disrepair, and made the neighborhood seem disorderly because of their numbers, poverty, and way of life. If Columbia could displace minorities who lived in Morningside Heights, then the police and private security guards who regulated the use of public space in the neighborhood would have an easier time sweeping away "questionable characters" who visited Morningside Heights. If the neighborhood became predominantly middle and upper class, poor visitors would stand out; because they would no longer live there, they would have no business being there. This calculation proved incorrect.

By the 1970s, Morningside Heights powerholders faced the following paradox: their neighborhood had been transformed into a middle-class enclave, yet its public space and image remained disorderly. The hope of simply exporting urban disorder elsewhere had failed. Columbia administrators failed to understand that low-income African Americans and Latinos had become too numerous in the areas neighboring Morningside Heights and in New York City in general to simply disappear from public space altogether. Another problem concerned crime. In the late 1960s, crime skyrocketed in New York and Morningside Heights, despite its partial fortification and conversion into a middle-class neighborhood, could not escape. In 1972, the high-profile robbery-murder three blocks away from the campus of Wolfgang G. Friedmann, a Columbia Professor of international law, received disproportionate attention from the press and showed that no one was immune from crime. Other press stories, such as the one in which a blind woman who ran a candy store in Morningside Heights was robbed five times in six months, further damaged the image of the neighborhood. By September of 1973, on the first day of registration for classes for the fall semester, Mayor Lindsay vowed to make Morningside Heights viable for its prestigious institutions by providing additional police protection. The police might have reduced criminal activity in the neighborhood but could not prevent low-income residents from surrounding neighborhoods from using the public space of Morningside Heights. Many of the people displaced from Morningside Heights had moved to west Harlem and Manhattan Valley, which maintained their SROs, and many former residents showed an extraordinary affinity for the parks, streets, and playgrounds of Morningside Heights. Moreover, people from west Harlem continued to go through Morningside Park to the Broadway subway line.[52]

Morningside Park continued to be a problem for Columbia University in the 1970s and the 1980s. Despite its promise, the university did not restore the portion of the park that it had excavated for the gymnasium. When the city encountered a fiscal crisis, the park remained neglected, representing another reminder of the decline of both Morningside Heights and New York City. In 1975, crime in the park persisted and the Morningside Area Alliance (MHI with a new name but fewer powers) requested that the New York Transit Authority post signs in several Broadway IRT station platforms warning passengers that if they stayed on the express trains they would end up in Harlem and not in Morningside Heights. Many confused subway riders had to walk to Columbia westward through a portion of Harlem and through Morningside Park. As Morningside Renewal Alliance officials explained, nineteen out of twenty-one attack victims in the park during that period had taken the wrong train uptown. In a related move in 1975, the institutions placed uniformed guards on top of Morningside Park to look down the park. Eugene McDermott, an ex-police officer and executive director of the Morningside Renewal Alliance, claimed that he allowed only his captain and himself to enter the park unarmed. Publicity over these incidents made outsiders wonder how safe they could be in Morningside Heights.[53]

The residents of the housing developments of Morningside Gardens and the General Grant Houses could not escape spatial conflict either. During hot summers, General Grant tenants could easily observe that apartments in Morningside Gardens had been equipped with terraces and outlets for air conditioners. The grass in Morningside Gardens remained well maintained while the green spaces in the Grant Houses disappeared. The Grant Houses were underfunded. The lack of contact between residents of the two projects did not help. Morningside Gardens residents preferred private schools for their children, something that made for even less interaction and greater bitterness between the two sides. By the 1970s, Morningside Gardens homeowners feared their General Grant neighbors and kept away from them; they were surprised by the hostility that Black children showed them. Grant renters called Morningside Gardens "Whitey's Hideaway."

The Failure of Urban Renewal as a Spatial Ordering Apparatus 55

Their children would sneak into Morningside Gardens and shoot at windows with BB guns and slash the tires of automobiles.[54]

Finally, Manhattan Valley, the neighborhood immediately south of Morningside Heights, became the home of African American and Latino housing refugees from adjacent areas that had been redeveloped. In reaction, middle-class residents of Manhattan Valley hired private guards to patrol the neighborhood, bought dogs to guard their homes, and turned their dwellings into "little private fortresses." By the mid-1970s, building abandonment by landlords and tenants became so widespread in Manhattan Valley that it became known as "a miniature South Bronx" with more than one hundred buildings abandoned. For Columbia, the situation in Manhattan Valley was disastrous.[55]

Beginning in 1972, Columbia entered a fiscal crisis precipitated by continuous budget shortfalls that had begun in 1966. Despite a nationwide crisis in higher education, many of the extra expenditures had to do with building acquisitions. At the same time, many wealthy alumni disturbed by the uprising of 1968 had become unwilling to donate money to Columbia. Between 1970 and 1980, the university decreased its faculty and spent $100 million of its endowment for operating costs. Because of deferred maintenance, in 1979 a cornice of a Columbia building fell and killed a Barnard student, and city inspectors fined Columbia for numerous building code violations. In 1980, an article in the *New York Times* claimed that many undergraduates attended Columbia only because they could not get into a better school, and that some of them intended to get straight As at Columbia and transfer to another Ivy League. Clearly, the spatial warfare of the 1950s and the 1960s had left the institution wounded.[56]

By the 1970s, it became clear that urban decline affected many sectors of New York, and even institutions like Columbia University suffered. What happened in previous decades affected how Columbia and Morningside Heights were able to cope with the urban decline. The distrust that developed between Columbia and its neighbors during the 1950s and the 1960s prevented the two sides from banding together to face their urban predicament. After 1968, Columbia and Harlem entered a period of noncooperation that lasted for at least three decades. Although Morningside Heights residents fared better than their neighbors because Morningside residents received better public services and security than Harlem residents, life became very difficult around Columbia University. Columbia's many attempts and failures proved that in New York City, complete withdrawal from social problems and complete spatial separation was impossible.

THE DECLINE OF GRAND-SCALE PHYSICAL SOLUTIONS

In the 1960s as physical solutions were compromised, the city government attempted to revive them in a modified form. During the John V. Lindsay

Administration (1966–1973), there were efforts to make urban redevelopment less controversial and more responsive to people's needs; to that end, there was a serious attempt to reform the way that the city government made land use and redevelopment decisions. The Lindsay Administration decided to adopt a comprehensive master plan for the city that would structure future redevelopment. The idea of a comprehensive plan was not new; Rexford Tugwell, the first chairman of the New York City Planning Commission, had proposed the development of such a comprehensive plan in 1938. The City Planning Commission drafted a master plan in 1940, and ideas of its utility continued to surface in the years that followed. However, Robert Moses opposed these master plans because he believed that they were unworkable and interfered with real urban planning. Moses never followed a master plan; he just pursued projects according to funding sources, the needs of private developers, and his own political requirements.[57]

In the 1960s, the federal government required New York to submit a comprehensive master plan before receiving any additional housing and urban renewal subsidies. The City Planning Commission conformed in 1969 and released a massive six-volume document entitled *Plan for New York City*. The plan was developed between 1964 and 1969 and was written by William H. Whyte. The *Plan for New York City* rejected the modernist urban renewal methods of Le Corbusier and Moses, the top-down approaches of urban redevelopment, and the separation of functions in urban space so that commercial, residential, and manufacturing areas existed separately. Though it retained some modernist ideas of urban planning, the plan advocated the inclusion of communities in urban planning, the practice of incremental redevelopment, and the respect of existing buildings and neighborhood uses. Implicit in the plan was an admission that physical solutions would not solve all of the city's problems and that education, welfare, job training, and social outreach would be needed in order to make the city more livable.[58]

The way that physical solutions were proposed in the *Plan for New York City* did not seem very effective in tackling what was considered to be urban disorder. Absent from these proposals was the removal of "undesirables" from certain neighborhoods, the ordering of people through urban design, the creation of restrictive zoning, and the elimination of physical disorder through its destruction. There were a few order-maintenance and disorder-eradication elements implied in the new proposals, but no one could believe that these new benevolent ways of rebuilding the city would achieve what Moses with extreme methods had failed to accomplish. The way that urban disorder was defined as an uncompromising scourge overrunning the city required forceful interventions by the government and those were largely absent from the *Plan for New York City*.

In the end, almost none of the proposals of the *Plan for New York City* were implemented. After 1969, physical solutions continued to be distrusted by neighborhood people, federal subsidies began to dry up, and New York's finances began to rapidly deteriorate. This failure to continue to implement physical solutions represented one of the biggest public policy failures of the ambitious Lindsay Administration. Without grand-scale physical redevelopment, urban liberalism became increasingly unfocused in the field of urban affairs. The irony is that this happened exactly at a moment that New York liberals finally got rid of Moses and had a chance to propose more humane versions of redevelopment.

3 Times Square
New York's Most Disorderly Place

> One of these streets, perhaps at the core of the Big Apple, is 42nd Street; song, motion picture and musical play have been dedicated to it. The street traverses midtown Manhattan; as one travels from east side to west side, the difference in economic standards is literally astonishing. On the east, arisen from the depths of what were teeming tenements and smell-sickening slaughter-houses are the world headquarters of the United Nations and the massive residential development called Tudor City. Going west, one passes the beautiful, park-like atmosphere of the Ford Foundation Building, the information centers of the Daily News Building and the New York Public Library, the modernity of the Grand Hyatt Hotel and the vastness of Grand Central Terminal and the Chrysler Building—once the tallest in the world *(AIA Guide to New York City* [1st ed.], p. 121). However, starting with what was once a potter's field, now known as Bryant Park, the tawdry, "honkey-tonk" part of New York, the Times Square area, begins. If the east side represents the zenith of New York, Times Square, with its flotsam and jetsam prostitutes, pimps, pornographers and other purveyors of poison, represents the nadir of our society. It is an area that has resisted one cleanup after another.[1]
>
> —Judge Jay Stuart Dankberg

On February 13, 1969, chief inspector Sanford D. Garelik of the New York Police Department (NYPD) lambasted the courts for convicting only twelve out of 292 people arrested in Times Square during a six-day crackdown of "undesirables." After the first day of the massive arrests, *The New York Times* reported that "the police began a crackdown on drunks, homosexuals, loiterers and other undesirables in the Times Square area last night, although the cold weather apparently kept many of them away."[2] *The New York Times* shared Garelik's frustration with the courts and agreed that Times Square had become a "nesting ground for muggers and degenerates." They contended that while "the right of every accused person to all the protections the Constitution provides to assure fair trial must never be infringed . . . the judges operating within those rules need not turn their courts into revolving doors that put hoodlums back on the streets almost as soon as they are picked up."[3] Days later, Frederick L. Strong, New York City Criminal Court Judge, characterized the police operation as a "dragnet."

He indicated that the great majority of the people were arrested for loitering and very few were arrested for any specific crime. In addressing the situation, he said that "a conviction for loitering on the street requires proof of doing so with an intent to engage in unlawful activity. Merely hanging around is not enough. In the majority of the cases to which you refer, no such intent was ever indicated, let alone proved."[4] City Council President Francis X. Smith also found the arrests to be problematic. He accused Mayor John V. Lindsay of encouraging the police to make a high number of baseless arrests to make his administration look tough on crime because of that year's mayoral election. But these criticisms did not deter the police from continuing their actions. By mid-June of that year, the police had made 4,731 arrests in Times Square, resulting in 1,603 convictions.[5]

While large-scale round-ups had occurred in Times Square before the late 1960s, once John V. Lindsay became mayor in 1966, police interventions intensified and became constant, reflecting a renewed emphasis on social solutions to disorder. This occurred not because Times Square was central to the city's actual spatial and economic organization but because of its centrality to the image of New York City. The city administration was responding to criticisms by the mass media that crime and disorder had overtaken Times Square and that this reflected the extent to which the city had declined. More than this, the image problem of Times Square was appended by an even more serious citywide crime problem. The homicide rate rose rapidly during the 1960s and other crimes such as robbery and burglary increased even more.

The massive arrests in Times Square resulted in a clash between the city government and the courts on constitutional grounds. With orders to improve the image of Times Square, the NYPD incorporated the routine violation of constitutional rights into its repertoire of spatial regulation. Since the majority of "undesirables" had committed no serious crime, the authorities charged them with vagrancy, loitering, or disorderly conduct violations. Local courts refused to convict people rounded up by the police under vagrancy, loitering, or disorderly conduct statutes. At the same time, the U.S. Supreme Court began to invalidate state vagrancy and loitering statutes because of their vague nature and because the police used them in order to arrest people who simply happened to be in public space. New York State courts followed the example of the U.S. Supreme Court, making the regulation of public space more of a challenge for authorities.[6]

In retrospect, police sweeps represented a specific type of regulatory policy in Times Square and were considered necessary in the absence of redevelopment. In residential areas such as Morningside Heights, public and private institutions resorted to the displacement of "undesirable" people who lived in the neighborhood though physical solutions in the hope that if these people did not live there they would also not frequent its public spaces. In Times Square, such a strategy seemed impossible since the "undesirables" lived elsewhere and since redevelopment plans were slow to come to fruition. Thus, city administrations believed that regular round-ups would displace "undesirables" from Times Square and make the area appear more orderly. As this hope was not realized, law enforcement officials blamed the courts for being too lenient.

Ironically, the eventual solution for Times Square included physical solutions in a limited form. After numerous failed campaigns against "undesirables" frequenting Times Square, the city government in an alliance with the private sector decided to redevelop portions of Times Square in order to attract middle- and upper-income visitors. This targeted redevelopment included a combination of physical and social solutions such as the building of towers that would function as anchors of redevelopment in the district, the spatial regulation of "undesirables," the displacement of unwanted businesses, the confiscation of properties through eminent domain, and various forms of zoning. However, the failure of social solutions to displace disorderly uses and users from Times Square delayed their comprehensive implementation in the city. After 1977, Mayor Koch decided that aggressive policing, antiloitering legislation, and morals squads had not been very effective and that the city government needed to invent other methods in order to fight social disorder. The relative success of targeted redevelopment in Times Square during the 1980s increased skepticism about the effectiveness of social solutions even more. Though applied in the late 1960s and early 1970s, aggressive policing was not emphasized as a mechanism of spatial regulation until the 1990s.

SOCIAL DISORDER IN TIMES SQUARE BEFORE THE 1960s

Throughout the twentieth century, Times Square has been one of the most popular entertainment and commercial districts in the United States. In the early part of the century the area came to symbolize consumer capitalism, the rise of the United States to a world economic and cultural power, and the golden era of New York City. The city- and nation-defining power of Times Square backfired in the post-1929 period as the redefinition of the district into a working-class space enraged the city's elites. During the Great Depression, powerholders and the mass media defined Times Square as a tawdry area taken over by morally questionable businesses that catered to "undesirables." They argued that the image of Times Square damaged that of New York City at large and they also resented the ability of ordinary people to dominate such a high-profile area. During this period, Times Square became one of the most comprehensive targets of local government intervention with a goal to make it a more mainstream consumption space. The city government used two different strategies in order to turn conditions in Times Square around. The first aimed to displace people whose sexuality, ethnicity, race, class, or age made Times Square seem disorderly when compared to white middle- and upper-class family standards. The second attacked the owners and operators of certain businesses because they cheapened the atmosphere of Times Square, degraded public morality, and prevented large corporations from investing in the area.[7]

The exceptional nature of New York's urban environment made the redevelopment of Times Square a complicated process. Other cities could simply concentrate on their downtown, enhance existing cultural institutions, and complement them with luxury housing, shopping malls, office buildings, and industrial parks. In New York City, however, numerous commercial centers with competing interests existed elsewhere. Despite the media attention that it received, Times Square was only one of many troubled high-profile locations.[8]

The strategy to transform Times Square into an upper-class entertainment center suffered a severe blow in the 1950s when the city's elites decided to build the Lincoln Center for the Performing Arts on the West Side of Manhattan. Although Times Square did not have the space for such a massive project, some of the cultural institutions that moved to Lincoln Center could perhaps have found a place in Times Square and complemented the theater sector, which, by itself, was not enough to revive the district. As it turned out, Times Square even lost its Metropolitan Opera House to Lincoln Center. With the city's premier performing arts center located somewhere else, Times Square struggled to find a desirable identity.[9]

Ambitious proposals that included Times Square and its surrounding areas existed but never materialized. For example, in the early 1940s Mayor Fiorello La Guardia felt that New York had the opportunity to supersede war-torn Paris as a fashion center and assembled a committee to plan a World Fashion Center in midtown Manhattan. The committee formulated a number of proposals that included the development of a series of buildings that would house design studios, showrooms, executive offices, a 25,000-seat convention auditorium, a 5,000-seat opera house, an underground garage, a rooftop heliport, and a school of industrial design. This complex would be located somewhere east of Broadway and south of 42nd Street. Apparel manufacturing would either remain in the garment district or relocate to the boroughs. Some of these ideas became reality in parts of the city, but the World Fashion Center itself was never realized. A proposal for a television city near Times Square with studios, office buildings, and theaters also failed. Although television networks entertained the idea, eventually, CBS moved most of its production facilities to Los Angeles, and ABC decided not to open substantial facilities in midtown New York.[10]

Despite these setbacks, many hoped that Times Square would benefit from a midtown office building boom. The arrival of corporations in Times Square could have replicated the excitement that surrounded the move of *The New York Times* headquarters to the Square in 1904. Many observers assumed that office development would not affect the entertainment character of the district since great theaters such as Loew's State and Paramount operated as parts of office buildings. But in the end, most office buildings took root either on the fringes of Times Square or in other parts of the midtown area. Construction that took place in Times Square not only failed to regenerate the area but also destroyed theaters, retail centers, and cultural institutions that might have functioned as anchors for future revival.[11]

While proposals to transform Times Square into a more desirable place failed, honky tonks dominated the cultural infrastructure of the district. Honky tonks sought to maximize profits with cheap amusements that attracted huge crowds around the clock. Business interests and the city government targeted honky tonks because they considered the people frequenting them to be menaces to the district's social order. While such forms of entertainment had been declining in Coney Island, their miniature version thrived in Times Square. The central location of Times Square proved indispensable for businesses focusing on amusement. Many tourists and New Yorkers were more likely to visit midtown Manhattan than the edge of Brooklyn where Coney Island was located. By the 1940s, boardwalk-type businesses had altered the atmosphere of Times Square into a working-class cultural space. The Broadway Association, which represented the mainstream business sector of the area, found this development disturbing. In 1948, the association presented Robert F. Wagner, Jr., chairman of the City Planning Commission, with proposals that called for the rezoning of the midtown area so that the "carnival atmosphere" of Times Square and Broadway would be eliminated.[12]

In 1952, frustration over disorderly conditions in Times Square resurfaced with honky tonks and other commercial establishments becoming the center of attention. The Broadway Association argued that Times Square could not survive as a penny arcade area and called upon the Planning Commission to approve its rezoning proposals. In a letter to *The New York Times,* Edgar Van expressed his dislike of street peddlers: "Pushcarts, canister wavers, socks salesmen, gardenia hawkers, bootblacks, accordion virtuosi, somnolent bums in theatre exits and just plain or garden variety of panhandlers make the sector a jungle of come-ons that would not be tolerated in the most chaotic community in the Orient."[13] Two days later, understanding that a campaign to remove peddlers had failed in the 1930s, the editors of *The New York Times* sought to channel indignation toward conditions in Times Square. The paper recalled the proposal of the Broadway Association, which sought to "protect Times Square from becoming a honky-tonk Coney Island," and provided an inventory of businesses causing urban disorder:

> On Broadway and Seventh Avenue alone up to Fifty-fourth Street (not attempting to make a side-street census) there are half dozen . . . arcades. There are eight dance palaces, some with canned music blaring into the streets over raucous loudspeakers. Eight record shops are committing the same loudspeaker nuisance, and several auction shops also pipe their blare to the streets. Contributing to a boardwalk atmosphere are shooting galleries, bazaars, gift shops of a junky nature, "last day" sales, "riot" sales, "alteration" sales, live turtle emporiums, shops for passport

photos, jokes, magic tricks, monogrammed cowboy hats, lurid, sexy and sadistic movie advertising (the latter more prevalent, however, on Forty-second Street between Broadway and Eighth Avenue).[14]

The attacks against these businesses seemed peculiar, given the fact that they had completely taken over Times Square. Furthermore, no one advanced any vision of what Times Square ought to be. The argument that Times Square could not survive as a penny arcade area made no business sense; penny arcades were among the few businesses able to afford the high rents.[15]

At the end of 1953, the City Planning Commission decided to redefine the three classifications of retail districts so that new businesses that contributed to Times Square's midway atmosphere would be prevented from opening. The Broadway Association hired the city planning firm of Harrison, Ballard & Allen to draft zoning revisions that favored the elimination of businesses considered to be disorderly. These zoning changes ensured that shooting galleries, flea circuses, penny arcades, wax museums, pinball gaming establishments, freak shows, skee-ball, open-front stores, sidewalk cafes, ground-floor auction rooms, and other amusements could no longer open anywhere in midtown. In the beginning of 1954, the Board of Estimate unanimously approved these zoning changes. Although businesses that already engaged in these activities were spared, whenever they closed, they could not be replaced. According to the editors of *The New York Times* in five editorials on the matter in about two years, "The Board of Estimate has taken an important initial step toward somehow remaking Times Square into the decent and respectable neighborhood we should have for one of our most famous name places."[16] The mentioning of "somehow" revealed the ambivalence centered around these zoning changes. After about a quarter of a century of dominating Times Square, honky tonks seemed to be on their way out for unclear reasons. What would replace them seemed even more unclear. Exclusionary zoning was a much more extreme regulatory mechanism than licensing and content objection. As it turned out, the 1954 Board of Estimate decision undermined the social order of Times Square even more.[17]

Although the city government had been targeting "undesirables" in Times Square since 1929, it resorted to exclusionary zoning at a time that African Americans increasingly frequented Times Square. This transition of people frequenting Times Square from white working class to Back working class seems to have made the difference. The need to change conditions in Times Square became more urgent than before.

THE CAMPAIGN AGAINST COMMERCIALIZED SEX

After the exclusionary zoning of 1954, sex-related businesses replaced the honky tonks, making Times Square even more disorderly. Real estate owners realized that they could double their profits if they leased to massage parlors, adult bookstores, peep show operators, movie theaters, and other adult-oriented establishments. Streetwalkers, prostitution houses, and other sexual enterprises complemented this newly rooted infrastructure, solidifying Times Square's reputation as the sleaziest place in the country. In 1969, ten grinders on West 42nd Street showing adult films attracted about nine million customers. Peep shows generated a weekly gross income of between $74,000 and $106,000, or about $5 million a year. This represented an enormous profit given that peep shows required a small square footage, needed very few low-paid employees, and were composed of a few booths with inexpensive film machines. These businesses operated under a lease system that put a distance between the actual owners of the properties and the operators of the porn shops, meaning that it was very difficult to blame anyone directly for their existence. Owners of the buildings—very often members of the city's elites—leased their properties for ten or more years to others, who in many cases were associated with organized crime. Sometimes those involved with organized crime operated the businesses themselves, though typically they sublet the properties on a short-term basis to small-time operators who assumed legal responsibility for whatever occurred on their premises. Besides subletting, organized crime also provided protection and legal aid. Many of the small-time operators sought to outsmart their leaseholders by making lots of money quickly and disappearing. In the meantime, the properties required nominal maintenance, meaning that costs associated with property ownership were minimized.[18]

As the incidence of prostitution increased in Times Square, the city government began to campaign against streetwalkers. Prostitutes overtook the streets of Midtown, especially those near Times Square. The city had tacitly admitted that it could not adequately control moral deviancy in 1964 when Mayor Wagner sealed the IRT subway entrance through the Rialto Arcade because it was a location where adult homosexuals picked up teenagers. In 1967, after complaints by business interests in midtown about the increase in the number of streetwalkers, the police department made 2,300 arrests in five weeks for disorderly conduct. This number represented a vast increase over that of 2,611 in the previous six months. However, the previous arrests were for prostitution since the women had solicited undercover policemen. Because the deployment of plainclothes officers in search of solicitation proved time consuming, the police department decided to start charging streetwalkers with disorderly conduct. When the courts disregarded the disorderly conduct charges, the police started to arrest streetwalkers on loitering charges under §240.35 (6). Criminal Court Judge Amos S. Basel characterized these arrests as a "disgrace" and dismissed the loitering charges. The New York Civil Liberties Union threatened to seek a federal injunction against the practice, and the dragnet operation of the police department seemed to be in shambles. In November of that same year, Judge Basel ruled that under New York State law, prostitution was a violation and not a crime and that prostitutes could not be arrested for loitering.[19]

This ruling did not prevent the police department from periodically reinstating street sweeps and making massive arrests of people suspected of prostitution. After 1967, the authorities began to arrest large numbers of suspected prostitutes under disorderly conduct section §240.20(5), which made it illegal for people to obstruct vehicular or pedestrian traffic. These arrests would never be accepted in the courts. The District Attorney did not prosecute the suspected prostitutes and released them the morning after their arrest. This practice sought to intimidate streetwalkers and cause them to move their operations into lower-profile areas. The city government went after prostitutes because their appearance in public space exemplified perceptions of social disorder. Prostitutes appeared on the sidewalks of Times Square in such great numbers that they often disrupted the flow of pedestrian traffic. Besides the way that they dressed, which made them easily identifiable, prostitutes pursued prospective clients aggressively. Their activities degraded the character of Times Square and made it a disagreeable location for families. In the views of powerholders, prostitution had no place in Times Square.[20]

In 1969, the film *Midnight Cowboy* explored the sexual politics of Times Square from a male homosexual perspective, tarnishing the image of the district and New York City even further. In the film, protagonist Joe Buck (Jon Voight) makes his way from rural Texas to New York City seeking his fortune as a heterosexual gigolo. Joe very quickly discovers that his cowboy image, which resembles a naive and self-commodifying image of John Wayne, appeals to gay men. His eventual sidekick, homeless Ratso Rizzo (Dustin Hoffman), tells Joe that "no rich lady with any class at all buys that cowboy crap anymore."[21] *Midnight Cowboy* was the first major Hollywood production to receive an X rating because of its blatant exploration of Times Square's sexual world. It angered Texas state legislators, who wanted to place a "dirty movie" tax on the film. It also angered many of New York's politicians, though they seemed more critical of actual conditions in Times Square. *Midnight Cowboy* was the first of a series of movies that reported the decline of New York City to the rest of the nation. After becoming the first X-rated film to win an Academy Award for Best Picture, it was re-released with an R rating and played to record audiences around the country.[22]

In the early 1970s, prostitution became even more of a problem in Times Square as large numbers of prostitutes turned to assault and robbery. Because of extreme competition and declining economic fortunes, many prostitutes started to rob unsuspecting clients or people simply walking by. On March 15, 1971, two women jumped from a car and stole the wallet of West German Defense Minister Franz Josef Strauss right outside his hotel. A few hours later, the police arrested the women and discovered that they had previous prostitution convictions. Weeks before, three prostitutes had murdered an

Italian industrialist at the doorstep of his hotel. Such incidents reflected streetwalkers' growing desperation for money. In many cases, this desperation was attributed to a growth of drug addiction among prostitutes; however, the economic slowdown of the period also greatly affected their behavior.[23]

The Lindsay Administration responded to this change in prostitution, and rising crime in Times Square, by launching an ambitious program in 1972 called the Midtown Project. This pilot program used funds from the federal government and created two super-precincts in the Police Department—Midtown North and Midtown South—which covered only commercial spaces. The program provided the officers with the latest equipment available for law enforcement such as scooters and video recorders. By 1973, the Midtown Project operated in full force by trying to clean up Times Square. That year, super-precinct officers arrested 1,945 people for direct solicitation of prostitution and 400 "johns" for patronizing streetwalkers. The police disrupted prostitution in more than thirty hotels, some of which shut down altogether. Officials also monitored and cited more than fifty massage parlor operators for various violations that included illicit sex. In targeting these establishments, the authorities hoped that they could reduce the number of prostitutes in Times Square by eliminating the trade infrastructure in the area. These police operations offered a glimmer of hope that prostitution could be displaced from Times Square. However, despite a more than 90% conviction rate, very few people served jail sentences for prostitution. Furthermore, by 1973 observers estimated that many thousands of prostitutes operated around Times Square each week. The arrest of almost 2,000 sex trade workers in a year did not mean much. To make things worse, many prostitutes began to consider police harassment and arrests as a necessary part of their trade.[24]

These two super-precincts represented the Lindsay Administration's endeavor to overcome the problems that it was experiencing with the NYPD. Efforts to make the police force more accountable and efficient had been opposed by the Patrolmen's Benevolent Association (PBA). In 1966, the PBA campaigned against the city administration's decision to create a civilian police review board and voters rejected the creation of such a board in a referendum. Although the Lindsay Administration succeeded in its efforts to create a fourth police platoon that would patrol the streets at night, transfer police officers performing civilian duties to patrol duties, and hire additional police officers, these plans fell apart because of inefficiency and corruption. In the late 1960s, charges that most police officers slept on the job at night and that there was widespread corruption undermined confidence in the police. The police commissioner took away power from local police precincts in dealing with prostitution and other violations and relied on specialized squads. The two super-precincts created in midtown Manhattan represented the new police approach of fighting crime and disorder. However, these specialized police units represented a small percentage of the entire police force. They were deployed in high-profile areas as well as high-crime areas with the hope that they could immediately solve problems and move to other neighborhoods. In Times Square, these problems was never adequately addressed.[25]

Because of repeated failures to clean up Times Square, the Lindsay Administration also attempted to dislodge sex-related businesses from the district, thinking that their elimination would displace "undesirables." The police department proceeded against peep show operators for maintaining premises of public amusement without licenses as required by the city's Administrative Code. By that time, peep shows had become the most numerous of the adult-oriented facilities in Times Square. Peep show machines could be found in specialized establishments but also in the back rooms of all kinds of businesses, including bookstores and gift shops. Peep show operators challenged this new licensing requirement in state and federal courts, arguing that it interfered with their First Amendment rights. State courts agreed and found the licensing sections of the city's Administrative Code to be unconstitutional because they tried to restrain the showing of motion pictures, which involved the exercise of First Amendment freedoms. The inability of the city government to require licensing meant that peep shows could operate throughout Times Square freely. Despite the possibility of harassment, the number of peep shows increased in Times Square after the early 1970s.[26]

The authorities also had difficulty regulating the showing of sexually explicit motion pictures in movie theaters, in spite of support by the courts. In 1973, in *Miller v. California*, the U.S. Supreme Court decided that a work could be considered obscene according to the following standards:

> (a) whether the average person, applying contemporary community standards, would find that the work, taken as a whole, appeals to the prurient interest, (b) whether the work depicts or describes, in a patently offensive way, sexual conduct specifically defined by the applicable state law, and (c) whether the work, taken as a whole, lacks serious literary, artistic, political, or scientific value—there being no requirement that the work be "utterly without redeeming social value" or "social importance"; if a state law that regulates obscene material is thus limited, as written or construed, the First Amendment values applicable to the states through the Fourteenth Amendment are adequately protected by the ultimate power of appellate courts to conduct an independent review of constitutional claims when necessary.[27]

Because of this decision, states and localities could ban motion pictures, magazines, plays, and books considered offensive to local standards, though such decisions could be subject to federal court review. After this decision, in Times Square city authorities successfully prosecuted a motion picture theater corporation for showing the movie *Deep Throat*. This was an indication that they could successfully go after movie theaters showing other "obscene" motion pictures. However, the police department had to bring each movie considered obscene before a panel of judges for review, which proved to be time consuming. Moreover, in fiscally hard-pressed New York, cases more serious than obscenity took priority. According to Manhattan District Attorney Robert M. Morgenthau, "when we have got more homicides, more rapes and more assaults, prosecuting prostitution or pornography has to be low in priority."[28]

Despite the city government's rhetoric and actions against Times Square's pornographic establishments, not much happened in terms of public policy, because no one knew what would replace these businesses. At the time, landlords thought that Times Square would somehow be redeveloped and that the sex shops were there only temporarily. The existence of these stores seemed preferential to empty storefronts or to legitimate businesses with long-term leases and legal rights. Despite attacks against sex-related businesses, there were questions about the intention of the government to remove them. One could argue that had the city government been serious about eliminating sex shops from Times Square in the 1970s, it could have zoned them out of existence in the same manner that it displaced the honky tonks during the 1950s. The City of Detroit, which was rarely innovative in city planning and zoning, passed two zoning ordinances in 1972 that prohibited the existence of adult entertainment establishments near each other. In 1976, the U.S. Supreme Court upheld these zoning restrictions, making it easier for any municipality in the country to avoid the overconcentration of sex-related businesses in any one location. In fact, the New York City government passed a zoning amendment in 1979 that effectively banned new massage parlors from operating in the city, but it did not zone out other sex-related businesses.[29]

Many non-sex-oriented businesses withdrew from Times Square in the 1970s, considering the future of the area to be bleak. In 1971, Ripley's Wax Museum, a fixture of Times Square for about twenty-three years, closed because of deplorable conditions that resulted in declining revenues. According to Charles Bristoll, Ripley's executive vice president, "in the last few years it got so depressing to go to New York that I found myself making excuses not to go. Times Square used to be the best tourist area of the world. But it's gone downhill severely. Now most people stay away from it. It's changed, the crowds have changed, and the people we cater to, the tourists and families—they've gone." Bristoll blamed conditions in the city and in Times Square for Ripley's decline of revenues since the late 1960s and characterized Broadway as the "Avenue of Perverts." Bristoll dismissed the idea that tourists and New Yorkers had become tired of Ripley's torture instruments and wax statues and argued that the Ripley's Wax Museum in Saint Petersburg, Florida, did quite well. Richard Caputo, the museum's manager in its last year, disputed Bristoll's account about declining tourism in Times Square and blamed Ripley's headquarters for the failure of its New York location. Caputo argued that Ripley's had failed to adequately publicize and move the museum to a more attractive location near Madison Square Garden and that the waxes there were not "elaborate enough." Caputo claimed that he could not convince his superiors to replicate the successful exhibits that Ripley's had in its other museums. Despite the disagreement, it seemed that Ripley's Corporation decided to focus on its branches in other parts of the country and disinvest from New York City.[30]

The departure of Ripley's Wax Museum was not the only high-profile commercial withdrawal from Times Square during that period. The Empire Theater, the Paramount, the Metropolitan Opera House, and even the Astor Hotel fell to the wrecking ball in the 1960s. In 1969, Times Square's only department store, Stern's, closed its doors to make room for an office building. Although Stern's could have tried to reopen in another location within Times Square, its executives decided to focus on its stores in the suburbs instead. In 1974, the very popular Woolworth store left Times Square after nearly forty years because it could not afford the costs of a new lease. During the same year, Jack Dempsey's restaurant, the Deli City restaurant, and the Royal Manhattan Hotel also closed their doors and these closures generated a public outcry that all legitimate businesses were abandoning Times Square. The departure or closure of these commercial establishments symbolized not only the decline of New York but also the unfettered exploitation of real estate, which destroyed everything considered legitimate. Private developers and real estate interests tried to maximize their profits without caring about the character of Times Square.[31]

In 1975, while a fiscal crisis was unfolding in the city, the Abe Beame Administration (1974–1977) continued to support the two super-precincts even though federal funding had expired. In anticipation of the bicentennial celebrations of 1976 and the Democratic National Convention of the same year, Mayor Beame spent a disproportionate amount of time worrying about Times Square. Hoping to at least displace prostitutes from public sight, the administration ended up proposing a new loitering statute against prostitution. The newly proposed statute was based on the British Street Offenses Act of 1959. It mandated ninety-day jail sentences for people loitering in public spaces for the purpose of prostitution and also empowered the police to arrest pimps for loitering. Beame, along with state senators from Manhattan and with the outspoken support of local business interests, staged a rally at the Majestic Theater demonstrating that the proposed legislation was tailored for Times Square. The State Legislature passed this bill in 1976. That year a criminal court declared the law unconstitutional because it was vague and inhibited free speech. However, upon appeal, higher courts reversed the decision and found it to be specific enough to satisfy constitutional standards. In April of 1977, the *Economist* reported that Beame's continuous campaign against vice in Times Square could be interpreted as "a clear signal that he is in the [mayoral] race," something that had been previously viewed as unlikely because of Beame's mishandling of the fiscal crisis.[32] Between 1976 and 1977, Beame relied on a special task force, the Mayor's Office of Midtown Enforcement, to return the district's real estate to "good commercial uses." The task force enforced obscenity laws but mostly shut down commercial establishments that did not conform to building, fire, and health codes. Beame lost in the Democratic primary for mayor in 1977 anyway. Inherited by the Koch Administration, between 1978 and 1984 this task force managed to almost eliminate massage parlors, most of which had become prostitution establishments.[33]

Having witnessed how the previous city administrations had failed to reestablish social order in Times Square, Mayor Ed Koch decided to change course in the late 1970s. Koch understood that a successful antiprostitution law in and by itself could not eliminate streetwalkers. Koch also understood that large-scale campaigns against "undesirables" and prostitutes had been tried and failed and that they could never succeed by themselves. Koch felt that middle- and upper-class populations would not return to Times Square unless the district had something to offer them beyond theaters, and he hoped that targeted redevelopment would create a new cultural infrastructure that could replace sex-oriented businesses. Koch also inaugurated a project called Operation Crossroads, which deployed eighty additional uniformed and twenty-five plainclothes officers in the area bounded by West 40th Street, West 50th Street, Broadway and Ninth Avenue in 1978. However, this project was part of Koch's effort to make New Yorkers feel safer by flooding high-profile areas with police officers and because of fears that conditions in Times Square could get out completely of control. Although spatial control via policing remained a public policy imperative, targeted redevelopment became a priority.[34]

THE EVENTUAL SOLUTION FOR TIMES SQUARE

In 1974, developer Richard Ravitch projected that Manhattan Plaza, a 1,700-resident upscale complex that he was building on the western edge of Times Square, would revive West 42nd Street and help displace porno shops, prostitutes, and massage parlors. By the 1970s, Times Square, which for many decades had functioned as New York's unofficial city center, had become a center of pornography and prostitution. Many observers associated conditions in Times Square with New York's decline. Manhattan Plaza represented a last-ditch effort to clean up and revitalize Times Square and make upper-class people a permanent presence in the area. Ravitch based his Manhattan Plaza optimism on the success of Tudor City, a multibuilding complex erected in the mid-1920s on East 42nd Street for the upper classes. Tudor City thrived in the midst of slaughterhouses and low-income neighborhoods because of its convenient location. However, there had been few other instances where expensive housing proved successful in less elegant surroundings and even fewer instances where upper-class housing revived complex areas such as Times Square. For example, despite

Tudor City, East 42nd Street did not become fashionable before the building of the United Nations headquarters in 1947–1953.[35]

As it turned out, upper- and middle-class people had no interest in moving next to Times Square in the 1970s. Inflation and construction mismanagement drove the costs of the development so high that it was cheaper to rent an apartment in the Upper East Side, New York's most affluent neighborhood. As a result, in 1975 the Beame Administration altered the original plan and secured federal assistance that amounted to $11.5 million a year for forty years in subsidies for low- and moderate-income families to move to Manhattan Plaza. Major real estate and business interests in the area sharply opposed the city plan, arguing that a low-income project on the edge of Time Square would hinder the upgrading of the district. The long-standing Broadway Association that represented big business and real estate interests in Times Square since the 1920s hoped that the thousands of upper-class residents who would move into Manhattan Plaza would induce the development of a cultural infrastructure in Times Square that would finally displace prostitution and pornography. However, affluent people viewed the area with suspicion. By the mid-1970s, the mass media represented Times Square as one of the most dangerous areas in New York. With many other options in safer, more comfortable areas, Manhattan Plaza proved unattractive. After much debate, the city government decided to rent most of Manhattan Plaza to people involved in the performing arts. Although many of them could not afford rents without subsidies, they at least resembled desirable people. So the city government decided to use Section 8 subsidies, which were generally used to assist low-income populations in renting housing, in order to attract entertainers and their offstage colleagues. In Manhattan Plaza 30% of the site was set aside for residents already in the area, even though many complained that the administrators of the site did not strictly observe waiting lists and that officials opted for tenants who had a desirable look. In 1980, the General Accounting Office of the U.S. Congress corroborated these accounts when it criticized Manhattan Plaza for using Section 8 funds intended for the poor in order to provide upper-class amenities to nonpoor groups.[36]

The Manhattan Plaza episode reflected the anxieties of the city government over conditions in Times Square. For many decades, Times Square had ceased to be a middle- and upper-class space of consumption and had been overtaken by many African Americans and Latinos. Until the 1940s, Blacks and Latinos were not welcome in Times Square unless they worked in the area's restaurants, hotels, or transportation stations. But as the number of minority populations increased in New York and as many whites withdrew to the suburbs, businesses started to cater to a diverse clientele by providing inexpensive merchandise and entertainment. Although hundreds of thousands of people visited Times Square every week, it did not project the kind of image that government officials and real estate interests hoped for. Times Square made New York seem like a city in decline, a city that had been overtaken by low-income people who acted in a disorderly fashion. The $95 million city-financed Manhattan Plaza represented an effort to stem the tide of urban disorder and to transform Times Square into a desirable area that conformed to mainstream business standards. Manhattan Plaza represented an effort to use a physical solution to social disorder in Times Square during a period in which such physical solutions were seldom employed. This experience showed the extent to which physical solutions were inadequate. It also showed the persistence of physical solutions in the hearts and minds of public officials and developers. Had government money been more plentiful in the 1970s, there would have seen many more such efforts.[37]

By the 1970s, Times Square epitomized the problems that city centers across the United States experienced, especially when compared to suburban shopping malls; for a while the idea of building a shopping mall was considered. As determined by the U.S. Supreme Court in 1972, shopping centers constituted private space, which meant that their owners could restrict many types of activities and evict objectionable people. In truth, shopping mall space remained quasipublic, meaning that people could freely enter as long as they behaved in ways that did not interfere with commerce. Despite efforts by New York's authorities to make Times Square inhospitable to "undesirables," the mere fact that its streets, sidewalks, and squares were public space meant that anyone could obtain access. Times Square could not be as exclusive as suburban shopping centers. Private interests reacted by proposing to restrict Times Square's urban character and separate affluent people from low-income populations through the construction of quasipublic entertainment spaces. In the early 1970s, city officials heralded a proposal for a major hotel on Broadway between West 45th and 46th as the beginning of "the renaissance of Times Square," as it would minimize street life of the area. Designed by Atlanta-based architect-developer John Portman, the Times Square hotel featured two fifty-six-story towers connected by several five-story-high bridges, an underground theater and parking garage, seven stories of indoor shops, and a glass-enclosed sidewalk café. Portman himself admitted that he designed a development that excluded the street with "control points," glass boxes, and other "protected environment" measures. Portman eliminated unrestricted access to the structure by pedestrians. At the same time, people using the sidewalk café could watch Times Square without having to come into direct contact with it. But the city officials wanted to clean up Times Square, not to avoid it with fortification. In their eyes, what made Times Square special was its open space, not the eradication of it. Portman's project also threatened to demolish three Broadway theaters. As Portman's proposal suggested, developers did not trust that the city government would ever be able to eradicate disorderly conditions in the public space of Times Square.[38]

The city administration insisted on its quest to improve the character of the area and salvage its public space, which required continuous campaigns against "undesirables" and prostitutes. As a compromise to the wishes of the developers, the city government flooded Times Square with police officers, trying to create a public space that was as well controlled as quasipublic space. In 1978, the Koch Administration offered Portman subsidies that amounted to $100 million to resurrect the hotel project that had stagnated during the uncertainty of the fiscal crisis. Portman accepted, and his hotel was completed in 1984, becoming the Marriot Marquis. Though not as originally planned, the hotel maintained many of its fortresslike elements. For example, there was no lobby or other facilities on the ground floor, making the point that the hotel wanted as little interaction with its surroundings as possible. The Marriot Marquis also displaced two popular historic Broadway theaters but never included the enclosed shopping center that was originally planned.[39]

After the fiscal crisis, a privately sponsored, ambitious proposal called The City at 42nd Street emerged with regard to Times Square. This plan, conceived in 1979, proposed to transform the area bounded by West 41st Street, West 43rd Street, Seventh Avenue and Eighth Avenue into a combined theme park. The development would include three office towers, a substantial fashion mart, and a 750,000-square-foot theme park featuring movie houses, theaters, a museum, rides, and other entertainment facilities. The project aimed squarely at attracting middle-class visitors with families. The quasipublic nature of this development meant that security guards could deny entry to "undesirables" or force out disorderly people. To everyone's surprise, two years after the initial proposal, and following expenditures of $1.2 million, Koch vetoed the plan. At first, it seemed that Koch disliked the plan's cultural vision. He announced that "New York cannot and should not compete with Disneyland—that's for Florida. . . . We've got to make sure [that Times Square visitors] have seltzer instead of orange juice." But besides the cultural issue, Koch opposed the plan because he wanted more control over the project. He understood that only the city and the state governments had the power to make the project a reality by mediating among various powerful interests involved in Times Square and by minimizing challenges through legislation. He also wanted to benefit politically from the project by including his real estate allies and taking credit for the renewal of the district. The city–state proposal that emerged in 1981 did not differ too much from The City at 42nd Street except that it was bigger, eliminated the amusement park, and called for the restoration of all nine historic theaters in the area. The city–state proposal borrowed from previous discourses of disorder about Times Square so that it could justify the magnitude of redevelopment. These discourses aimed at gaining the support of the public and justifying controversial actions such as the displacement of many legitimate businesses from the area. In the end, the city and state governments were convinced that the redevelopment of Times Square was the only way to eradicate disorder from the area and make it attractive to affluent visitors.[40]

In 1984, the New York State Urban Development Corporation along with private consultants released an environmental-impact statement that defined the Times Square redevelopment project as an effort to take back the area from undesirable and offensive forces. The statement considered "hustlers and loiterers" as the most disorderly elements on West 42nd Street: "In a real sense, 42nd Street is their territory, and others venturing through it perceive that they do so at their own risk." The statement added that economic and social forces in the area had created an atmosphere devoid of any positive forces that could make competing claims over space, leaving "sidewalks . . . free and available to loiterers and over time 42nd Street has become their turf."[41] On a somewhat contradictory note, this statement found that only 3% of the area's pedestrians could be characterized as loiterers despite a very liberal definition of loitering. The statement ended up defining the constant presence of large minority populations in Times Square as the real problem. It suggested that many young African Americans and Latinos hanging out in Times Square or waiting outside action movie theaters represented a problem for the area because it was hard for middle-class visitors to distinguish them from hustlers, loiterers, and criminals:

> Thus, a large (over 30% on the weekend) group of like people were on the street. Most of these came for legitimate purposes; however, the distinction between legitimate and illegitimate users of the street is not easily made and, in the ebb and flow of the 42nd Street crowds, those standing around or congregating in front of a movie often appear as ominous as the pushers, solicitors and others "doing business" on the street.[42]

The statement declared that this group was overwhelmingly young, male (89 to 100%), and Black or Hispanic (over 60%). It downplayed the fact that as much as 40% of this group could be white, reinforcing the idea that African Americans and Latinos, not whites, made public spaces disorderly. This state-sanctioned document asserted that the 1980s redevelopment project would reclaim the turf of Times Square from disorderly populations and from the businesses that attracted them. The idea was that once a critical mass of mainstream businesses moved to the area, they would provide a counterweight to the social world of the illegitimate businesses and, with the help of the authorities, would change the character of the area. Both public and private interests were determined to make Times Square visitors more white and more affluent.[43]

This environmental-impact statement revealed how efforts to spatially regulate Times Square in the postwar period were to a great extent tied to the racial background of people frequenting it. In 1987, Jim Sleeper summed up the redevelopment process of Times Square when he wrote: "It's as if politicians and developers wanted to 'whiten' the complexion of Manhattan and, more broadly, to get rid of the wage-earning poor."[44] Times

Square experienced many problems in the post–World War II period, but even during its darkest hours it represented a major destination for millions of Americans. Despite the emphasis on commercialized sex, the district also functioned as an entertainment destination for young African Americans and Latinos who found the cultural infrastructures of their neighborhoods wanting. The great majority of these young people went to Times Square in order to see action movies and frequent inexpensive restaurants, pool rooms, and bars. As it turned out, the city government and mainstream business sector considered the proliferation of such a great number of young minority people in Times Square to be antithetical to New York's image. They also viewed the proliferation of such populations to be damaging to real estate prospects. Thus, by the late 1980s, they displaced them in order to make Times Square a more attractive place for more affluent white visitors. The displacement of young African Americans and Latinos from Times Square preceded that of the sex-oriented businesses.

Columbia University sociologist Herbert Gans advanced the most scathing rebuttal against the claims of the environmental-impact statement. In a report that he prepared on behalf of the Brandt Corporation, which controlled many of the area's theaters, Gans argued that the authors of the environmental-impact statement had manipulated statistics so that they could prove ideas that the city and the state had been advancing about Times Square. Gans particularly took issue with the section of the state document that discussed the disorderly street conditions:

> This entire sector of the EIS is an attempt to justify class-displacement in the project area: to move out lower-income citizens and taxpayers and to replace them with more affluent ones. This bias is so extensive that it even pervades the architectural jargon. For example, the bright lights that are now condemned as "garish," will after redevelopment supply "glitter and excitement"; and at that time, the project area will exhibit "an active pedestrian environment," the report's architectural euphemism for affluent loitering.[45]

Gans concluded that the statement was a "commercial" for the project and if anyone was to accept the statement's definitions of loitering, then "New York is full of loiterers."[46]

Many critics and scholars characterized the redevelopment trends of Times Square in the 1980s as part of what they considered to be the "Disneyfication" of public space. Brendan Gill, who opposed the city–state redevelopment plan of Times Square, characterized the project as "architectural Disneyitis," which he defined as the removal of disorderly cultural elements that disturbed "the members of the prosperous white middle class." Sharon Zukin pointed out how Walt Disney recreated desirable small-town images by screening out of the design potentially "negative, unwanted elements." Michael Sorkin went as far as to lament the end of public space because of interventions such as Disneyfication. Such critiques gained even more credibility once it became clear that Disney Corporation would become one of the protagonists of redevelopment in Times Square.[47]

An important step in the redevelopment process involved the taking of Times Square properties through eminent domain. States and some localities can use eminent domain to unilaterally acquire property from a private owner for a legitimate public purpose. Although the state must pay a fair price, eminent domain means that the buyer and not the seller sets the price. The Board of Estimate justified its decision to use eminent domain in Times Square by arguing that the project area was physically, economically, and socially blighted and that its redevelopment would better the area and the city in general. The owners of the properties to be taken over by the city disagreed with the blight assessment; in fact, proprietors such as the Brandt Organization that Gans attempted to defend had restored two theaters for legitimate use and proposed to restore others at their own expense. The most significant legal challenges against the taking over of Times Square properties by the city and the state surrounded the issue of legitimate public purpose. Opponents of eminent domain argued that the city's plan would simply transfer the properties from one set of private owners to another and that such action did not constitute a legitimate public purpose. The courts accepted the superiority of eminent domain over all private property rights. They also accepted the city's argument that the area was blighted and agreed that the transfer of the properties taken through eminent domain could serve the public interest even though they would be transferred to private developers.[48]

In the end, the project succeeded because of government flexibility and improving economic prospects. In the early 1990s, the project had slowed down because of an economic recession and an office space glut in Manhattan. State and city officials agreed to requests by the developers to postpone some of the office tower construction and sought a low-rise solution to the site. In the mid-1990s, however, as the economy improved, many corporations and retailers that were not included in the original plan agreed to open facilities in Times Square and construct new buildings. For the first time in seventy years, Times Square became a landscape that showcased contemporary global and national capitalism. Corporate symbols had always dominated the billboards and towers of Times Square, but now global corporate entities actually relocated to Times Square. For example, the presence of financial companies such as Prudential Financial, Nasdaq Marketplace, and Reuters gave Times Square a legitimate corporate look. MTV, with its studios on location, made the area popular among teenagers and other music lovers. Restaurant chains such as Chevy's, Applebee's, Chili's, McDonald's, and T.G.I. Friday's, which were usually located in the suburbs, flooded Times Square, making the area comfortable for suburbanites. ESPN Zone and a New York Yankees store appealed to sports fans, while stores and entertainment venues like Toys 'R' Us, Planet Hollywood,

Virgin Megastore, Bar Code, and Loews Theaters provided the area with a mainstream retail character. Restored theaters, many of which were taken over by large corporations, continued the theatrical tradition of the Great White Way. Ironically, Madame Tussaud's opened a wax museum in a location very close to where Ripley's had operated a wax museum before it closed in the early 1970s. The combination of retailers, media empires, financial companies, and theaters that appeared in Times Square in the 1990s made the area attractive to white middle- and upper-class visitors.

A final touch included a zoning amendment that eliminated sex businesses. As the Rudolph Giuliani Administration (1994–2001) discovered, the sex industry also benefitted from the recovery of the area, serving suburban visitors and office workers. The number of adult-oriented businesses increased from 131 in 1984 to 177 in 1993. However, such a vibrant, commercialized sex activity tarnished the white, suburban, family vision of Times Square. In 1995, the City of New York enacted a zoning resolution that banned "adult establishments" from residential and most commercial areas. The resolution also mandated that adult establishments must be located at least 500 feet away from residential or commercial areas and 500 feet from schools, churches, and one another. This zoning resolution shut down almost 90% of existing sex-oriented businesses in New York City. Legal challenges failed, since the courts usually upheld land use decisions by municipalities. Because of this resolution, Times Square could once again rid itself of commercialized sex and other areas would not have to become the recipients of fleeing Times Square operators.[49]

4 Neoliberalism, Neoconservatism, and Spatial Regulation

After the fiscal crisis, New York City became the neoliberal city par excellence, though many of its politicians used neoconservative ideology in order to win elections and create policy. Neoliberalism and neoconservatism are two complicated and distinct late-twentieth-century political ideologies with many elements of convergence in the United States. Both neoliberalism and neoconservatism matured as social theories in the 1960s and became intellectual movements that by the late 1970s were able to influence public policy. Both were also used by politicians in order to advance their political careers, attack New Deal liberalism and its legacy, and propose solutions to festering social and economic conditions. Furthermore, both have sought to radically reorganize the political sphere, shape principles of governance, and redefine citizenship. Neoliberalism is a theory of political–economic practices that promotes the deregulation of capitalist markets, the reduction of international trade barriers, the privatization of state companies, the growth of private investment, and the withdrawal of the state from public provision. Neoconservatism as a theory embraces family values, promotes traditional gender roles, values conservative religious movements, and encourages patriotism. Neoconservatives view the alliance of the state with the business sector as the best way for the capitalist economy to grow, though they want the state and not the corporations to be in command. Neoconservatives view the Republican Party as a vehicle for their policies, though some Democratic politicians have also embraced these ideas. Since at least the 1970s, neoconservatism has profoundly influenced American conservatism; however, most conservatives continue to use the conservative label and avoid the term "neoconservative," which is considered more of an intellectual position.[1]

Ed Koch, David Dinkins, and Rudy Giuliani were New York's first three mayors during the city's neoliberal era. Both Koch, whose administration spanned between 1978 and 1989, and Giuliani, whose administration lasted between 1994 and 2001, embraced neoconservatism and neoliberalism and used elements of these two political ideologies in order to run the government, manage the economy, maintain order, fight crime, and gain the electoral support of white ethnics. They cultivated a culture of racial intolerance in the city's outer boroughs, attacked portions of the city's Black and Latino populations for receiving public assistance and for being disorderly, and reformed the city government into a business-friendly entity that subsidized the expansion of the corporate and real estate sectors. Without their neoconservative rhetoric and actions, Giuliani and Koch would have been unable to gain the electoral support of their core white ethnic supporters. Without their neoliberal policies, both mayors would have been unable to gain the support of the corporate sector. The combination of neoliberalism and neoconservatism by these two mayors and their administrations proved winning electoral formulas in a city that was politically very challenging. Their fight against urban disorder also strengthened their neoliberal and neoconservative credentials. David Dinkins, whose mayoralty was between 1990 and 1993, was considered a liberal. He attempted to distance his administration from the prevailing political–economic structure of the city but failed. The corporate and real estate sectors did not allow him to reverse the neoliberal economic and social reforms that had taken place since the fiscal crisis. Dinkins was also against neoconservatism and its discourse on race relations, and this contributed to the strengthening of the conservative coalition that supported Giuliani.

The neoliberal reforms of the post-1975 period displaced many poor people and generated an increasingly disorderly public space. This was catastrophic for New York because the city government had shrunk its size and did not have the resources to deal with this displacement of the poor or with public disorderly conditions. Although proponents of neoliberalism argue that the state should reduce its size and scope so that capitalist accumulation can occur freely, the state needs to guarantee that this capital accumulation can occur without interference from groups that are unable to conform to this new order. Neoconservative criminology, with its prescription of an unforgiving law and order apparatus, came to the rescue of the neoliberal city. The police force was enlarged at the expense of other governmental functions because powerholders decided that there was a need for a more comprehensive and efficient regulation of urban space.

AMERICAN LIBERALISM AND CONSERVATISM

The period between the New Deal in the 1930s and the Great Society in the 1960s is viewed as the twentieth-century heyday of the Democratic Party and American liberalism. During this period, a Democratic political order emerged, matured, and held power. Progressive liberalism became the political philosophy that distinguished this Democratic order from previous dominant political regimes and their ideologies. Despite the difficulty of clearly defining liberalism, it contained the following general characteristics: (1) a commitment to the maintenance and expansion of a welfare state established during the New Deal; (2) a belief that the government should regulate the market on behalf of middle- and working-class people; and (3) a positive view of the state's role in promoting racial equal opportunity. Liberalism became so dominant during the 1932–1968 period that many Republican politicians also accepted its basic principles. In New York, liberalism constituted a major ideological part of both the Democratic and Republican political parties. Nelson Rockefeller, who was governor of New York between 1959 and 1973, was a liberal Republican even though he became increasingly conservative in the late 1960s and early 1970s. Many observers consider John V. Lindsay to have been the most liberal postwar mayor of New York City; he switched to the Democratic Party in 1971, though he was originally elected to the office of mayor as a Republican.[2]

Conservatives, who were politically marginalized since the late 1920s when they were held responsible for the Great Depression, began to make a comeback in the 1960s by focusing on crime, social disorder, and race. Conservatives blamed liberals for the breakdown of social order in the United States. In particular, they accused liberals of encouraging disrespect for law and authority through civil disobedience, which had been popularized by the civil rights movement. Conservatives also blamed the Supreme Court for decisions that enhanced the rights of criminal defendants and resented what appeared to be the rewarding of criminal behavior by urban rioters through Great Society programs. Conservatives successfully blurred street crime with protest actions. Many of these ideas were advanced by neoconservative thinkers who were increasingly influencing the conservative movement. Law and order as a central campaign issue propelled Ronald Reagan to the office of governor of California, allowed the Patrolmen's Benevolent Association (PBA) to win a referendum against the civilian police review board in New York City, and helped Richard Nixon become president of the United States. In New York, Governor Rockefeller, who had presidential ambitions, began to move to the right so that he could be in sync with the national Republican Party and began to advocate a tougher treatment of criminals. The enactment of the Rockefeller Drug Laws in 1973 by the state legislature was part of this conservative transformation. Conservative politicians continued to exploit the law and order issue in the 1970s and the 1980s, which retained its racial overtones.[3]

THE NEOLIBERALIZATION OF NEW YORK CITY

Neoliberal prescriptions are based on the idea of a liberalized financial and trade regime that encourages direct foreign investment, unrestricted capital flows, and a competitive exchange rate. These economic principles are enhanced and safeguarded by a smaller government that reduces taxes, privatizes public services, establishes fiscal discipline, and deregulates the private sector. Although neoliberalism as a political–economic system was not as obvious before the 1990s, a number of political–economic reforms based on neoclassical economic theories that embraced free market principles have occurred since the 1970s. In the 1990s, neoliberalism as an economic orthodoxy was articulated as the "Washington Consensus" and was enthusiastically embraced by President Bill Clinton and Prime Minister Tony Blair. As an economic blueprint, neoliberalism was promoted globally by the International Monetary Fund and the World Bank. In terms of economic theory, neoliberal economics developed in the 1950s and the 1960s and was based on the ideas of political philosopher Friedrich von Hayek and economist Milton Friedman. Both Friedman and Hayek viewed themselves as liberals in the traditional European sense because of their belief in freedom. The term "neoliberalism" gradually appeared after Hayek and Friedman embraced the free market imperatives of neoclassical economics. Although Hayek, Friedman, and their associates were considered to be mavericks in the economics profession in the 1950s and 1960s, they entered the academic mainstream in the mid-1970s when Hayek won the Nobel Prize in economics in 1974 and Friedman in 1976. Both Friedman and Hayek grew skeptical of Keynesian economics, which constituted the economic orthodoxy of the capitalist world between the New Deal and the early 1970s and advocated the withdrawal of the state from the market. Influenced by Adam Smith, Friedman argued that the main function of the government "must be to protect our freedom both from the enemies outside our gates and from our fellow-citizens: to preserve law and order, to enforce private contracts, to foster competitive markets."[4] This meant that the basic purpose of the government was to maintain a military and a police force. Eventually this idea was adopted by neoliberal proponents, who suggested that the primary function of the state is to guarantee private property rights. In the 1970s, neoliberalism replaced embedded liberalism—the post–World War II international political economic system of the industrialized west wherein states minimized the harmful effects of open markets through regulation, social provision, and the maintenance of social safety nets. As the principles guiding embedded capitalism began to falter and a crisis of capital accumulation threatened the economic power of the elites in many parts of the world, neoliberalism emerged as the predominant theory of political economy. Neoliberalization was a way for elites to maintain their social and economic power and ensure the subjugation of restless middle- and low-income populations in a period of profound crisis. David Harvey has contended that above all, "neoliberalization has been a vehicle for the restoration of class power."[5] Unlike the more egalitarian political–economic system that it replaced, neoliberalism redistributed wealth upward and increasing social inequality became one of its main characteristics. In the United States, neoliberal reforms since the 1970s created a spectacular concentration of wealth among few families, a phenomenon that has not been encountered since the Gilded Age, the period before World War I. In the 2000s, the term "New Gilded Age" was invented to characterize this new superaffluent class and its fortunes.[6]

New York City was one of the first locations in the world to experience a neoliberal intervention. It was in 1975 when the business elites of New York, dissatisfied with the direction of the city and its political leadership, refused to continue lending the municipal government money and forced it into a technical bankruptcy. According to Joshua Freeman, this maneuver amounted to the overthrow of the elected government of the city by the financial elites, which used the fiscal crisis to dictate their vision of New York:

> In the recession and the budget crisis, financial leaders saw an opportunity to undo the past, to restructure New York along lines more to their liking than those drawn by decades of liberalism and labor action. They wanted less and less costly government, fiscal probity, and the desocialization of services and protections for the working class and the poor. They also wanted humbled municipal unions that no longer would enable government workers to have superior benefits and a less intense pace of work than private-sector workers. The banks had not been able to effect such a program during the post–World War II years, a testament to the strength of labor and its allies. But as the city began sliding toward insolvency, they saw a greater need and a greater possibility of carrying out their financial and social agenda.[7]

To that end, the leaders of the city's financial community—men such as David Rockefeller, chairman of the Chase Manhattan Bank, William Salomon, managing partner of Salomon Brothers, Ellmore Patterson, chairman of the Morgan Guaranty Trust, Donald T. Regan, chairman of Merrill Lynch, John F. McGillicuddy, president of Manufacturers Hanover, and William T. Spencer, president of First National City Bank (later renamed Citibank)—formed the Financial Community Liaison Group in order to pressure political leaders to make the right kinds of reforms and to guarantee investors the city's solvency. In late 1972, Secretary of the Treasury William Simon headed the municipal bond division at Salomon Brothers and was implicated in the debt creation of New York. In 1975 he turned down Mayor Abe Beame's requests for short-term federal loan guarantees because he despised the city's social policies that went against the free market. Simon believed that the causes of New York's fiscal crisis were liberal municipal policies that generously subsidized the middle class such as: rent control, middle-income housing, free public universities, inexpensive public health, and excellent public employee benefits along with high wages. In response to the fiscal crisis, the State of New York created the Municipal Assistance Corporation and the Emergency Financial Control Board, public organizations dominated by business leaders. These organizations took over the city's budget and debt payment. New York's mayor Abe Beame and the city council remained in office, though their power was seriously diminished.[8]

Elected in 1977, Ed Koch was New York's first neoliberal mayor and quickly became a favorite of the financial community. Once he had taken office, Koch indicated that his main priority would be to revitalize the city's economy by creating an administration that would support the expansion of the business sector and balance the local government's budget with a reduction of public employment. In the beginning of his administration, Koch said that "the main job of municipal government is to create a climate in which private business can expand in the city to provide jobs and profits. It's not the function of government to create jobs on the public payroll."[9] Besides increasing the developmental functions of the city government so that it could assist the expansion of the corporate sectors, the Koch Administration attempted to lower the operating costs of its agencies though efficiency measures, tough negotiations with municipal unions, and the replacement of higher-paid workers with ones who were paid much less. Under Koch's stewardship and with the aid of an economic recovery, the City of New York was able to repay its fiscal crisis debts in 1981, one year ahead of schedule. After this recovery, the city government began to subsidize a real estate expansion of Manhattan through the building of offices and luxury condominiums. The city government also became involved in public–private partnerships such as the redevelopment of Times Square and took financial responsibility for projects that benefitted the private sector. These actions made Koch very popular in the business community, which supported his reelection efforts handily. Many observers have credited Koch with making New York a leader of the new global economy, with an agglomeration of financial, banking, media, real estate, and culture industries thriving there. Many individuals working in top positions of these corporations benefitted markedly and pulled away financially from the middle and lower classes.[10]

In contrast, the city's poor suffered disproportionately from the fiscal retrenchment and the upward redistribution of resources that accompanied the fiscal crisis. In the 1981 volume of their annual survey of the city's economy, Charles Brecher and Raymond Horton wrote: "These policies yielded a balanced budget, but at what cost? And for whom? The greatest burden was borne by the city's poor, whose standard of living was reduced."[11] On the one hand, the proportion of the city's population living under the poverty level increased from 15% in 1975 to 23.4% in 1985, meaning that the number of people with incomes below 75% of the poverty line went from 560,000 to 1,100,000. On the other hand, the top 10% of the city's population received almost a third of all income increases, while the top 20% gained half of all income increases. The Koch Administration continued to curtail social services but increased spending in the form of property tax reductions for corporations that promised to create more jobs and tax breaks for luxury residential housing. Consequently, entities such as AT&T, the Rockefeller Center, and the Park Avenue Trump Tower received tax breaks that amounted to hundreds of millions. Under Koch, the city government oriented itself toward subsidizing the large corporate sector and continued to withdraw from social services that assisted the poor.[12]

After the fiscal crisis, the city's leaders of banking and finance continued to influence city governance. Not only did they oversee New York's budget decisions through the state's public organizations, they also formed and strengthened their own public policy interest groups. In 1979, David Rockefeller founded the New York City Partnership and affiliated it with the Chamber of Commerce; Rockefeller's vision of the Partnership was "to allow business leaders to work more directly with government and other civic groups to address broader social and economic problems in a 'hands on' way."[13] This more direct approach of the business sector to government guided public policy in the decades that followed. Mayors were increasingly required to consult the business community for major decisions, including the distribution of resources in the city. Moreover, business interests began to remake the image of the city according to their liking.[14]

In these early days of neoliberalization, Koch proved to be indispensable because he cultivated an existing culture of intolerance and kept it in focus. His neoconservative rants against welfare kingpins, graffiti writers, and the underclass were always racially coded. Koch praised multinational corporations, Wall Street, and real estate companies and developers for their role in providing middle-class jobs and improving the city's economy and argued that the only way to economic well-being was the expansion of intensified capital accumulation. As displaced poor people became more visible in public space, Koch attempted to move against them. His failure to make these populations vanish from high-profile public spaces led in many ways to his defeat in 1989.

The election of David Dinkins in 1989 to the office of mayor was viewed as a rejection to the business- and real estate-friendly regime that had prevailed since the fiscal crisis, but almost immediately, the reality of neoliberal pressures set in. Dinkins had the bad luck of inheriting a local economy that had declined since the stock market crash of 1987 and worsened in 1990 because of the national recession of 1990–1991. In addition, by 1991 the city's financial elites began to demand substantial budget cuts and Governor Mario Cuomo threatened that if the 1991 city budget facing a $1.8 billion deficit was not balanced, he would ask the state's Financial Control Board to take over the city's finances. Dinkins capitulated to these demands, reduced social and other municipal services, and was never able to adequately address the worsening condition of low-income households. Meanwhile, the New York City Partnership along with other business and real estate interests pressured Dinkins to continue Koch's probusiness policies and provide hundreds of millions of dollars in commercial and real estate incentives. While Dinkins had repeatedly criticized the developmental tax incentive programs under Koch during his campaign, his pledge to eliminate them was never realized. If anything, the Dinkins Administration increased existing tax incentives and created new ones, realizing that there was probably no alternative. This business-friendly approach did not help Dinkins electorally because members of his coalition became frustrated with his inability to engender substantive changes.[15]

In the 1990s under Mayor Rudolph Giuliani—who replaced Dinkins and created a new electoral coalition with an emphasis on crime fighting, welfare reduction, and racial scapegoating—inequality continued to increase and the city government kept on pursuing fiscal and land use policies that benefitted the corporate and the real estate sectors. It is remarkable to consider that during the amazing economic growth of the 1990s when the real personal income of city residents rose by $72.63 billion, 80% of the city's families saw their income drop. In the outer boroughs of Queens, The Bronx, and Brooklyn, the median family income declined by more than 7%. Middle-class households declined significantly in the city and the structure of inequality began to resemble that of Brazil, which at the time was one of the most unequal societies in the world. The top fifth of the city's income earners made fifty-two times the income of the lowest fifth. The average yearly income of families in the East Midtown of Manhattan was $825,267, while households in the Wagner Houses in East Harlem had a median income of $9,320. The Giuliani Administration continued to provide tax benefits to corporations such as ABC, CBS, CS First Boston, Smith Barney, and many others; in return, these corporations promised to maintain their workforce in the city and, if possible, expand it. In many cases these promises were not kept. Many of these jobs were held by people living outside of the city, but this did not seem to matter in terms of business policy. Moreover, the city government provided tax breaks for leases and renovations mostly for office buildings in downtown Manhattan; some of these benefits were extended to midtown Manhattan. Hundreds of millions of dollars were devoted to these developmental projects each year at a time when the city was facing severe budgetary problems. In fact, the New York City Partnership requested that Giuliani cut 50,000 municipal jobs because of the city's financial woes. By 1997, the city administration had cut 36,000 jobs through layoffs or attrition.[16]

THE RISE OF NEOCONSERVATIVE CRIMINOLOGY

Although neoconservatism is not easy to define and is often blurred with movements and entities such as traditional conservatism, the Republican Party, and the American right, it is safe to say that the proliferation of neoconservative ideas in the 1960s and the 1970s helped to attract many people to the conservative movement. In common parlance, since at least the 1970s, there has been a conflation of conservatism with neoconservatism. This is because neoconservative ideas have influenced the conservative movement to the extent that traditional conservatism is no longer as prominent or understood by many people who consider themselves conservatives.

Irving Kristol, who has been "the godfather of neoconservatism," has outlined a number of basic tenets that define neoconservatism. He claims that unlike traditional conservatives and neoliberals, neoconservatives are comfortable with the growth of the state in the twentieth century and that they only object to the concentration of welfare services within that state and would like to see a diversification of welfare providers. Kristol also argues that neoconservatives believe in tax cuts so that the economy can continue to grow steadily; that they agree with traditional conservatives that modern American mass culture is vulgar and that the government should take a role in influencing the proliferation of American values; that they view patriotism to a be a natural sentiment that should be promoted by the public and private sectors; and that they are comfortable with U.S. intervention abroad, especially when it comes to defending a democratic nation under attack from antidemocratic entities.[17]

Although New York City cannot be adequately defined as neoconservative city, many white ethnic voters, among others, were attracted to neoconservative ideas in the 1960s and 1970s. Ed Koch used some of these neoconservative ideas in order to differentiate himself in the crowded field for the office of mayor in 1977 and continued to use neoconservative ideology in order to scapegoat racial minorities when it came to issues of crime and welfare throughout his mayoralty. Rudy Giuliani was also increasingly guided by neoconservative ideology.

Contemporary neoconservative approaches to crime, disorder, and urban development are influenced by the writings of Edward C. Banfield. Regarding the urban crisis of the 1960s and the 1970s, Banfield explained urban decline as an evolutionary process that he referred to as the "logic of metropolitan growth." According to his argument, well-to-do downtown residents abandoned the central cities not because of white flight, crime, or urban decay, but because of their desire to live in larger, more luxurious homes. Given that these populations could afford the cost of commuting, they chose to move to suburban locations around the city. They were replaced by low-income people who valued downtown's proximity to jobs, stores, and public infrastructures. The affluent people who left the central city viewed this process of population change as neighborhood decay. The lower-income newcomers did not. Banfield argued that low-income people did not care about unkempt lawns or broken bottles. In fact, they welcomed some of the disrepair of their immediate environment because they understood that low rents depended on a degree of physical disorder. They were more interested in houses with decent plumbing and heating systems rather than in the appearance of their neighborhoods. For Banfield, this meant that lower-class families were culturally different from middle- and upper-class families who were paying attention to cosmetic neighborhood factors such as grass lawns and the absence of sidewalk garbage.[18]

Although the logic of metropolitan growth explained the process of central city decline, Banfield admitted that it did not fully explain why low-income people generated such disorderly conditions in their new neighborhoods; he turned to social class in order to explain this phenomenon. Banfield argued that social class was a complicated concept and that American sociologists defined it in differing ways. Some of these definitions relied on objective criteria such as "income, schooling, occupation," some on subjective criteria such as "attitudes, tastes, values," and some on the position that a group of people held in a "deference hierarchy." Banfield's concept of class emphasized the cultural traits of lower-class people and was deeply influenced by arguments found in the "culture of poverty" literature.[19]

The culture-of-poverty argument of the 1960s and the 1970s was based on the early ideas set forth by anthropologist Oscar Lewis. A Marxist who believed that the cultural traits of the poor could be transformed by revolutionary processes such as the socialist revolution in Cuba, the civil rights movement in the United States, or the independence movement in Algeria, Lewis made many arguments about poor people in Latin America that others were able to exploit. He argued that the poor were disorganized, lazy, unambitious, and fatalistic. There were two important characteristics that defined this culture of poverty: (1) the poor were present minded to a fault and were unable to postpone instant gratification; and (2) the poor were caught in a cycle of poverty that was familial and intergenerational. This meant that unlike middle- and upper-class people, poor people could not plan for the future and, as a result, their situation would remain the same. This also implied that they would be unable to defer gratification even if that meant that they would have to suffer in the future and that upward mobility did not apply to the poor because the culture of poverty influenced children, who reproduced the behavior of their parents.[20]

Banfield developed a social class typology based on the orientation of certain groups toward the future. He argued that upper-class individuals had a tendency of being the most future oriented, that they looked forward to the future of not only their family but also of mankind, nation, and the community, and that they felt that they could influence the future according to their ideas. According Banfield's typology, middle-class individuals were less future oriented than the upper classes and working-class individuals even less. Lower-class individuals were present minded to a fault, had no conception of the future, could not discipline themselves, and sought action and instant gratification. Banfield blamed lower-class individuals for generating many social problems, including crime and urban disorder:

> Although he has more "leisure" than almost anyone, the indifference ("apathy" if one prefers) of the lower-class person is such that he seldom makes even the simplest repairs to the place that he lives in. He is not troubled by dirt or dilapidation and he does not mind the inadequacy of public facilities such as schools, parks, hospitals, and libraries; indeed, where such things exist he may destroy them by carelessness or even by vandalism.[21]

Banfield found the slum to be the perfect place for the lower-class individual because most things there happened by chance, everything was disorganized, and social disorder was the norm. Because of these factors, lower-class individuals did not attract as much attention in these neighborhoods, could engage in irresponsible behavior, and could get involved in criminal activities. Even if these criminal activities took place in a different neighborhood, lower-class individuals could always withdraw back into the chaos of their own neighborhoods.

James Q. Wilson, who was originally Banfield's student and eventually his collaborator and colleague, also attempted to explain urban decline by examining urban disorder. As early as 1969, Wilson wrote about how the function of the police gradually changed from that of order maintenance to crime fighting and how this development damaged the social and physical fabric of certain neighborhoods. Wilson argued that powerholders originally entrusted the police with maintaining order, leaving crime fighting to private detectives, often ex-criminals who worked for people who suffered losses on a contingency-fee basis. In time, the police absorbed these detectives and their crime-fighting objectives while professional prosecutors took over the responsibility of prosecuting criminals. In the 1960s, the developments of urban rioting and a steep rise in crime further weakened the everyday order-maintenance function of the police. Instead of focusing on how to make the streets safer, police departments in the wake of the riots concentrated on preventing and reducing the incidence of mass violence. Because of the crime wave, police departments had to increase crime-fighting activities and show results based on the number of arrests of criminals and the number of crimes solved.[22]

In the 1970s, Wilson, who became the founder of neoconservative criminology, contended that public policy makers should stop worrying about the causes of crime such as present-orientedness and poverty and focus on situational factors that made crime a rewarding activity. This argument was based on the disdain that neoconservatives had for the legacy of New Deal liberalism and the presidency of Lyndon Johnson in particular. In 1964, responding to attacks that he was doing nothing about crime, President Johnson proclaimed that the War on Poverty was an anticrime measure. In 1965, Johnson launched an actual war on crime, but conservatives kept accusing him of being soft on crime. In the 1970s, Wilson advocated the return of order-maintenance policing coupled with changes in the criminal justice system that included aggressive policing and arrest practices, longer prison sentences, mandatory sentencing, rapid trials, and a reduction of prosecutorial and judicial discretion. Like Banfield, Wilson rejected the emphasis of the New Deal and the Great Society on fighting poverty but unlike Banfield, he recommended an activist criminal justice system that maintained strict order in low-income neighborhoods that would ultimately find and punish criminals. For Wilson, the reduction of serious crime would also allow the police to devote more time to order maintenance.[23]

Wilson's view of the necessity of a tougher criminal justice system coincided with the development of the concept of the underclass, which cast young, low-income minority populations as problematic for cities and their public space. The discourse on the underclass began to obscure the differences between social disorder and serious crime and began to emphasize the similarity of offenders in terms of race, class, gender, and age. Young African Americans and Latinos were branded as disorderly people with a high propensity for crime. Many writers on the underclass found the groups to be different from the poor of the past and recommended that the only effective intervention government could make was with stricter law enforcement. Banfield and Wilson already considered low-income people problematic before these underclass theories even existed. In the late 1970s, their writings merged with theories on the underclass, producing a more coherent body of literature that encouraged the banishment of certain low-income people who were considered unruly.[24]

As neoconservatives soon discovered, the enactment of legislation that established a draconian criminal justice system did not solve problems associated with social disorder. People who were considered objectionable and committed minor violations or no violations at all were not the serious criminals that neoconservatives wanted to imprison. The spatial regulation of these populations required a different criminal justice approach—one that branded certain kinds of appearance in public or behavior as unacceptable. The "broken windows" theory provided this approach in conceptual terms. It attempted to collapse the difference between serious crime and social disorder when it came to spatial regulation. In 1982, Wilson and George L. Kelling advanced this theory, which proved influential in the way in which authorities tried to reclaim New York's public space for the middle and upper classes. In an article that appeared in *The Atlantic*, Wilson and Kelling claimed that the appearance of disorder caused more damage than crime itself and cited the results of a New Jersey state program that targeted urban neighborhoods in the 1970s. The centerpiece of the program had consisted of the deployment of foot patrols instead of vehicle patrols. Five years into the program, foot patrols had not reduced crime; in fact, crime statistics rose in most of the neighborhoods under the program. However, many residents perceived a decrease in crime because of the appearance of officers walking their streets. These officers had an effect on ordering public space in a recognizable pattern. Wilson and Kelling argued that the program succeeded because many people feared "being bothered by disorderly people." Wilson and Kelling admitted that some of the methods employed by the foot patrols in order to discipline disorderly populations would not withstand legal challenge but viewed them as necessary for the well-being of the community. In the "broken windows" theory, Wilson and Kelling explained the post–World War II decline of American cities in similar ways that Wilson had previously done. They claimed that in earlier times, everyone in the community had an intrinsic interest in retaking neighborhoods from disorderly people because exit options such as suburbanization did not exist. The police supported the "reassertion of authority by acting, sometimes violently, on behalf of the community." Thus, after events threatened the order of a neighborhood, "Young toughs were roughed up, people were arrested on 'suspicion' or for vagrancy, and prostitutes and petty thieves were routed." Eventually this practice vanished because many neighborhood families did not put up a fight and simply abandoned the old neighborhood and its problems. Unless residents showed that they cared, the police force could not maintain order by itself.[25]

Order maintenance became a key strategy in the efforts of the city government to regulate low-income people in public space and to transform portions of New York into desirable locations for white middle- and upper-class populations. In that sense, order maintenance replaced urban renewal as a way to rebuild neighborhoods. This does not mean that physical solutions were completely discarded but that social solutions were emphasized. As the city recovered financially, its government began to focus on ways to dominate public space comprehensively and began to dismantle mechanisms that used to provide public assistance to low-income people. This meant that there was a redistribution of resources that went from social welfare to spatial regulation. The "broken windows" theory and its public policy application became the blueprint for taming urban disorder in New York City. From the early 1980s onward, order-maintenance activities by the police increased and intensified, though not continuously because of budget problems. However, the number of police officers increased substantially in the early 1990s under Mayor Dinkins and the police department was significantly reformed during the Giuliani Administration. Mayor Giuliani and his police commissioners began to use the terms "order maintenance," "quality-of-life policing," "broken windows," and "zero tolerance" in order to describe policing strategies and goals in the 1990s. The decline of crime rates during the period offered order maintenance the credibility that it needed and made it the preferred way of tackling crime and urban disorder.

5 Graffiti as a Manifestation of Social Disorder

"The perception of space is not what space *is* but one of its representations; in this sense built space has no more authority than drawings, photographs, or descriptions."[1]

—Beatriz Colomina, Architect

"A clean car [of a subway train] is a symbol of an authority in control of its environment . . . It is a direct communication to passengers that the system is orderly."[2]

—David L. Gunn, New York City Transit Authority President

In the 1970s and the 1980s, the authorities of New York City designated hip-hop culture as a threat to urban order and sought to regulate it. City administrations targeted all three principal manifestations of hip-hop culture: graffiti, breakdancing, and rap music. However, most of the attention was paid to graffiti writing because of its disorderly appearance in space. Inscriptions by young Latinos and African Americans began to dominate public space in the 1970s and challenged notions of social and physical order. Although the result of writing was defined as physical disorder because quasipermanent inscriptions became part of the physical infrastructure, the act of writing graffiti was defined as social disorder. As efforts to erase graffiti from buildings, subways, and other facades could not keep up with new inscriptions, the authorities attempted to regulate the mobility of potential graffiti writers.

The persistence of graffiti gave the impression that the authorities had completely lost control of the city. During a 1983 visit to New York City, James Reynolds, who had not ridden the New York subway since he moved to the suburbs in Connecticut in the early 1970s, said "the graffiti makes you wonder just who is in charge down here anyway."[3] A *New York Times* editorial confirmed Reynolds' sentiments by saying that subway graffiti signified "the spiraling loss of public authority."[4] Another editorial in the *Chicago Tribune* attested that "the presence of graffiti . . . creates an atmosphere conducive to vandalism and crime against riders. It can turn the daily commute into a Hieronymous Bosch vision of hell."[5] U.S. Senator Alfonse D'Amato (R-NY), a Long Islander, said "I'm afraid to get in that subway system even when I'm with my bodyguard."[6] On several occasions,

Figure 5.1 Graffiti piece in the southern Bronx. (Photograph by Themis Chronopoulos, 1997.)

Metropolitan Transportation Authority (MTA) president David Gunn mentioned that graffiti created a perception of disorder and that the subway system seemed to be out of control.[7] A *New York Times* reporter argued that "the onslaught of graffiti gave passengers the sense that the public realm was not a place of order but a jungle."[8] After graffiti writers began to scrawl on garbage trucks, the following was written: "White trucks that once were rolling symbols of efficiency and cleanliness now convey messages of disorder and dirt."[9] In an article on social ills, Nathan Glazer wrote that "Crime is believed to lurk everywhere and the graffiti reminds one that the unsocialized are everywhere."[10]

The spatial and discursive war that emerged during the campaign against graffiti targeted African American and Latino youths, who had functioned as scapegoats for many of the problems the city experienced during the postwar period. City powerholders used antigraffiti efforts as part of a strategy that sought restrict the activities of people of color in public spaces. Many whites supported these efforts, since graffiti in their neighborhoods and business districts symbolized the presence of Blacks and Latinos and illustrated stagnant property values and devalued spatial status.

Graffiti writing and hip-hop culture irked both neoconservatives and neoliberals. Neoconservatives who had taken over the underclass debate viewed hip-hop culture as a manifestation of juvenile delinquency that could easily mutate to criminality. Neoliberals in government and the private sector who

Figure 5.2 Mural of Notorious B.I.G. in the Bronx after his untimely death. (Photograph by Themis Chronopoulos, 1997.)

wanted to improve the image of the city after the fiscal crisis, did not want New York to be viewed as the capital of hip-hop. Both groups blamed the John V. Lindsay Administration (1966–1973) for failing to discipline graffiti writers and protect subway trains and public spaces from their inscriptions. After a decline in aggressive policing actions because of the fiscal crisis, the Ed Koch Administration (1978–1989) combined the justifications provided by neoliberalism and neoconservatism in order to declare a new war against the spatial manifestations of hip-hop culture in the 1980s.

THE EMERGENCE OF GRAFFITI WRITING AND HIP-HOP CULTURE

In the 1950s and the 1960s, graffiti acquired a symbolic meaning associated with young people and their efforts to dominate space. Urban graffiti originated when street gangs began to demarcate their territories. The most threatening gang graffiti appeared at street junctures where neighborhoods of different ethnic and racial backgrounds met, with messages such as "Keep Out," "You Are Now Entering Dragons Territory," "White Power," "Dominicans Not Allowed," and "Down to Kill." Graffiti inscriptions also appeared in parks, around pools, and in other public facilities that gangs sought to dominate. Boundary graffiti functioned both as a device to dissuade competing groups from venturing into claimed turf and as a way to affirm a gang's power.[11]

In the 1960s, as gang activity declined, partly as a result of government-supported outreach programs and the influence of social movements, political graffiti began to replace gang graffiti. Messages advocating civil rights, welfare rights, and the end of the Vietnam War appeared on government buildings and university campuses. Morningside Heights was especially hard hit by graffiti because students there resented the relationship between Columbia University and the Institute of Defense Analysis. In addition, Harlem youngsters opposed the expansion of Columbia toward Harlem. The boundaries between gangs within Harlem became less important than those between Harlem and Morningside Heights. Graffiti with messages such as "Soul Nation, Brothers Only," "Harlem is Mecca, Blood Brothers Only," and "No Whites Wanted, This is Our Community," appeared with regularity at the boundaries of Harlem and along major thoroughfares.[12]

During the same period, another form of graffiti similar in style to that of gangs emerged in Philadelphia. Individual writers, who were not affiliated with gangs, wrote their names all over the city. These writers claimed space for themselves alone. They followed the main transportation routes and labeled spaces that gang members would consider impractical for defense purposes. They understood that moving surfaces such as subway trains and buses provided maximum exposure. This style of graffiti matured in New York City during the early 1970s.[13]

The most influential early graffiti writer in New York went by the name of "TAKI 183." He used this name because he lived on 183rd Street and because his family and friends called him Taki, which is the diminutive of Demetrios. He was of Greek American descent and grew up in Washington Heights at a time when the neighborhood was changing from a predominantly white to a multiracial community. In the 1960s, Taki and his friends observed Washington Heights gang members demarcating their territories with graffiti and witnessed many of their peers becoming addicted to drugs. Instead of getting involved in gangs or drugs, Taki and his close associates decided to write their names in their neighborhood and in subway trains. By 1970, the name Taki could be seen in many parts of the city and received widespread attention. Taki explained how his job as a delivery boy motivated him to make his name known citywide and how he intentionally targeted affluent neighborhoods:

> I used to write in the areas where influential people would see it, like I would go into a fancy building—I used to deliver cosmetics. All those guys that write for newspapers, publishers, they all live in nice neighborhoods. So they would see it and they'd say "Aw God," but they'd write about it the next day. If a guy like, I don't know, Junior, wrote up in Harlem—nobody goes there, only the people in the area. That's why I got the most publicity.[14]

Taki's strategy worked. His job as a delivery boy allowed him to write his name with regularity in affluent neighborhoods and business districts. He gained acclaim among his peers and even attention by *The New York Times*, which published a feature article on him in 1971. In that article, Taki explained that the practice of writing his name in public spaces was influenced by the political stickers that were plastered everywhere before elections. In fact, Taki lamented the concern that authorities had shown to the type of graffiti he had been writing: "Why they go after the little guy? Why not the campaign organizations that put stickers all over the subways at election time?"[15]

Graffiti writers exploited the power of name recognition through graffiti's frequent appearance in public space. They were influenced by commercial advertisements and posters that inundated New York City bearing the names and images of products and owners, that appeared on billboards, buildings, subways, and vehicles. According to writer Iz the WIZ,

> Mr. Mobil, Mr. Amoco, Mr. Exxon. They're rich. They can put their name on any sign, any place. Build a gas station and there's their *name*. . . . OK, now you're on a poorer economic level and what do you have? Years ago, and even today, a boxer makes a name for himself in the boxing ring. So when this art form starts developing, why would it be any different? It's all in the name. When you're poor, that's all you got.[16]

In other words, writers felt that they could escape invisibility through a radical intervention with writing. By 1972, inscriptions by adolescents rivaled even the most high-profile advertising campaigns in the public spaces of New York City. These inscriptions also appeared on television shows, in advertising campaigns, and in movies. For example, Taki's signature on a wall near the Statue of Liberty appeared in a frequently run national antismoking commercial. The names P-NUT, JESTER, and DIABLO made it to the opening sequence of the television show *Welcome Back Kotter*. John Travolta's night of soul searching in *Saturday Night Fever* occurs against a backdrop of graffiti.[17]

After the appearance of *The New York Times* article on Taki, graffiti writing continued to gain popularity among adolescents and evolved in form. Graffiti originally existed only in the form of a tag, which consisted of the name of the writer in the style of a logo. In 1972, some writers adopted a new form of inscription called a "throw-up," which looked like a very large tag with thick letters and included more colors than black. Unlike tags, throw-ups appeared on the outside of subway trains and their practitioners used spray paint, not pens. Gradually, graffiti writers with artistic ambition painted "pieces," short for masterpieces, which usually contained at least four letters, were multicolor and covered a considerably larger area than tags and throw-ups. Pieces were succeeded by "top-to-bottoms," which extended from the bottom of a subway car to its top;

"end-to-ends," which extended from one side of a subway car to the other; and "whole cars," which covered entire subway cars including the windows. Pieces, top-to-bottoms, end-to-ends, and whole cars contained embellishments in addition to the name of the writer and often required the collaboration of many artists. These forms of graffiti also appeared on walls, trucks, and other surfaces, making graffiti visible everywhere throughout the city.[18]

Graffiti writing, like gang activity, depended on performance, and during the heyday of the graffiti movement in the 1970s and the 1980s, graffiti writers gained more status in proportion to the number of times they wrote their name. Thus, because they appeared on the outside of trains, throw-ups became the most common and significant forms of writing. People who painted the most throw-ups on certain subway lines were known as the "kings" of those lines. While most graffiti was done by individuals seeking recognition, graffiti inscriptions taken as a whole, nevertheless, represented the community. Thus, the focus on the number of times that graffiti writers "got up" exemplified the desire of communities of young people, writers and nonwriters alike, to dominate their environment through personal symbols.[19]

In the 1970s, graffiti merged with DJ-ing, breakdancing, and rapping and formed what has been termed hip-hop culture. The elements that comprised hip-hop represented a revolution in the way that young residents of cities appropriated space. First, instead of deploring the blighted conditions of their neighborhoods, African American and Latino youths from the South Bronx claimed them for creative purposes. They turned abandoned buildings, empty lots, shabby streets, neglected parks, and rusting subway trains into vibrant performance spaces. Second, they rejected the violent turf wars that had previously defined young people of working-class New York. Many popular DJs created spheres of influence in the South Bronx and typically resolved differences through competitions based on performance. Graffiti writers gathered in coffee shops and subway stations to compare their art and exchange ideas. DJs united young people from many parts of the city and allowed them to interact. They also created a cultural infrastructure for inner city youths who had very few outlets for entertainment in their neighborhoods. Finally, members of radical African American and Latino organizations provided participants with a political philosophy. In the course of time, hip-hop participants exported the manifestations of a movement to the rest of the city and spaces that did not initially belong to them. Graffiti writers made art with their names throughout the city. DJ crews distributed fliers that advertised gigs. Music fans used ghetto blasters to disseminate music in public space. Automobile drivers did the same, playing music loudly and risking fines. Aspiring MCs went to subway stations and public parks and practiced their rhymes for donations. Breakdancers did the same, and, for a period of time, became the main attractions in public parks, shopping areas, and street corners.

Figure 5.3 Graffiti on an anchorage of Williamsburg Bridge. Many writers targeted visible surfaces in well-traveled areas, contributing to the anxieties of the authorities. (Photograph by Themis Chronopoulos, 1997.)

Many of the participants also adapted and refined old gang attire and created a new fashion that became popular around the world. By the late 1970s, people associated with hip-hop had managed to take over much of New York City's public space with symbols, inscriptions, advertisements, sounds, performances, and fashion.[20]

THE INITIAL GOVERNMENT REACTION

When graffiti first appeared in high-profile public spaces in 1971, the Lindsay Administration was trying to recover from a perception that it could not govern New York. Between 1967 and 1969, a transit strike made movement in the city virtually impossible; a sanitation strike brought about the threat of health epidemics in some poor neighborhoods; a long confrontation between the teachers' union and African American neighborhood groups shut down public schools; and a snowstorm paralyzed life in the boroughs for weeks. Combined with a steep rise in crime and social disorder, these issues prompted many New Yorkers to question the adequacy of their city government. Of course, many of these events were out of the ordinary, and despite mishandlings and setbacks, the Lindsay Administration paid little attention to such perceptions. City officials expected that the dust from all these extraordinary events would settle and that a sense of normality would gradually reemerge. The appearance of graffiti in the early 1970s challenged that hope, not because it represented a momentous event but because it reinforced the perception that the local government was not, in fact, in control.[21]

Because graffiti was so difficult to erase, it accumulated on a daily basis and began to overtake advertisements, government signs, and other public displays. Although graffiti did not inconvenience New Yorkers to the extent that a transit strike, a subway fare increase, or a severe snowstorm had, it still represented a serious problem. Since graffiti was visible everywhere, it magnified public anxieties about New York's urban environment. This uneasiness intensified as graffiti artists painted larger and multicolor pieces in defiance of law and order. Gradually, graffiti became one of the most potent symbols of New York City's decline and disorder. Unlike the devastating conditions in the South Bronx, which most middle- and upper-class New Yorkers would encounter only on their television sets, graffiti appeared throughout the city on subway cars, the walls of buildings, public signs, highway overpasses, sanitation trucks, commercial trucks, highway overpasses, and subway stations. Graffiti did not discriminate between poor and wealthy neighborhoods, commercial and residential places, public and private spaces. More importantly, it undermined the promise of public order that the government had been accustomed to use as a source of legitimacy. Graffiti bolstered the belief that the city government had lost control of public space and that it could not govern New York.

The authorities reacted by claiming that graffiti had reached "epidemic proportions" and that something had to be done. In 1972, City Council President Sanford D. Garelik declared a war on graffiti, announcing that "graffiti pollutes the eye and mind and might be one of the worst forms of pollution we have to combat."[22] Mayor Lindsay and his administration soon took over the campaign of antigraffiti proclamations. In 1973, in a report that discussed the rising incidence of graffiti, Lindsay remarked on the "ugliness of graffiti," arguing that "the situation was getting worse" and ridiculed those who called this "vandalism" an art form. In the same report, Steven L. Isenberg, chief of staff for Lindsay, asserted that "the most important notion to be discredited publicly is that graffiti vandalism and defacement of property can be cloaked with the justification or excuse that it is an acceptable form of pop art."[23] The above statements defined the parameters of the debate in aesthetic terms. Government officials rejected outright the notion that graffiti might be a form of artistic expression and designated graffiti as vandalism, pollution, and defacement. Clearly, traditional and unquestioned attitudes of class superiority toward vernacular forms of art in the city informed these arguments. However, the aesthetic argument alone was not sufficient to justify a full-fledged war.[24]

The authorities also attempted to name, define, and characterize graffiti practitioners by tapping into narratives of youth and developmental abnormalities. "Psychologists say graffiti are an attempt by insignificant people to impose their identity on others, if only until the wall is cleaned," claimed an article that appeared in *The New York Times* in 1972.[25] "Should there not be, besides the rather lenient and unworkable penalties, methods by which the destruction of our subway system by ravaging, mentally ill 'artists' can be prevented?" wondered a Flushing, Queens, resident a year later.[26] In another article, the mayor declared that "it was 'the Lindsay theory' that graffiti writing was 'related to mental health problems' and that graffiti artists were 'insecure cowards.'"[27] A report on the elimination of graffiti released by the City Bureau of the Budget suggested that the city should perform psychological experiments on graffiti artists so that it could locate the motivations for their writing. In this report, graffiti writers were called "disturbed vandals."[28] In his attempt to defend the inability of the courts to effectively deal with the "problem," Bronx Family Court Chief Judge Reginald Matthews said that "Graffiti is an expression of social maladjustment, but the courts cannot cure all of society's ills."[29] Clearly, the argument that graffiti writers were mentally ill was not made so that they could seek professional help, but in order to discredit their actions.

Despite the heavy-handed rhetoric, the credibility of the city government suffered because graffiti writing continued to increase. The situation was exacerbated by Lindsay, who gave the appearance of running a personal but failing crusade against graffiti. Isenberg, who was chief of staff for Lindsay and in charge of the administration's graffiti-fighting effort, remembered when Lindsay went into his office using four-letter words and ordering him to "clean up the mess." On one occasion the mayor attended an opening ceremony of a Brooklyn swimming pool that had already been hit by graffiti writers. "I certainly got reamed out," Isenberg recalled. The pool incident was especially telling. In the early 1970s, public pools were prized facilities that communities cherished but that the government could not maintain. On the rare occasion when Lindsay could open a new swimming pool, graffiti stole the thunder, and urban disorder became the focus of attention. Two weeks before he moved out of Gracie Mansion (the official house of New York's mayor), Lindsay tried to explain his sometimes erratic behavior to Norman Mailer:

> People would come into new [subway] cars and suddenly they'd see them all marked up, covered inside and out, and it depressed people terribly. You know, we have to be a kind of nerve center to the city. Reports came in from everywhere. The graffiti was profoundly depressing—it truly hurt people's moods. The life would go out of everybody when they saw the cars defaced, they saw it as defacement, no question of that.[30]

Despite this justification, Lindsay's agitation contributed to a climate that associated lack of security and maintenance with graffiti, while Lindsay's inability to do anything about it contributed to a climate of hopelessness. Mailer, in his book *The Faith of Graffiti,* offered his own interpretation of Lindsay's actions:

> In the framework of that time in the Summer of '71 and the Winter and Spring of '72 when Lindsay was looking to get the Democratic nomination for President, what an upset to his fortunes, what a vermin of catastrophe that these writings had sprouted like weeds all over the misery of Fun City, a new monkey of unmanageables to sit on Lindsay's overloaded political back. He must have sensed the Presidency draining away from him as the months went by, the graffiti grew, and the millions of tourists who passed through the city brought the word out to the rest of the nation: "Filth is sprouting on the walls."[31]

It would be an exaggeration to claim that graffiti brought about the downfall of Lindsay's political fortunes, as the mayor had been in trouble since at least 1969 when he won a surprising reelection as a third-party candidate. But in many ways, his inability to solve the problem of graffiti contributed to his failures. It effectively ended his career as the most articulate spokesperson of cities, since under his watch graffiti artists had taken over the subway system, which many considered the backbone of urban life.[32]

Almost immediately, the atmosphere created by the discourse on graffiti began to pervade the mass media in other parts of the world. According to an article in the *Toronto Star,*

> There are those who believe that the decline and fall of New York City is reflected these days on its monuments; subway cars, buses, school buildings and playgrounds. In each case, the structures or rolling stock are defaced with a multi-colored assortment of scrawls—some neat, some sloppy—generally lumped under the heading of "graffiti," and applied with either felt-tipped pen or spray paint.[33]

Of course, the *Toronto Star* took its cue from prominent New Yorkers who associated graffiti with decline and disorder. The problem of the image of the city in relation to graffiti kept reemerging during subsequent years. However, for middle- and upper-class New York residents, the dilemma was more than just a problem of image. As early as 1972, many of these citizens linked graffiti directly with serious crime. In a letter to *The New York Times,* Paul Seligman remarked on a press photograph that depicted the body of murdered Columbia Professor Wolfgang G. Friedmann in front of a graffiti-painted wall that belonged to Public School 36 in Morningside Heights. Seligman suggested that "this desecration and crime against property may have contributed to the shocking killing and other crimes. If children and young adults think they can get away with defacing property, perhaps in their fragile minds they feel they can get away with more. Boys will be boys—and boys will be murderers."[34] The following year, Blandinia B. Ijams in a letter to *The New York Times* wrote that "millions of New Yorkers . . . are forced to ponder . . . [the] graphic assault on their sensibilities daily," and attacked the city government for doing nothing against the "graffiti nightmare," and the "barbarians" who "keep the city in a state of siege."[35] The equation of graffiti writing with serious crime and the perception that authorities could no more stop graffiti than fight violent crime persisted in the years that followed Lindsay's failed war.

The emergence of the graffiti movement coincided with a comeback of gangs, and the connections among individuals associated with either gangs or graffiti art seemed straightforward—at least to outsiders. In the early 1970s, the mass media paid enormous attention to this rebirth of gangs, especially those located in the South Bronx. The police claimed that South Bronx gangs had about 20,000 members, that they terrorized shopkeepers, students, and women, and that they were involved in deadly clashes against competing gangs. Although many South Bronx residents credited gangs with routing drug dealers and forcing junkies out of their neighborhoods, others argued that drug dealers used gangs as their own private armies for turf wars.[36]

In reality, graffiti writers resented the restriction of movement that gangs imposed on them and they sought to subvert it. Several of the early influential writers terminated their gang membership, citing irreconcilable differences between writing and belonging to a gang. Testimonials by Taki 183, Wasp I, Cornbread, and Tracy 168 show that graffiti artists viewed their writing as a way to avoid drug and gang involvement and as a way to abolish the rigid spatial boundaries that gang fighting created. In the Bronx, large gangs allowed graffiti artists to move about their territories out of respect for their courage. However, smaller gangs all over the city and larger gangs in Brooklyn attacked graffiti writers, who in reaction formed their own writing gangs. The first and largest writing gang, the Ex-Vandals, formed in 1971 in Brooklyn, where groups such as the Jolly Stompers and the Tomahawks attacked not only competing gang members but also individuals they found wandering in their territories. The Ex-Vandals adopted the idea of "safety in numbers," rejected violence, and existed for the purpose of writing. By 1972, because of their numbers and diligence, the Ex-Vandals enjoyed citywide fame and respect because their name could be seen all over New York City. However, this fame made members of the Ex-Vandals targets for other gangs, which eventually forced the Ex-Vandals to disband. Whatever the case, in the mid-1970s street gangs were weakened and had problems maintaining membership. On the other hand, the graffiti movement had more participants than ever, many of whom painted large masterpieces and became cultural heroes of their communities.[37]

The public proclamations on graffiti writing contributed to the racial antipathy that many whites felt toward African Americans and Latinos. Although the Lindsay Administration had no interest in encouraging the demonization of minority youth of color, its discourse against graffiti had exactly that result in many segments of New York. Whites, insecure about their economic position in the city, interpreted Lindsay's anxiety about graffiti as an assault on the urban order. Jonathan Rieder, in his study of Canarsie, found that graffiti and murals by African Americans generated anger and resentfulness among white residents in the mid-1970s. For example, an Italian worker from Canarsie considered a mural with scenes from slavery as the invasion of an alien people into his neighborhood:

> I seen one painting of a girl with a slit in her dress and hustling two dudes. But that's not drawings of a middle class area. A lot of this stuff is displayed as art, they said that people are expressing themselves or saying something. But I can't read it. It's not what I want to see. They even have black schools where kids paint pictures of kids picking cotton! But this is 1976, not 1876.[38]

Another Canarsian argued that "we never had this graffiti stuff when we were growing up, and we didn't have muggings either." Canarsians dreaded African American murals and graffiti, associating them with neighborhood decline and disorder. The discourse that equated graffiti with crime and ghetto culture exploded over the following decades and was integrated with the mainstream media.

Figure 5.4 Graffiti mural in the Bronx. The colors of this piece are those of the Puerto Rican flag. (Photograph by Themis Chronopoulos, 2006.)

The official discourse against graffiti was accompanied by legislation intended to deter offenders and police crackdowns that brought the number of arrests of graffiti writers into the thousands each year. In 1972, the City Council passed an antigraffiti ordinance, originally authored by Lindsay's staff, which banned open markers and spray cans in public buildings and made the act punishable with a maximum fine of $500, three months in jail, or both. Moreover, New York Housing Authority officials threatened public housing tenants that any graffiti convictions incurred by their children would result in eviction hearings. New York and Transit police officers stepped up arrest efforts at the cost of ignoring more serious crimes. Judges sentenced writers to clean-up duty in subway stations and trains. In spite of these measures, graffiti grew in frequency and size during this period, in subways and on walls.[39]

After Lindsay left office in 1974, the mass media began to focus on more threatening problems in New York such as the fiscal crisis, and the discourse against graffiti faded. In 1974, the editors of *The New York Times* chastised the MTA when it announced an expensive plan to use attack dogs to guard subway yards and suggested that "the service in general [be] improved to the level of the transit system in Baghdad or Kabul" before focusing efforts on fighting graffiti. The editorial also argued that the money could be used to place readable maps on the subways or to hire more transit police who could help curtail muggings. This editorial indicated that the failed antigraffiti effort of the early 1970s ended with the departure of Lindsay from the political scene.[40]

In 1975, the fiscal crisis caused severe municipal employee cuts and the fiscal austerity that ensued trivialized the antigraffiti effort. That year, John G. De Roos, senior executive officer of the MTA, announced that the numerous campaigns against graffiti had failed and that "crackdowns were no longer top priority." He blamed lenient judges who nullified arrest efforts and a media that offered extensive coverage to graffiti writers even when they performed court-ordered clean-up duty. However, with a reduction in the transit police force that approached 20%, the MTA could not possibly have continued a war against graffiti. Instead, the MTA had to focus on basic transit service. In times of crisis, image problems became a low priority.[41]

Despite continuous budgetary shortfalls, some antigraffiti measures persisted through the late 1970s. The Abraham Beame Administration (1974–1977) established an antigraffiti police squad of about ten plainclothes officers with citywide jurisdiction in 1975. The squad gathered information about graffiti at informal meetings and by socializing with writers. The unit aimed at getting information that would allow them to apprehend major graffiti artists. Although the squad amassed information on thousands of writers, the arrests never occurred because they lacked manpower. Indeed, the number of arrests of graffiti writers, which had been around 4,500 between 1972 and 1974, went down to 998 in 1976, 578 in 1977,

272 in 1978, and 205 in 1979. Graffiti no longer represented a priority law enforcement issue. With reduced police personnel in 1977, the MTA turned its attention to a petroleum hydroxide-based solvent that would make cleaning graffiti from subway trains easier. Graffiti artists promptly repainted their art on subway cars, making the wash seem futile. In addition, transit workers and riders suspected that the cleaning fluid caused health problems. In 1977, John Dewey High School principal Jack Metzger announced that teachers and students complained about the fumes coming from the adjacent subway yard in Coney Island. MTA officials denied that the cleaning chemical caused any health problems.[42]

THE NEOCONSERVATIVE AND NEOLIBERAL RESPONSES

On July 13, 1977, at the height of a heat wave, there was a massive power failure in New York that lasted for twenty-five hours and affected more than nine million people. Almost immediately there were reports of widespread looting, burglarizing, and arson in sections of Brooklyn, Manhattan, Queens, and the Bronx. Thousands of people broke into stores and carried away all kinds of merchandise including food, furniture, and television sets; some of them even drove away cars from dealerships. Police officers trying to restore order came under attack from brick and bottle throwers; there were also reports of snipers. There were so many people arrested that the city's jails and criminal justice system were overwhelmed, and people detained began to riot. At the Bronx House of Detention, those who were incarcerated jammed toilets to cause flooding, started fires in their cells, and broke television sets and furniture. Mayor Beame reopened the Tombs in Manhattan, formally known as the Men's House of Detention, in order to accommodate the large number of people arrested. By the end of the disturbances, the damages were estimated at about $1 billion with 3,700 people arrested and 2,000 stores looted.[43]

The popular disturbances of New York in 1977 signaled a number of issues that had to be taken seriously. They represented the first riot in the city since 1964 and occurred two years after the beginning of the fiscal crisis. They dispelled the expectation that municipal labor unions would be the greatest challenge to fiscal retrenchment. Almost all of the occurrences happened in low-income areas of the city that suffered disproportionately from the greatest recession since the Great Depression. These were the first popular disturbances to be initiated by the underclass, which soon became a proof for some that everything had gone wrong with inner city populations in the United States.

A few weeks later, *Time* magazine announced the emergence of this new underclass in a cover story. The authors claimed that inner city neighborhoods contain a "large group of people who are more intractable, more socially alien and more hostile than almost anyone had imagined.

They are the unreachables: the American underclass."[44] The article added that the underclass, which was composed mostly of urban African Americans, "produces a highly disproportionate number of the nation's juvenile delinquents, school dropouts, drug addicts and welfare mothers, and much of the adult crime, family disruption, urban decay and demand for social expenditures."[45] Thus, the emphasis was not on poverty but on unemployment, criminality, addiction, single motherhood, dependency, and lack of motivation.

In 1982, Ken Auletta wrote a book in which he presented the characteristics of the underclass more systematically and divided them into four distinct categories:

> (a) *the passive poor*, usually long time welfare recipients; (b) the *hostile* street criminals who terrorize most cities, and who are often school dropouts and drug addicts; (c) the *hustlers*, who, like street criminals, may not be poor and who earn their livelihood in an underground economy, but rarely commit violent crimes; (d) the *traumatized* drunks, drifters, homeless shopping-bag ladies and released mental patients who frequently roam or collapse on city streets.[46]

Auletta's "hostile street criminals" were mostly responsible for crime, the "traumatized" individuals were mostly responsible for social disorder, and the "hustlers" for both. All of these populations represented a burden to the state, some of them because of welfare dependency, some of them because of demands on social and medical services, and some because of pressures on the criminal justice system.

The underclass thesis reflected the preeminence of neoconservative intellectuals during this period on issues of race, poverty, culture, family, crime, and personal responsibility. Liberal intellectuals were unable to provide explanations for the decline of inner-city neighborhoods and the problems that they were experiencing, and for a period of time they uncritically acquiesced to the concept of the underclass. Meanwhile, neoconservative academics continued to build on the concept of the underclass and use it as a way to discredit social policy. In *Losing Ground*, Charles Murray blamed generous public social programs for eroding poor people's incentives to work and maintain a nuclear family. In *Beyond Entitlement*, Lawrence Mead argued that the solution to the problem of the underclass was work and recommended that the government should force its dependents to work. The contrast between Murray and Mead was telling. Like classical conservatives, Murray found the problem of dependency widespread in big government and thought that a smaller, thriftier government would force welfare recipients to change their behavior. Like neoconservatives, Mead found the idea of a small government to be out of step with the late twentieth century. He believed in the existence of a strong, autocratic government that forced poor people to work.[47]

Unlike the events of the 1977 blackout, which represented the underclasses' infrequent tendencies to riot, graffiti writing represented a more permanent disorderly behavior. Regardless, both were symptoms of social disorder generated by young African Americans and Latinos that had to be met with law-and-order initiatives. Despite the inclusion of people of all ages and genders in this underclass, young minority males represented its most feared members. This was the group considered to be the backbone of hip-hop culture and highlighted during the uprisings of 1977.

In New York City, neoconservatives branded graffiti as the cultural production of the criminal underclass. This thesis dominated the mainstream public sphere. As graffiti became a common occurrence, more people began to believe in the mainstream connotations of graffiti—crime, urban decline, and juvenile delinquency—as a structure that functioned in opposition to themselves. Graffiti replaced the pervasiveness of government and its promise of maintaining order. Graffiti seemed to be everywhere, and each piece was an original. If the people who wrote graffiti were in a particular site, they could always come back. If they were criminals, they might pose a threat to anyone. Nathan Glazer was one of the first to articulate this position in a 1979 article for *The Public Interest*:

> I have not interviewed the subway riders; but I am one myself, and while I do not find myself consciously making the connection between the graffiti-makers and the criminals who occasionally rob, rape, assault, and murder passengers, the sense that all are part of one world of uncontrollable predators seems inescapable. Even if the graffitists are the least dangerous of these, their ever-present markings serve to persuade the passenger that, indeed, the subway is a dangerous place—a mode of transportation to be used only when one has no alternative.[48]

Glazer's argument proved influential. In 1980, a psychologist argued that "People see graffiti as a symbolic assault."[49] During the same year, one subway rider expressed a similar sentiment: "I am tired of being crammed like a piece of livestock into a litter-strewn, dark, graffiti-laden subway car. I am tired of paying 60 cents for the privilege of looking around me like a paranoiac, fearful of being attacked."[50] A *New York Post* editorial affirmed that "the problem is primarily a symbolic symptom of uncontrolled underground lawlessness."[51] Mayor Koch acknowledged that late trains, crime, and defective doors represented more serious subway problems but claimed that the elimination of graffiti would have a "positive psychological impact" on straphangers.[52] Another article suggested that no one wanted to "spend up to two hours a day unwillingly inserted into someone else's mural."[53] Joseph P. Fried, in a *New York Times* article, agreed that "defacement by graffiti, breeds cynicism among those responsible for such acts and may lead them to more serious crimes."[54] At the same time, city and transit officials insisted "that the perception of crime as a problem in the subway system is far greater than the reality."[55] Mark H. Moore, professor of criminal justice policy and management, agreed that "the average level of risk in the society ... is relatively low. Nonetheless, people are afraid, and their fear is triggered by instances of disorder." Moore cited graffiti as one of those instances.[56] As late as 1987, Richard Cohen made a statement similar to that of Glazer ten years before:

> [Graffiti] signified that the subways were not safe. If someone could deface a train and get away with it, then that same someone could enter the train and rob the people on it. The graffiti meant that New York City could no longer guarantee the safety of the people who rode the trains. The person who left a mark on a train could leave a mark on a passenger too.[57]

As Atlanta and Alexander wrote, graffiti sought "to dominate urban space with the same totality with which drugs dominate perception," ultimately disrupting "the white consumer culture dream" by providing a "nightmare flipside" of ghetto expressions and representations.[58]

Figure 5.5 Mural located in the Lower East Side depicting Mike Tyson after his infamous boxing match with Evander Holyfield. (Photograph by Themis Chronopoulos, 1997.)

The neoconservative critique on graffiti writing as the cultural expression of the underclass also emphasized the significance of race. In 1980, Daniel Seligman in *Fortune* magazine summarized what he perceived as the connection between race and graffiti:

> In the period around 1970, when the prevailing ethos in New York mandated a certain reverence for all young, poor, minority persons—a lot of the paint-sprayers seemed to be Hispanic—one reaction to the graffiti was to view them as an admirable new form of folk art.... In the latter 1970s, a darker perception took hold. The new view was that the city had a god-awful problem but that nothing could be done about it. It was now accepted that the spectacle of an entire subway fleet awash in graffiti was an insistent reminder of the decline of law in New York.[59]

Seligman selectively ignored Lindsay's campaign against graffiti and focused on changing perceptions about graffiti writing that were inaccurate. On another occasion, Gordon J. Davis, a Koch-appointed parks commissioner, explained that "Nine out of 10 times, what people mean when they say that the park is lousy is not only that it's not clean, but that there are kids smoking dope and there are graffiti and there are Blacks and Hispanics where there were once Italians and Jews."[60] In this case, many people blamed the terrible conditions that existed in parks in 1980 not on deferred maintenance but on perceptions of their disorderly uses by minority youth. As the menacing youth-of-color discourse merged with that of the underclass, Mayor Koch made sure to construct the underclass in opposition to the middle class and urged the Democratic party to stop being the party of the poor. Graffiti became known as the scrawls of the underclass in public spaces and its eradication became equated with the discipline and control of disrupting populations. Although during his tenure as mayor Koch accommodated middle-class populations of color, his oratory often reinforced racialized perceptions of African Americans and Latinos. As Gay Talese wrote in 1984, Koch was "the first white man in New York in 10 years to talk back to a black."[61]

Despite its success in influencing public opinion, the neoconservative response to graffiti writing and hip-hop culture had its limits. On the one hand, this neoconservative rhetoric prolonged a climate hostile to young African Americans and Latinos and united many whites under an electoral coalition led by Mayor Koch. On the other hand, the narrative that hip-hop was the culture of a criminal underclass and that graffiti paintings were the unauthorized inscriptions of disorderly young people of color was too uncompromising and provided no solutions. The tough law-and-order approach against graffiti failed, and it undermined the perception that law enforcement agencies were actually controlling the city's territory. If graffiti was such an unacceptable behavior, then why did it appear everywhere, and what did that say about the state of the city? The "broken windows" theory, which very well could have been named the "graffiti scrawls" theory given that "broken windows" functioned as a metaphor to neighborhood disorder and disrepair in the same way as graffiti writing, provided recommendations against graffiti that were difficult to implement. Order-maintenance policing as well as other aggressive policing methods failed to eradicate graffiti writing. A more proactive solution came from neoliberals, who were better equipped to deal with matters of culture and image.

The biggest difference between neoliberals and neoconservatives in the United States is that neoliberals embrace popular culture, the arts, cultural experimentation, and the mass media—aspects of culture that neoconservatives often consider to be vulgar and morally bankrupt. Some neoliberals accommodate alternative culture and experimental art because they can improve urban life and they represent innovations that can translate into profits. Hip-hop culture had made the city a more exciting place and had the potential for such profits. This does not mean, however, that neoliberals were thrilled to see New York City overtaken by hip-hop culture and its participants in the 1970s. The popular disturbances of 1977 put an end to such notions, if they ever existed, since they damaged the image of the city even more.

The city's political and business elites wanted to distance the image of the city from the fiscal crisis, crime, the South Bronx, and the underclass. New York City was undergoing a severe image crisis, and hip-hop culture was held responsible because of the sizable number of young African Americans and Latinos active in public space and because of neoconservative arguments about hip-hop's connection to the underclass. The neoliberal city required an urban culture hospitable to middle and upper managers as well as their families so that corporations would have no difficulty recruiting the best possible associates. In fact, the inability of corporations to recruit such people meant that there was something wrong with the location, and this is exactly what happened in New York City during the 1960s and 1970s, when there was an exodus of large businesses. By the late 1970s, New York was competing with other world cities such as Tokyo, London, Hong Kong, and Los Angeles. Its image problem undermined its competitive edge.

After the fiscal crisis, the state and city governments restructured their economic and tourist development agencies and began to promote New York City as a business- and tourist-friendly destination. Governor Hugh Carey appointed John S. Dyson, president of Dymer Communications, to be commissioner of the New York State Department of Commerce and Bill Doyle, marketing manager of Chase Manhattan Bank, to be his deputy commissioner. Dyson became a controversial figure almost immediately for picking a verbal argument with the state's education commissioner, calling state legislators liars, promoting tax breaks for the rich, advocating sizable cuts in spending, and viewing projects such as the environmental cleanup of polluted rivers to be a low priority. Dyson and Doyle wanted to package

New York City as an attractive destination for corporations and for tourists. In their marketing campaigns, they emphasized the city as a tourist destination because they were convinced that businesses would not relocate to the area if tourists were not willing to visit. Moreover, many New Yorkers faulted the city's corporations for the fiscal crisis, and promoting tourism became less controversial than encouraging the arrival of big businesses. John Dyson is credited with the "I Love New York" campaign, which marketed the city as an attractive location to visit and make money. The campaign emphasized theaters on Broadway, shopping on Fifth Avenue, and nightlife near the World Trade Center. It de-emphasized the fiscal crisis, neighborhood collapse, working-class culture, labor strife, political radicalism, the outer boroughs, and racial diversity. Gradually, other campaigns focused on Manhattan's skyline, luxury hotels, art museums, Wall Street, corporate vibrancy, high-end shopping, and famous restaurants and nightclubs.[62]

Despite their dominance, hip-hop culture and graffiti writing were not included in these campaigns. The spatial takeover that hip-hop followers and performers engaged in challenged the kind of image that New York powerholders tried to project. These elites could not possibly welcome the idea that the symbols and images of teenage African Americans and Latinos dominated the public space of their city. As Ira Katznelson has written:

> Ordinarily, the cultural patterns of most working and poor people are hidden from view. They neither control nor find themselves recognized by the society's mechanisms of communication and schooling. Their neighborhoods are theirs alone. Only fragments of their lives appear in the public domain, often as the stuff of human-interest tales. So long as they are politically quiet (political scientists have seen their apathy as a bulwark of stability) and do not disturb the regular routines of other people, they can be absent from the calculations of middle- and upper-class America.[63]

Hip-hop culture, with its intense public space presence, disrupted the mainstream symbolic order of New York City. As long as minority manifestations of art and dissent remained in areas like the Bronx, they were tolerated. The minute that their creators exported them to the rest of the city, they became a problem. According to neoliberal sensitivities, graffiti appeared in the wrong places. If graffiti was art, then it belonged in a museum or an art gallery. Art was something too valuable to arbitrarily appear on public walls and subway trains. Graffiti writers were unable to commodify their creations and penetrate "legitimate" cultural spaces. The rest of hip-hop culture was also slow in achieving a mainstream cultural status that would translate into profits. This was the paradox of hip-hop culture; a seemingly anticapitalist and arbitrary popular culture had taken over public spaces in ways that the best marketing campaigns and government efforts had failed.[64]

Although the campaigns to make New York attractive to tourists and corporations were successful, and although graffiti was eventually eliminated from the subways, the city continued to experience image problems. In 1989, Walt Disney Co. exhibited a New York City subway car at its new MGM theme park in Orlando, Florida. Such an exhibition would have gone unnoticed by New York transportation officials except that the replica train was covered with graffiti. A few months before the MGM display, the New York City Transit Authority (NYCTA) had succeeded in eradicating graffiti from the subway system. David Gunn, president of the NYCTA, sent a letter to Michael Eisner, chairman of the Walt Disney Co., arguing that Disney World perpetuated an "unfair and inaccurate" image of New York. Some New York media outlets ridiculed Gunn's gesture and advised him to focus on improving the performance of the transportation system. But Gunn's reaction was not as unreasonable as it may have seemed. Gunn, who became president of the NYCTA in 1984, had been considered the savior of the transportation system for a period of time because of the improvements in service that occurred during his tenure. However, by 1989, problems returned. Gunn could not avoid a fare increase, frequent subway breakdowns, dirty cars, and persistent crime. The eradication of graffiti represented one of the few things the NYCTA president could take credit for. After the Disney World incident, even that achievement was questioned. Other New York powerholders shared Gunn's sensitivity about the image of their city.[65]

THE GOVERNMENT RESPONSE AFTER THE FISCAL CRISIS

By the late 1970s, graffiti became associated with New York's fiscal crisis, infrastructure decline, rising crime statistics, and urban disorder. The Koch Administration, which equated the eradication of graffiti with New York's economic recovery, rallied against graffiti writers even more swiftly than previous administrations. The reduction of graffiti was an important prerequisite for the credibility of the business-friendly climate Koch wanted to create. In the context of the city's transportation system, efforts to eradicate graffiti acquired additional importance. At a time when the subway system experienced frequent derailments, fires, breakdowns, perpetual delays, and rising crime, the emphasis on eradicating graffiti seemed misplaced. However, since the city government cared most about repairing New York's image, graffiti and its racial associations had to disappear. The city government had to take back the public spaces of the city symbolically and return them to whiter, more affluent populations.[66]

Graffiti did not appear as an issue in the 1977 mayoral campaign. During the campaign, Koch advocated the return of the death penalty, promised fiscal discipline, and articulated his position against the power of municipal unions. Koch declared himself the champion of middle-class New York and won the overwhelming support of whites. Koch spent most of his first term (1978–1981) in a campaign to convince corporations to invest in the city and regain fiscal autonomy from the state. A series of balanced budgets and economic growth during the late 1970s enhanced Koch's popularity. A wholesale war against graffiti did not resume until 1980, a year that signaled the beginning of another campaign: that of repairing the image of New York City after the damage that the fiscal crisis created. In the worst days of the fiscal crisis, graffiti seemed to be a relatively small problem since the city appeared to be visibly collapsing. However, a rebuilding effort returned attention to the image problems of New York City. The elimination of graffiti became equated with the distancing of New York City from the fiscal crisis, and this strategy had a racial component. Many observers blamed the fiscal crisis on the liberal policies of Lindsay and Beame, which failed to promote economic growth by embracing redistributive policies that benefitted low-income minorities. This sentiment against welfare combined with a perception of minority youth out of control helped forge Koch's conservative political coalition.[67]

In 1979, responding to criticisms that the subway system was unsafe, the Koch Administration invented a symbolic intervention to make riders feel safer. At the time, serious crime had overshadowed graffiti as a problem in the subways. Consequently, the city government decided to flood the system with uniformed officers with the hope that their high visibility would comfort passengers. Beyond this, the city government encouraged uniformed police officers and fire fighters to take public transportation to and from work, while the MTA extended free ridership to uniformed corrections and auxiliary officers. This policy of ensuring the high visibility of uniformed personnel failed to reduce crime. However, the Koch Administration insisted on this policy and placed even more uniformed officers in the subways in 1982 by adding officers to the transit police and by putting undercover detectives into uniform. This strategy focused on the appearance of order rather than actual order and was designed to reassure riders rather than to actually protect them.[68]

The Koch Administration's war against graffiti began in 1980 when the mayor proposed that subway yards be surrounded by fences and patrolled by unescorted guard dogs. The MTA had previously been lukewarm to such proposals, assuming that fences could not protect the entire subway fleet and that dogs were costly. Although initially rebuffed by the MTA, Koch succeeded in fencing all subway yards. In fact, after a public relations campaign with heavy media coverage, Koch forced the MTA to place German shepherds at the Corona subway yard in Queens. Koch even went as far as to suggest that the MTA use wolves to guard its yards, a comment that proved controversial but that nonetheless put even more pressure on the MTA to take action. A year later, Koch decided to enclose the rest of the subway yards using razor-edged-metal-coiled fences. Koch preferred to think of these fences as "steel dogs with razor teeth," but he admitted that "you don't have to feed steel dogs." As it turned out, it cost about $18,000 a year for the upkeep of the six dogs that patrolled the Corona yard, a quite expensive undertaking. In the years that followed, Koch continued his public proclamations against graffiti by periodically announcing new anti graffiti measures. In 1982, he suggested that the city should build a prison work camp on Rikers Island for minor criminal defendants including graffiti writers. During the same year, the city government unleashed an ad campaign in which celebrities, such as boxing champions Hector Camacho and Alex Ramos, Yankees player Dave Winfield, and singer Irene Cara, participated in antigraffiti advertisements. This ad campaign failed as a graffiti deterrent just like the idea of the prison work camp. Frustrated, Koch accused criminal court judges of refusing to send minor criminals to the city's prison work camp. In 1985, the City Council followed the mayor's recommendation and passed legislation that prohibited the sale of spray paint and markers to anyone under the age of 18. In 1989, while running for a fourth term, Koch threatened to sue parents of graffiti writers for damages and urged them to "beat the hell out" of their kids if they wrote graffiti. At the same time, the city government came under fire by labor unions after making prisoners clean graffiti from the overpasses of the Long Island Expressway.[69]

Koch's continuous campaign against graffiti aggravated an already harmful atmosphere for African American and Latino youths and resulted in high-profile violent incidents. In 1983, a twenty-five-year-old African American from Brooklyn named Michael Stewart died at the hands of a Transit Police after he was caught writing graffiti in a subway station. Initially, the medical examiner, Dr. Elliot Gross, determined that the injuries Stewart suffered while in custody did not cause his death. However, a month later, and after a citywide uproar, Gross amended his report and admitted that Stewart collapsed while in police custody and that he died because of a physical injury to the spinal cord in the upper neck. Gross refused to say what may have caused the injury. In 1984, a grand jury indicted three of the transit police officers for second-degree manslaughter and criminal negligence. Yet a judge nullified the decision of the grand jury, citing the improper conduct of one juror. A second grand jury acquitted all officers of all charges in 1985. An audit report released in January of 1987 by the city comptroller concluded that the transit police officers involved in the Stewart death acted with excessive force. The audit report also found that an arresting officer lied and that Transit Police Chief James Meehan did nothing to investigate the tragedy. Immediately after the release of the report, Meehan resigned. In October of 1987, Koch fired Gross from his post as chief medical examiner. In 1990, the NYCTA agreed to pay Stewart's family $1.7 million. Gross's dismissal and Meehan's resignation came at a time when race relations in New York City were at an all-time low. On Friday, December 19, 1986, a gang of whites holding bats and sticks and yelling racial epithets attacked and beat three

African American men whose automobile had broken down in Howard Beach, Queens. After two beatings, Michael Griffith, an Afro-Caribbean construction worker from Bedford Stuyvesant, Brooklyn, ran onto the Shore Parkway, was struck by oncoming traffic, and died. In the aftermath of the beatings, Koch came under fire from many sectors of the city. Many African Americans argued that Koch's rhetoric toward people of color contributed to the climate that led to Griffith's death. They pointed to other racially motivated violent acts during the 1980s, including the death of William Turks in 1982, whose car stalled in the Gravesend section of Brooklyn and who was attacked by fifteen to twenty whites; the death of Michael Stewart in the hands of Transit Police; and the shooting of four Black teenagers in 1984 by the so-called "subway vigilante," Bernhard Goetz. Goetz claimed that the teenagers tried to mug him and that he shot them in self-defense. All these violent incidents are examples of attempts by white residents to defend the public space of their neighborhoods and take back the subways. In the 1980s, white ethnics sought to consolidate their dominance of certain areas in the boroughs, and they became the backbone for Koch's electoral coalition. Because the city still had not fully recovered from the fiscal crisis, white ethnics felt that until the level of policing reached adequate levels, they had to protect their public spaces themselves from people they considered criminals. As the Stewart and Goetz incidents showed, the subways were considered contested territory; the discourse against graffiti writing and disorder in the subways worsened during an already tense climate.[70]

Rhetoric aside, a consistent strategy to eradicate graffiti from the subways did not emerge until 1984. That year, MTA chairman Robert R. Kiley and NYCTA president David L. Gunn unveiled a program focused on keeping an increasing number of trains completely free of graffiti. At first, the program targeted lines with new and overhauled subway cars. Workers stationed at both ends of the subway line removed graffiti immediately and maintained the goal of graffiti-free trains even if they had to withdraw the trains from service and take them to subway car washes. The city government placed transit police officers in the trains covered under the program so that graffiti writers would be discouraged. This approach worked. By the end of 1985, approximately one-third of subway trains had no graffiti; by the end of 1986 about half, and by May of 1989, the entire fleet was graffiti free. In order to see this program through, the NYCTA increased its budget for cleaning, and the enclosure of subway yards with fences made the writing of large pieces significantly challenging.[71]

As the Koch Administration discovered, the focus on appearances that the "broken windows" approach prescribed had many drawbacks. Nothing illustrates this better than what happened when graffiti was almost eradicated from the subways in 1989. The "graffiti problem" became increasingly replaced by the "homeless problem." According to NYCTA president Gunn in 1989, the subway problems were divided into "physical things" such as graffiti and "human–environmental things" such as the homeless. Gunn saw success on the physical front since graffiti shortly became eradicated. He was not as optimistic on "coping with social ills that spill into the subway. . . . If a homeless person is sitting on a bench, you can't just tell them to leave. They've got a token, they put it in the turnstile, they've got a right."[72] Koch attacked this new "menace" by announcing the following: "In most cases, in my judgment, the money that you give to beggars goes for booze and drugs. . . . It is not in the best interest of this city to encourage people to panhandle instead of looking for jobs."[73] In another article, Jim Dwyer of *Newsday* detected problems more important than graffiti in the subways: "They [subway technical workers] are under the supervision of a chief mechanical officer who is an accountant and who has announced he does not know how to use a wrench. All these folks have done a splendid job cleaning graffiti. However, engines are needed to run the trains." The fact that 72% of respondents to a 1989 *Newsday* poll claimed that city life worsened under Koch illustrates the fact that what was perceived as the "graffiti problem" was more complex. A war against unpleasant appearances would not appease the general population forever.[74]

At the same time, the train wash that the NYCTA used to clean graffiti came under fire. Since the late 1970s, the MTA had ignored the complaints of workers and people who lived nearby subway yards where the chemical solutions used were releasing harmful fumes. However, in 1988, John S. Pritchard, 3d, Inspector General of the MTA, concluded after a 26-month investigation that the train wash adversely affected the health of employees. By 1989, hundreds of people experienced health problems because of the subway car wash. That year, the mass media began to attack the MTA and the NYCTA for their train wash oversight, mentioning the death of one NYCTA maintenance employee and the health problems of another two hundred. Throughout the 1980s, MTA officials refused to provide yard workers with masks and other safety equipment, citing lack of money.[75]

Despite these shortcomings, in the 1990s, George Kelling revised the effect of "broken windows" policies and credited himself with efforts that aimed at "taking back the subways." At the time that the Koch Administration attacked the homeless for making the subways disorderly, Kelling worked as consultant for the MTA on matters of disorder. Although Koch lost the 1989 Democratic primary for mayor, his successor David N. Dinkins (1990–1993) continued the war against the homeless in transportation facilities. In 1990, Dinkins hired William Bratton to head the Transit Police. Bratton followed Kelling's proposals and targeted youths, the homeless, and people who may have been under the influence of drugs and alcohol in an attempt to restore order in the subways. Bratton viewed farebeating, disorder, and robbery as one and the same problem. Given that Kelling and Wilson had already argued that many of the people considered disorderly did nothing illegal, this meant that Transit Police treated whoever they considered disorderly like serious criminals. Citing statistics of crime reduction, Kelling and Bratton credited themselves and the "broken windows" theory as saviors of the subway system.[76]

In reality, order-maintenance tactics employed in the subways during the early 1990s were not as effective as advertized. Graffiti never quite reemerged, but it was replaced by scratchiti. Aspiring graffiti writers seeking to make their tags permanent scratched subway surfaces with sharp objects. By 1996, 99% of subway windows were covered with scratchiti. Had Kelling's and Bratton's tactics worked to the extent that they had claimed, scratchiti would not even exist. In addition, panhandlers continued to request assistance from subway riders. However, Bratton's strategies were aimed at destroying the open defiance to the authorities that homeless people in groups practiced in the late 1980s and early 1990s. Despite claims to the contrary, the "broken windows" approaches had political means and ends.[77]

Graffiti evolved in style, form, and message despite wars against it. Many graffiti pieces resembled murals and political pieces against certain politicians and the authorities appeared frequently. Sometimes graffiti artists memorialized someone from the neighborhood who died, while other times they commented on contemporary events. Abstract pieces that revolved around the name of the writer persisted and represented some of the best works. After its elimination from the subways, graffiti persisted in low-income neighborhoods. In such areas, most people considered graffiti a positive contribution to their communities. Many businesses outside the

Figure 5.6 Graffiti piece in Queens. (Photograph by Themis Chronopoulos, 2008.)

main commercial districts frequently hired graffiti artists to beautify their exteriors. Some public schools commissioned graffiti artists to make their shabby yards look more colorful. In fact, in the 1990s, the only spaces where active clean-up campaigns against graffiti existed were business improvement districts such as Times Square and Wall Street.

Most elements of hip-hop culture took a road different than that of graffiti. After the city government reclaimed areas such as the South Bronx, DJs withdrew from public spaces. As hip-hop gained widespread popularity, many of the DJs happily moved their operations to night clubs, bars, and other indoors spaces where they could make more money. Breakdancing declined just as the outdoor performances did. Some of the older breakdancers became absorbed by theater and other performance outlets. Hip-hop music became one of the most popular forms of music in the United States and the world. Hip-hop combined with music videos and movies exported the symbols and images of the ghetto to the rest of the world. By the 1990s, hip-hop had once again taken over the public sphere, though this time without a need to dominate public spaces.

6 The Declining Appearance of Order, 1978–1993

In the summer of 1989, a *New York Times*/WCBS-TV News poll showed that an overwhelming majority of registered voters had an unfavorable opinion of Mayor Ed Koch. These voters considered the incidence of crime, the trade of crack, and the number of homeless people to have overtaken the city. They blamed Koch for having failed to address these issues and for not deploying an adequate number of police officers. Koch had actually tried to deal with all of these matters; he increased the number of police officers, opened a number of new homeless shelters, and fought a war on drugs. However, this did not translate into visible improvements, and crime rates, the number of the homeless in public spaces, and the use of crack cocaine increased during his long tenure as mayor (1978–1989).[1]

Becoming mayor after the extreme economic decline of New York in the mid-1970s, Koch did not anticipate that his prodevelopment neoliberal economic policies would create any additional displacement among the poor. With the most visible effect of this displacement being homelessness, the Koch Administration found itself under siege. The courts forced the city government to assist the homeless. This represented the kind of policy that Koch was trying to avoid. Even half-hearted ways of providing assistance to the homeless cost lots of money and diverted resources from what the city government viewed as more worthwhile causes that would solidify white working- and middle-class support for the mayor. At the same time, the crack cocaine trade also devastated portions of the city's population and worsened perceptions of public spaces. Physical and social disorder became common encounters even for residents in middle- and upper-class neighborhoods. Koch understood that eventually he could not survive politically if he did not tackle many of the problems associated with urban disorder. Over the course of time, he reversed his initial policies and began to enlarge certain city agencies that dealt with spatial matters, though most of this expansion occurred in the police force. However, the problems associated with urban disorder worsened during his mayoralty. His third term from 1986 to 1989 was disastrous. Many of Koch's opponents criticized him for failing to plan for the long run and not anticipating New York's economic slowdown after 1987, which strained the city's ability to respond to everyday problems.

David Dinkins, who replaced Koch as mayor, attempted to move away from the neoliberal policies of his predecessor, but a poor economy combined with rising crime rates limited his choices. Dinkins hired approximately ten thousand additional police officers at the expense of social programs and changed the way the NYPD operated. The police expansion and operational reforms began to show results and crime rates declined. However, Dinkins was unable to benefit from these positive changes and was defeated by Rudolph Giuliani in 1993. Many of Dinkins's core supporters did not turn out to the polls in his reelection bid because they were disappointed by his failure to provide an alternative to neoliberal economics. Moreover, Giuliani successfully portrayed Dinkins as someone not tough enough to do the job required by a crime fighter.

POLICING IN THE POST-FISCAL CRISIS PERIOD

Problems with policing in the city worsened after the fiscal crisis of 1975. That year the police department lost about 5,000 police officers because of fear of fiscal default, and the numbers of the force remained constant in their decreased state until the early 1980s. Hoping to avert the shrinkage of the police department, the Police Benevolent Association (PBA) published a leaflet entitled "Welcome to Fear City" that urged visitors to stay away from New York because of crime and violence. This tactic failed, however, and with the numbers of its officers diminished, the NYPD reduced efforts to enforce traffic, littering, loitering, and other "quality-of-life" violations and focused on violent crime. The number of total arrests fell one fifth between 1975 and 1979. Felony arrests actually increased by 11%, but arrests for misdemeanors and violations decreased by 27% and 75% respectively. Even the fight against serious crime became selective. The narcotics unit stopped operating during the weekend, while investigations against organized crime all but disappeared. The police department made the arrest of muggers its priority during this period. According to statistics, 85% of the 100,550 reported robberies that occurred in 1981 took place in public spaces, costing the victims about $59.1 million in money and valuables. The police had to focus on street crime because its frequency compromised the movement of people in public spaces. However, this focus on robberies along with efforts to control other violent crime diverted attention from most quality-of-life offenses.[2]

After the difficult years of the late 1970s, the Koch Administration decided to spend a substantial portion of the budget in order to revamp the police department. This came as a direct contradiction to Koch's vows that he would not enlarge the city government and represented a challenge to his beliefs that aggressive policing could not displace social disorder.

In the 1980s, he ended up presiding over the greatest expansion of the three police forces in the city up until that time. This expansion of policing complemented the business-friendly climate that Koch wanted to create since more police officers could now pay attention to quality-of-life offenses. By June of 1988, the police force reached the 32,600 mark, which was about 10,000 larger than the low point of 22,542 officers in June of 1980. In 1984, the NYPD reorganized itself so that its officers could go after quality-of-life crimes such as vandalism, prostitution, drug dealing, and gambling. The mayor contended that this change reflected requests by neighborhood residents and argued that the stripping of a car was not much different from playing music loudly at night. This expansion signified the mayor's priority in policing and his belief that crime fighting and order maintenance were more important for his political fortunes than other services such as sanitation.[3]

Despite this attention to urban disorder, the situation worsened after 1985 because many of the city's populations were still suffering from the effects of the fiscal crisis and the implementation of neoliberal economic policies. The perception that the 1970s represented the worst period for the city in terms of poverty and human displacement may have been true with the decline and collapse of certain areas such as the South Bronx. However, for many people citywide, living conditions worsened in the 1980s and urban disorder began to affect middle- and upper-class neighborhoods even more. This is because it became impossible for affluent neighborhoods to isolate themselves from the problems of the city, which were achieving a state of quasipermanence. In the 1980s, the number of the homeless increased rapidly and reached staggering levels. Drug use became more prominent. Cheaper and more addictive forms of cocaine began to devastate the populations of many city sections. Violent crime also rose, as did the incidence of ugly crimes that received media attention and made people feel unsafe. The number of poor people doubled.

Mayor Koch was caught in a conundrum. His experiences in Times Square had taught him that social solutions were not effective. As misbehavior in public spaces persisted, Koch continued to believe that the police could not eliminate social disorder. Yet many New Yorkers were demanding more police officers and felt that social solutions could work. Eventually Koch capitulated to their wishes and enlarged his police agencies.

THE WAR ON DRUGS

As drug use and its side effects reached epidemic proportions, the police department undertook a campaign against drugs. The Koch Administration focused on a law-and-order drug solution, following a trend that had been initiated by Governor Nelson Rockefeller in the early 1970s when the state legislature passed his draconian drug laws. These laws called for severe mandatory penalties for drug offenders. Koch's war on drugs contained both a crime-fighting and an order-maintenance component. The crime-fighting component was obvious; since drug dealing and using had been branded as illegal and targeted by national and state administrations, its regularity in the city streets was unacceptable from a criminal justice point of view. The order-maintenance component became obvious over the course of time; drug dealers and users took over sizable portions of city neighborhoods and their behavior in public disrupted whatever appearance of order there had been in the past. Because of these factors, the city administration appeared unable to effectively dominate its territory, which was true. Furthermore, many of the people addicted to drugs engaged in panhandling, petty crime, and other activities viewed as nuisances. Gradually some of the addicts lost their homes and began to lead a nomadic lifestyle, which was highly visible in public space.[4]

Beginning in 1980, the police department in its antidrug operations focused on the Lower East Side, claiming that it was the retail drug capital of the city. In the 1970s, drug dealers took advantage of the relative withdrawal of the city government from the Lower East Side and established sizable operations and defense mechanisms there. Dealers operated from vacant buildings owned by the city. Inside, they installed layers of steel doors so that they could resist the police and other intruders, and they constructed tunnels so that they could escape or hide drugs and money. In many cases, the drug transactions took place through cracks in brick walls and other extemporaneous protective designs so that the customers would never see the sellers who operated safely from behind the barriers. The dealers employed a great number of steerers who attracted customers and led them to the right places. The sale of cocaine and heroin in the Lower East Side attracted all kinds of people from all over the city, including many whites from Long Island, New Jersey, and Connecticut who were afraid to venture into Harlem or the South Bronx for their purchases. Some blocks turned into drug supermarkets with long lines of people waiting to purchase drugs, street vendors selling them hot dogs and sodas, individuals offering express service for a small fee, and cars double parking without interference. Local police officers were unable to disrupt the drug trade because of a lack of personnel; between 1976 and 1984, the number of police officers working in the Lower East Side precincts went down from 733 officers to 492. By the early 1980s, dozens of dealers occupied more than twenty buildings in the Lower East Side and cleared about $100 million each year. Considering this state of affairs to be unacceptable, the city government deployed special squads to fight the drug trade.[5]

Although drug dealing in areas like Harlem and the South Bronx had also reached vast proportions, the city government could not invade them as easily as the Lower East Side because of Koch's already strained relations with communities of color. Throughout his mayoralty, Koch used divisive racial rhetoric and actions against minority populations so that he could maintain his popularity among whites. In the election of 1977, Koch prevailed because of this extreme rhetoric and because he represented himself as the champion of the city's white middle class. In that year's campaign, Koch highlighted his support of the death penalty, repeatedly characterized minority candidates as "poverty pimps," and aligned himself "against ripoffs that exist in some [public employee labor] contracts." His rhetoric appealed to many whites who believed that minorities received too much attention and too many resources from the local government. Public opinion polls suggested that 31% of New Yorkers considered the welfare system, which they associated with African Americans and Latinos, to be the main reason for New York's fiscal crisis. Another 20% considered the minority-friendly policies of Mayor Lindsay as a main reason behind the fiscal shortfalls. In the years that followed, it seemed that working-class and middle-class whites were willing to tolerate reduced service delivery and a disorderly environment as long as the mayor appeared to articulate their feelings when it came to issues of race and class. This rhetoric made large-scale police interventions in upper Manhattan, the South Bronx, or central Brooklyn unlikely. The Lower East Side was a much smaller and higher-profile area for such purposes. The Lower East Side received so much attention not only because it was a drug capital but also because such activities prevented its gentrification. As the city was recovering from the fiscal crisis of the 1970s, many parts of Manhattan were being renewed. The Lower East Side seemed to be the only neighborhood resisting this trend even though it was sandwiched by prime real estate locations.[6]

Despite serious efforts to dislodge drug dealing in the Lower East Side between 1980 and 1984, there were no improvements; this led the city administration to inaugurate Operation Pressure Point in 1984, which was an invasion of the area by more than 200 uniformed and undercover police officers and a helicopter. The NYPD adopted two procedures that regulated the proliferation of individuals and potentially that of drug dealers in public. The first concerned the elimination of the Desk Appearance Ticket system that usually allowed people charged with misdemeanors to be immediately released from custody upon receiving a notice of their court appearance date; individuals arrested in Operation Pressure Point for any violation were kept in jail, usually for several days, until they appeared before a judge. The second was a stop-and-frisk procedure; the police harassed suspicious individuals by stopping them, questioning and searching them, and arresting them or telling them to move on. After eighteen days, the police arrested 1,362 people and claimed that the area appeared to be more orderly. Although 416 people were arrested for the sale of narcotics and another 626 for possession, 159 were arrested for loitering and 161 for other minor offenses. A month into Operation Pressure Point, only one-third of the 1,780 arrests were for felonies. Parts of the Lower East Side became deserted because people who lived there had no desire to be harassed by the police. Two years later, the police declared Operation Pressure Point a success. More than 21,000 suspects had been arrested in the Lower East Side even though fewer than 500 ever served prison terms. Police officers also seized drugs worth $3 million, though that quantity seemed low for the duration of two years. After those two years, however, in 1986, the police force withdrew unceremoniously from the Lower East Side, hoping that residents would report drug offenses and watch the neighborhood for themselves. It was obvious that the police department could not sustain such a sizable force in the Lower East Side any longer. After the police withdrew, drug dealing and other offenses returned to pre-1984 levels.[7]

Operation Pressure Point failed, but it provided some important lessons. The public nature of drug dealing was disrupted because drug dealers had to operate more covertly. The Lower East Side appeared to be more orderly because many people who were considered to be suspects were arrested or harassed. As arrests for loitering and other offenses of dubious legal character continued and stop-and-frisk operations became constant, many populations who felt targeted were more reluctant to spend as much time outdoors. In its effort to fight crime, the city administration discovered the benefits of order maintenance. The problem with this practice was that it was unsustainable at a time when the police department lacked adequate personnel. The marketing and consumption of drugs increased and serious crime was on the rise. Crack undermined Koch and his efforts to seek reelection for a fourth time in 1989.

Despite police interventions such as Operation Pressure Point, many neighborhoods began to find themselves increasingly overwhelmed by street-corner crack cocaine salesmen and their customers. The concern with the drug trade was greater than before because crack cocaine was a cheaper substance that generated a more intense high than traditional cocaine consumption. Since most of the new users were low income and had fewer resources to cope with their drug problem, crack use reached epidemic proportions and became visible in public space. Addicts bought crack as often as four times an hour in order to satisfy their craving for the drug. Multiple transactions created a back-and-forth movement of addicts to places of distribution and consumption that made many neighborhoods seem disorderly. Moreover, addicts spent lots of their time in search of money to support their habit, contributing to the rise of petty crimes. Many abandoned properties were transformed into crack houses where addicts would go to consume the drug. Furthermore, unlike cocaine or heroin, which required sophisticated processing techniques, crack was produced in hundreds of back rooms and kitchens throughout the city. Because of decentralized production, law-enforcement officials had great difficulty disrupting the supply.[8]

The city government, sensing that the crack problem destroyed any pretense that the war on drugs was successful, intensified its antidrug efforts. In 1986, the police expanded the use of a sixteen-year-old federal law and started to confiscate the cars of people caught with crack. Koch said that officials should aim to seize 5,000 cars and that the city would provide additional garage space for these vehicles. City officials targeted the Lower East Side under this policy so that they could discourage outsiders from driving into the area to purchase drugs. The police also raided hundreds of stores, most of which were located in Greenwich Village and the Lower East Side, and seized over 39,000 pipes that could be used to smoke crack. The most far-reaching change in police behavior was the arrest of large numbers of street-level dealers and buyers. Unable to catch big-time dealers, the police tried to sweep the streets of anyone engaged in the drug market. This policy sought to displace people involved in the drug trade from the streets so that many neighborhoods could once again reflect an image of order. Initially, the police were surprised by the success of these operations, but as it turned out, the enforcement failed to reduce the trade and consumption of crack. In September of 1988, correction officials declared a jail emergency because of overcrowding. The continuous arrests also overwhelmed the courts.[9]

In 1989, statistics showed that the crack epidemic had devastated large portions of the city's population and that it contributed to perceptions of urban disorder. Crack contributed to the city's rising murder rate; from 1987 to 1988 the number of homicides in New York rose by 10.4%. The number of cocaine users tripled between 1986 and 1989, while drug consumption contributed to three times as many parents abusing or neglecting their children. Between 1985 and 1989, the city's jail population had almost doubled. Crack use contributed to such a general feeling of disorder that the Koch Administration seemed to be in serious trouble. By 1988, the city spent more than $500 million a year for the control of drugs without any visible effects. That year, Koch admitted that the growth of narcotic consumption impinged on city services. Although the city's workforce surpassed the pre–fiscal crisis levels in the late 1980s, unexpected demands including drug-related offenses made municipal service provision suffer. Many New Yorkers who had patiently waited for the return of decent municipal service in the years of the fiscal crisis realized that this would perhaps never happen under Koch. Of course, people who lived in neighborhoods swamped by crack users and dealers lost faith in government altogether. Even basic services such as sanitation and firefighting seemed to matter very little during this period.[10]

THE PERSISTENCE OF PHYSICAL DISORDER

By the 1970s, conditions in the South Bronx had deteriorated to such a level that it became an international metaphor for urban disaster. Responding to allegations by the Bronx Model Cities director that contractors used public money to build substandard housing that crumbled, in 1973 contractor Gerald Weintraub claimed that to "maintain a building [in the South

Bronx], you have to have armed guards and a super who's a murderer." Martin Tolchin in a *New York Times* article entitled "South Bronx: A Jungle Stalked by Fear, Seized by Rage," wrote, "this is the South Bronx today—violent, drugged, burned out, graffiti splattered and abandoned." Tolchin also claimed that "even for a native New Yorker, the voyage across the Willis Avenue Bridge is a journey to a foreign country where fear is the overriding emotion in a landscape of despair."[11] This implied that native New Yorkers did not live in the South Bronx. In 1977, a Bill Moyers CBS News documentary called *The Fire Next Door* and an ABC News close-up entitled *Youth Terror* depicted the South Bronx as a landscape where most urban violence and arson in the United States occurred. When Pope John Paul II visited the South Bronx in 1979, newspaper and television reports bemoaned alleys "where drugs are forever bought and sold," and how the pope "ventured down mean streets . . . where cabdrivers and garbagemen fear to tred."[12] In 1980 the nation's top census official, Vincent P. Barabba, asked South Bronx census takers to take enumeration in groups rather than follow the typical one-census-taker-per household routine citing safety reasons. In 1987, a Japanese government-sponsored guidebook warned tourists that New York is "a dangerous place, filled with muggers, con artists, thieves and cheats waiting to take advantage of unsuspecting visitors from Japan." It suggested that visitors "steer clear of the South Bronx, Central Park at night and Manhattan neighborhoods north of 100th Street and west of Eighth Avenue."[13] Television crews, filmmakers, and journalists reinforced these depictions with visual representations of rubble-strewn empty lots, burnt-out buildings, shabby streets, sidewalks with overgrown grass, and suffering residents.[14]

The statistical picture of the South Bronx corresponded with popular perception. Between 1970 and 1975, the South Bronx lost approximately 43,000 apartments to fire and other destructive forces. By 1977, upward of 3,000 vacant lots and buildings occupied over 500 acres in the South Bronx while 6,900 residential parcels owed property taxes for more than one year. From 1965 to 1977, the South Bronx lost more than 40% of its manufacturing jobs, resulting in an unemployment rate that surpassed the 25% of those eligible for work. Some areas lost as much as 60% of their population.[15]

The lamentable conditions that became commonplace in the South Bronx after the 1960s are rooted in a series of public policies that used racial preconceptions as their guide. On the one hand, for most of the post–World War II period, the city government neglected large portions of the South Bronx settled by African Americans and Puerto Ricans and minimized municipal services for these groups. On the other hand, city administrations spent money on projects that sought to maintain the whiteness of certain neighborhoods at a time when many whites were moving away to the suburbs, and that same money could have helped to stabilize neighborhoods that were on the brink of collapse. These policies influenced landlords' indifference and they neglected their properties and the people who lived in them. As deplorable spatial and social conditions in the South Bronx reached a climax during the 1970s, the area became an international symbol of urban decay. Representations of the South Bronx indicated the failure of New York City's postwar urban policy and reproduced racial stereotypes that guided that policy. In the end, representations of the South Bronx damaged the image of New York City and its government. By the 1980s, conditions in the South Bronx brought city administration pronouncements that the city was making a comeback into question.

In 1983, New York City officials decided to spruce up the windows of abandoned buildings visible from the Cross Bronx Expressway with color vinyl decals that depicted curtains, shutters, flowerpots, and venetian blinds. This beautification scheme aimed at improving the Bronx's image by giving the abandoned buildings a lived-in look. According to Anthony B. Gliedman, Commissioner of the city's Housing Preservation and Development (HPD), "perception is reality," and since the city government lacked the funds to structurally restore these buildings, window dressing seemed the only way to rehabilitate them, at least in the minds of commuters. Robert Jacobson, director of the Bronx office of the City Planning Commission, argued that "the image that the Bronx projects—and projects to potential investors—is the image you see from that expressway, and our goal is to soften that image so people will be willing to invest."[16] Jacobson added that most people knew the Bronx only from what they saw when they drove on the Cross Bronx Expressway and that they prayed that their vehicles could pass through without breakdowns. By making the windows of buildings presentable, it was believed by some that negative perceptions would diminish.[17]

Immediately after the announcement, the city's window-dressing plan became subject to extreme criticism and ridicule. Residents of the Crotona Park neighborhood suggested that "while the city was at it, why not expand the program to provide designer clothing decals to place over the tattered apparel of impoverished residents, large Mercedes-Benz decals to strap to their sides and decals of strip sirloins for them to eat."[18] The editors of *The New York Times* wrote that "the $100,000 so invested would symbolize not Government's interest in struggling neighborhoods but its desire to hide unpleasant realities."[19] Even newspaper articles that sought to put a positive spin on the story could not avoid questions over the rationale of this decision. Mayor Koch and other city officials adamantly defended the vinyl decal window beautification, and this defense heralded a new approach toward the South Bronx and its problems. Although the critics were correct that window dressing symbolized the withdrawal of the Ronald Reagan Administration from urban policy, more importantly, it exemplified the determination of the New York City government to rehabilitate the image of the South Bronx. City officials arrived at the conclusion that in the absence of money to rebuild the South Bronx, they could at least make efforts to improve its image since the entire city suffered from the bad image of the South Bronx. Moreover, an improved image could provide much-needed bases for the physical and social rehabilitation of the area when the funds for such an undertaking became available.[20]

The assumptions that guided the authors of the "broken windows" theory were similar to those that guided the Koch Administration officials in their attempt to hide urban disrepair in the South Bronx. The early 1980s were understood as a period of fiscal retrenchment. The days of the government providing substantial funding to fight urban disorder seemed to be gone. Urban renewal had been discredited and shelved. Other efforts that sought to displace "undesirables" from commercial districts had also failed. Public officials and social scientists concluded that the way to control urban disorder would have to depend on less ambitious programs of image making and focus on the creation of individuals who were more civic minded and cared about their neighborhoods. Ambitious mayors like Koch could not accept the idea that image making and efforts to change the meaning of behavior in public space were the only solutions left for government. Public officials began to experiment with strategies that would allow them to dominate the public space of urban neighborhoods once again and defeat urban disorder along with serious crime. The Koch Administration set these strategies in motion in the late 1980s. However, it was not until the 1990s that the order-maintenance approach appeared to work.

In the case of the South Bronx and certain other parts of the city, there would be no improvement without a physical rebuilding. The Koch Administration recognized this and waited for the funds to become available. Once it became clear that the federal government would not provide much-needed assistance, the municipal government decided to spend city funds. In the late 1980s, the Koch Administration announced a $4.5 billion (later to become $5.1 billion) ten-year citywide reconstruction plan that would provide affordable housing. In this plan, the rebuilding of the South Bronx had the highest priority. Besides easing housing shortages, the city administration viewed this plan as a way to provide housing for tens of thousands of homeless people who flooded the streets of Manhattan daily and made the image of the city suffer. In order to succeed, city agencies tapped into local knowledge by embracing local community organizations and allowing them to sponsor the rebuilding efforts. Organizations such as Banana Kelly, the Catholic Church, the South Bronx Churches, and other local community corporations took advantage of government funding and provided local expertise in order to revive neighborhoods that had failed. The program did not benefit Koch politically since it began to show results in the 1990s. However, many previously abandoned neighborhoods were brought back to life to a great extent because of this ten-year plan. This effort to rebuild the South Bronx and other parts of the city such as Bushwick and East New York in Brooklyn represented the most far-reaching physical solution in New York since the 1950s. In this case, there was no slum clearance involved since many neighborhood buildings had been destroyed and the city owned all of the vacant lots and abandoned buildings. Some sizable buildings were rehabilitated rather than destroyed while others that were beyond repair were taken down and rebuilt. Even the demolition of buildings was viewed as a positive step at the time because many observers argued that empty lots appeared to be more orderly than abandoned buildings, which frequently functioned as shooting galleries and housing for squatters.[21]

Koch was not credited for this housing plan because it came too late during his mayoralty. In 1989 when his reelection effort for a fourth term failed, there was no evidence that areas like the South Bronx would turn around. Instead, many people looked at their neighborhoods and saw few improvements. Neighborhoods that had collapsed remained collapsed. Marginalized neighborhoods remained marginalized, and conditions in middle- or upper-class neighborhoods actually worsened.

HOMELESSNESS AND GENTRIFICATION

On August 7, 1988, hundreds of people clashed throughout the night with approximately 450 police officers in Tompkins Square Park. Police officers, in their effort to enforce a 1 a.m. park curfew, miscalculated the determination of certain groups of people and the homeless to remain in the park and the symbolic significance of that resistance. In the melee that ensued, hundreds were injured. Angered by the resistance, police officers ended up rioting as well. After forcibly evicting everyone from the park, police officers mounted numerous baton charges against groups assembled on the edge of the park. Many of the officers involved wore riot gear and concealed their badges. Despite cavalry charges and other police attacks, the crowds kept growing and refused to leave the streets adjacent to the park. After failing to defeat the civilians, the police withdrew shortly after 4 a.m. At that point, protesters, homeless, activists, punks, squatters, and other Lower East Side residents reentered the park and celebrated their victory until the morning.[22]

In the days that followed, the city administration unsuccessfully blamed groups of dissenters from the Lower East Side for the Tompkins Square Park events. Mayor Koch blamed the riot on "anarchists" and described the park as a "cesspool." The head of the PBA argued that an "insipid conglomeration of human misfits" caused the riot and that the area was full of "social parasites, druggies, skinheads, and communists." Police commissioner Benjamin Ward agreed with the official city line, but he also faulted police actions in the park and dismissed two police supervisors. The Civilian Complaint Review Board received hundreds of police brutality complaints. Despite efforts at damage control, the event proved a public relations disaster for Mayor Koch, who was preparing to run for a fourth term in 1989. The mayor seemed unable to impose some kind of order on the Lower East Side. Moreover, many New Yorkers realized that the confrontation between the police and protesters in Tompkins Square Park was the direct outcome of prodevelopment neoliberal public policies enacted in New York City in the 1980s.[23]

The riot signified a conflict in the Lower East Side that originated in the 1970s over public space and real estate. The Lower East Side was the only area in lower Manhattan to experience a dramatic decline similar to that of the South Bronx. However, there were some important differences. The Lower East Side, sandwiched between midtown and downtown Manhattan, represented the last sizable underdeveloped area south of 96th Street where there was ample money to be made by exploiting real estate. In addition, many of the people who lived in the Lower East Side were well-organized members of radical community movements with a determination to oppose intrusions unfavorable to their causes. In the 1970s, the appropriation of vacant lots and their transformation into community gardens signaled the first community mobilization in the Lower East Side with regard to urban space. The neighborhood gardeners cleaned up vacant lots full of garbage, construction materials, old appliances, and disemboweled cars and transformed them into green spaces. The first community garden was created in 1973 when a group called Green Guerillas helped local residents throw balloons containing plant seeds into a fenced-in parcel of land

Figure 6.1 One of numerous Puerto Rican pieces in the Lower East Side. (Photograph by Themis Chronopoulos, 2008.)

located on Houston Street near the Bowery. As the number of abandoned lots increased in the Lower East Side, a full-fledged community garden movement developed. Some of the gardens were created and cared for by individual families, others by organized neighborhood groups. Many Puerto Ricans created *casitas,* which were lot gardens with small wooden shacks and featured benches, tables, murals, and shrines besides the planted areas. *Casitas* operated as social clubs and meeting spaces for the community. By the 1990s, more than seventy community gardens had been established in the Lower East Side, more than in any other area in New York.[24]

An urban homesteading movement that appropriated abandoned buildings and made them into homes for neighborhood people also flowered in the Lower East Side during the 1970s. The city government, having taken over too many buildings from landlords who walked away from them, found itself in the embarrassing situation of trying to sell them off, often unsuccessfully, to developers and other real estate interests. As community organizations protested the transfer of buildings to commercial interests that did not care about the well-being of the neighborhood, the city allowed tenants to manage their own buildings temporarily and to own them eventually as cooperatives. Many programs that sought the orderly transfer of abandoned buildings to local residents were developed in the late 1970s and the 1980s. Among homesteaders, women constituted a slight majority. Over 70% of homesteaders were Puerto Rican with the remainder white (17%), Asian (9.5%), and African American (3.1%). Homesteaders managed to rehabilitate more than 100 buildings between the late 1970s and the 1990s. However, the difficulty of rebuilding properties according to city code and the reluctance of the city government to place all of its buildings in the hands of nonprofit groups meant that thousands of properties were never part of the program. This encouraged the antagonistic relationship of certain neighborhood groups with the authorities.[25]

With homesteading being a limited option, urban squatting represented the most radical and lasting appropriation of buildings in the Lower East Side. Although urban squatting predated homesteading, it was a highly controversial activity, with activists taking over abandoned buildings and rebuilding them outside of formal and legal channels. Unlike homesteaders, squatters did not cooperate with government agencies because of practical or ideological motivations. In the late 1970s and early 1980s, when the decline of neighborhoods like the Lower East Side reached extreme levels, activities like squatting did not seem to matter. However, as the economy improved in the 1980s and mainstream real estate interests became involved in the redevelopment of the Lower East Side, squatters became a big problem. They personified the most extreme case of land appropriation. By the 1980s, these groups of people had appropriated over twenty multistory buildings, had opened community, art, and nonprofit commercial spaces, and had made Tompkins Square Park an epicenter of political and recreational activity. When one combined the squatters with the organizations that built community gardens, the Lower East Side appeared as an area in Manhattan that refused to participate in the capitalist real estate market almost completely.[26]

In the 1980s, real estate speculators became attracted to the Lower East Side by the extreme devaluation of property and land and by the sizeable real estate growth that adjacent neighborhoods experienced. Small-scale speculators bought land and buildings, waited for a few years, resold those properties and made tens of thousands of dollars. Gradually, more capital-intensive developers entered the game. They profited by upgrading the properties in order to attract people willing to pay higher rents. Large development firms could take advantage of tax breaks and discounts provided by the government for reconstructing properties. These developers sought to displace residents of rent-regulated apartments through intimidation. In many cases, they hired people to terrorize residents, torch empty apartments and withhold heat and hot water in the winter months. As buildings reached various stages of gentrification and such tactics became impossible, developers simply paid off families in rent-controlled apartments to move. Each time someone moved from a rent-controlled apartment, the owners renovated it cheaply and then placed it on the market for higher rent. In many cases, they preferred students and other mobile populations as tenants because they moved out quickly, allowing the developers to renovate or pretend to renovate the apartments and collect even higher rent.[27]

During this period, what was termed "gentrification" occurred in the Lower East Side as well as in many other parts of the city. This resulted in the displacement of thousands of people, many of whom became homeless. Using methods similar to those of Columbia in Morningside Heights during the 1960s, developers terrorized low-income residents so that they would evacuate their apartments. In fact, many of those apartments were located in single-room occupancies in the Upper West Side immediately south of Morningside Heights. As *New York Times* columnist Sydney Schanberg wrote, "for it is here [Upper West Side] that large numbers of sturdy buildings including many S.R.O. . . . became occupied by citizens who did not qualify as 'Beautiful People' and who, in our age of disposable everything, became the discardable humans." Those displaced were almost always low income, elderly, or disabled. Developers became interested in renovating such apartments because they were located in neighborhoods that were making a comeback and because the city granted generous "conversion" tax abatements. After renovation, these apartments were rented to affluent people. Although the city administration distanced itself from developers employing questionable methods to remove tenants, it also blocked all legislative attempts in the city council to deny tax abatements to any landlord found guilty of harassment. The people who became homeless because of gentrification joined the ranks of other homeless populations such as Vietnam War veterans, the mentally ill, people whose housing had burned down, and other types of low-income individuals.[28]

As homelessness substantially increased in the late 1970s and in the 1980s, the Koch Administration found itself under siege by the courts, which forced the city government to provide shelters to qualified homeless people; by liberal and homeless advocacy groups, which criticized and monitored the administration's treatment of the homeless; by the homeless themselves, who flooded the public spaces of the city and made them seem disorderly; and by working- and middle-class New Yorkers who resented the opening of homeless shelters in their neighborhoods, the disorderly conditions that homeless people were generating, and the inability of the city to articulate a coherent policy on homelessness.

Between 1979 and 1984, a number of lawsuits brought by homeless advocates forced the city and state to provide shelters for the homeless and established minimum shelter standards. In 1979, the Coalition for the Homeless brought a class action suit on behalf of homeless men, arguing that the available homeless shelters were unhealthy and dangerous and that there was a shortage of beds. In this case, known as *Callahan v. Carey*, the court accepted the claim that the New York State Constitution had a provision stating that the state should come to the "aid, care, and support of the needy," and concluded that the city and state had the responsibility of providing shelters for the homeless. Under the auspices of the court, a decree of consent was negotiated between the city and the homeless advocates. The decree required the city's shelters to accept any homeless man meeting criteria established by the state. It also set minimum requirements for the condition of homeless shelters and voucher hotels on access, recreation time, capacity, size of the beds, and the availability of trained staff. It also required the city to provide laundry facilities, storage lockers, showers, soap, and towels, as well as mail and telephone services. Two years later, in *Eldredge v. Koch*, the courts agreed that women should be provided shelter facilities that were equal in quality to those of men. Finally, in *McCain v. Koch*, the courts forced the city to provide adequate shelter to families in a timely fashion instead of having them sleep on the floors, chairs, and countertops of welfare offices. The city government did not meet many of the stipulations found in these court decisions; however, its agencies made an effort to provide shelter to the homeless even if it was inadequate.[29]

In order to avoid an influx of people, the Koch Administration made the shelters that it provided unpleasant. The city government relied on congregate shelters in gymnasiums, armories, and other warehouselike buildings in order to shelter the homeless. People who stayed in these shelters complained of squalid conditions, lack of privacy, and problems with security. For families, the city chartered rooms in run-down hotels. The courts, which had already required the provision of shelters for the homeless, began to force the city to improve conditions in hotels as well. The federal and state governments, which subsidized a large portion of these costs, also pressured the city to improve conditions. In 1987, Manhattan Borough President David Dinkins attacked Koch's reliance on temporary shelters and urged the administration to provide more permanent housing to homeless families. The Koch Administration responded by moving some families to permanent housing after instituting an eighteen-month waiting rule so that families with other options would not claim to be homeless in order to obtain decent apartments. According to J. Phillip Thompson, this expensive shelter policy diverted resources from low-income neighborhoods and from those who were not homeless. The homeless problem, however, was so great that there were few other solutions.[30]

As gentrification became a controversial issue in New York and homelessness increased, the Koch Administration asserted that the two were not linked. Human Resources Commissioner George Gross argued in 1986 that the gentrification of neighborhoods was not the primary reason for homelessness. He supported his argument by stating that a recent study done by his department found that most homeless surveyed were from the South Bronx and northern Brooklyn, which were areas not undergoing gentrification. Fred Greisbach, director of the Coalition for the Homeless, questioned this assertion and said that the surveys reported the last place the homeless lived, not their original neighborhoods. Many of the homeless moved around with family members and friends before they ended up in the streets. Despite Gross's claims, thousands of people with fixed income lost their apartments during the 1980s and many of them ended up living in the streets. Lack of affordable housing was definitely one of the reasons for homelessness. In the Lower East Side, a significant number of people were skeptical of claims that gentrification did not create homelessness.[31]

The Lower East Side represented not only a neighborhood whose low-income residents suffered from gentrification but also a neighborhood that received many displaced people from other areas who were now homeless. The Bowery had historically been a destination for the down and out of New York City. However, many of the 1980s homeless relocated to the Lower East Side because they enjoyed a higher degree of toleration there and because of the proximity of many soup kitchens, shelters, and cheap hotels. As a result, in the 1980s, the Lower East Side experienced two contradictory processes: extreme gentrification and a great influx of the homeless. Some homeless people lived in Tompkins Square Park throughout the decade. In fact, their presence triggered the riot of 1988.

The sixteen-story Christodora building located across the street from Tompkins Square Park on Avenue B represented what was wrong with gentrification in the 1980s for many Lower East Side activists. In 1975, the City of New York tried to sell this dilapidated building but attracted no bidders. This attested to the decline of the neighborhood and the deterioration of the building, since the city had paid $1.3 million for Christodora in 1947. After the failed auction, the city managed to sell the building to George Jaffee, a real estate developer, for $62,500. In the early 1980s, Jaffee received offers between $200,000 and $800,000 for Christodora. He finally sold it in 1983 to developer Harry Skydell for $1.3 million. A year later, Skydell sold the building for $3 million. In 1986, Skydell recouped the building along with another developer named Samuel Glasser. They renovated the Christodora, transformed it into a luxury building, and sold eighty-six condominiums. The top-floor penthouse sold for $1.2 million. It was the only building to be attacked the night of the park riot in 1988. Demonstrators used a police barricade to crash the glass and brass doors of the Christodora after the police withdrew. The Christodora represented one early example of what was happening with hundreds of properties in the Lower East Side in the late 1980s.[32]

Despite a high degree of urban homesteading and gardening, by 1987 the city government owned about 500 buildings and lots in the Lower East Side. As the Lower East Side slowly became fashionable in the 1980s, these parcels of land became the object of conflict between local groups and real estate interests. Neighborhood groups wanted the city to turn over many of these properties to nonprofit corporations so that they could build community and tenant-controlled housing. Public officials did exactly this in the South Bronx and other parts of the city but were no longer willing to give up properties in the Lower East Side for low-income groups. Instead, they wanted to sell the land for profit to private developers who would in turn build luxury condominiums and contribute to the gentrification of the neighborhood. The Tompkins Square Park riot was the most dramatic confrontation between neighborhood groups and the city government in the 1980s over gentrification.[33]

Throughout the 1980s, HPD policies tried to weaken community organizations in the Lower East Side and transfer properties to real estate interests. In 1982, the department started to ignore the rising number of applications of neighborhood people to participate in a tenant interim lease program that would eventually lead to their ownership of buildings. Instead, the department recruited real estate managers to run some of its properties. The city government also refused to improve the structures and demolished many buildings, arguing that drug dealers used these spaces. In the same year, the city government attempted to create a progentrification coalition by encouraging artists with incomes much higher than those of the neighborhood to move to buildings renovated by large developers. Lower East Side activists, including most of the artists in the area, campaigned against the Artists' Home Ownership Program and defeated it in 1983. Eventually, large corporate interests became involved in the Lower East Side's development market. Toward the late 1980s, the HPD agreed to demands by the local community board to set aside housing for low- and moderate-income groups equal to that developed for market purposes. However, this program did not move quickly enough to match the construction rate of housing for market purposes. As mainstream development interests became involved, many local residents felt that the area would rapidly gentrify no matter what.[34]

Real estate interests were more successful in attracting artists to the Lower East Side than the city government had been. In the early 1980s, management companies offered artificially low rents to artists in order to attract galleries that would make the area appear hip and desirable. The Lower East Side became the cheap alternative to SOHO, which by then had become one of the epicenters of the mainstream art world. Once a sizable artist community became established in the Lower East Side, the management companies substantially increased the rents of cheap spaces. By then, demand for the Lower East Side allowed for the payment of higher rents. Meanwhile, the activity of artists in the Lower East Side elevated its desirability. Although the area had already developed an attractive cultural infrastructure, the opening of many more nightclubs, bars, and coffee shops in the 1980s made the area even more exciting for outsiders.[35]

Homeless people had lived in Tompkins Square Park since the late 1970s, though they did not get much attention before the neighborhood started to gentrify. In 1980, about fifty people lived in the park and most of them were white. In contrast, by the late 1980s, about 200 people lived in the park, the majority of them Black and Latino. Throughout the decade, residents of Tompkins Square Park formed alliances with squatters, anarchists, and other groups of young people who appropriated space in the Lower East Side. Although many observers considered homeless people to be disorganized and politically inactive, the opposite was true in the Lower East Side and New York City at large. There were a number of protest actions by homeless people throughout the 1980s in New York—the largest in August of 1987 when thousands of people marched against homelessness through midtown Manhattan. The failure of the police to remove homeless people from Tompkins Square Park in 1988 represented a great victory for the homeless in regards to public space in New York.[36]

Throughout the 1980s, prodevelopment city policies went hand in hand with the intense regulation of public spaces. The city government tried to redefine the use of streets, parks, empty lots, and appropriated buildings. In the Lower East Side, these policies failed because of the determination of squatters, homeless, and other community groups that rejected such heavy governmental interference. After the 1988 riot, the Lower East Side continued to resist official city policies.

As their number rose into the tens of thousands in the 1980s, homeless people interfered with city government development programs that sought to make the city desirable for corporations and affluent people. The homeless effectively replaced graffiti as the symbol of urban disorder in the subways, sidewalks, and parks. Their proliferation in the commercial districts of Manhattan served as a constant reminder of the city's decline. There were many reports that the homeless who had flooded Grand Central Terminal, the Port Authority bus station, and Penn Station shocked tourists who were not accustomed to them. Locals and commuters who were accustomed to the homeless were more likely to be outraged rather than shocked.[37]

During Koch's third term, efforts to regulate the presence of homeless people in transportation facilities intensified. This occurred because the number of homeless rose, crime rates increased, and many New Yorkers felt that the city administration lost its way in combating issues of social disorder. Encouraged by a court ruling that convicted a homeless man who was charged with loitering at the Port Authority Bus Terminal in 1985, the authorities attempted to dissuade homeless people who caused problems from frequenting the Grand Central Terminal and the Port Authority Bus Terminal. In 1987 in a unanimous decision, the State Supreme Court's Appellate Term found a state law prohibiting loitering in transit areas to be unconstitutionally vague and overturned the 1985 conviction. The judges argued that because they contained shops and other businesses, transportation facilities were public spaces that no longer qualified as places solely used for travel. Nonetheless, two days later the Metro-North police arrested a number of people in Grand Central Station for criminal trespassing. Although these charges were dismissed, the authorities showed their determination to evict the homeless from these transportation facilities. In 1988, the New York Court of Appeals in another unanimous decision also found loitering legislation governing transportation facilities to be unconstitutional, but efforts to regulate homeless people in transit areas continued. In the election year of 1989, transit police began to enforce rules of conduct in the subways and target homeless people begging or lying down on train seats. MTA chairman Robert Kiley claimed that the rules were enforced because many passengers complained that the subways were increasingly becoming disorderly.[38]

By the late 1980s in the eyes of the public, the homeless had become indistinguishable from the nomadic population of crack users. People who used crack also begged for money, collected cans, and constantly moved about public spaces. They looked like homeless people, and indeed many of them eventually became homeless. The homeless became part of the undeserving poor in the eyes of many, and the Koch Administration was blamed from all political sides for being unable to have a coherent homeless policy and to restrict the movement of the homeless in public space. For a period of time, transportation facilities had become the most restricted public spaces because of a loitering law that had prevented people from hanging out there. However, the court decisions eliminated that law. The city administration also tried to regulate public parks. City Parks Commissioner Henry J. Stern contended that public parks could not be both spaces of recreation and habitation and that the city needed to clarify their function. The problem with carrying out a plan of evicting the homeless from public parks was that it failed badly in Tompkins Square Park and the city was reluctant to escalate potential conflicts.

What happened in New York during the Koch years is puzzling. Koch pursued neoliberal economic policies and was very successful in the beginning of his mayoralty. The problem with this success is that after the near default of 1975 and the severe reduction of municipal services from much of the city, expectations were low. Many New Yorkers credited City Hall with slight improvements between 1978 and 1985 and thought that the city was on the right track. Koch was also a mayor who said the right things and emphasized middle-class job creation in the private sector as the road to prosperity. To that end, he offered tax subsidies to many corporations and real estate interests, hoping that these businesses would become the economic engines of the city. What Koch did not expect was the remarkable increase of homeless people. Over the course of time, it became clear that the neoliberal policies that Koch pursued created an extreme upward redistribution of wealth. The elites of the city definitely benefitted. Middle-class people did not do as well, though they held their own. The number of people falling below the poverty line increased. For example, populations with fixed incomes, such as retirees, the disabled, or women with young children, found themselves with higher bills for housing, energy, food, and other basic necessities. People with low-paying jobs began to suffer because inexpensive housing options such as SROs began to disappear. As the number of homeless people increased in public space and as the courts pressured the city, Koch began to pursue policies that contradicted his neoliberal agenda. As it turned out, it became difficult from a human rights point of view to pursue a neoliberal agenda that discarded the needs of the poor completely.

Figure 6.2 Memorial mural depicting Tupac Shakur in the Lower East Side. Homeless people continued to frequent the Lower East Side despite crackdowns. (Photograph by Themis Chronopoulos, 1997.)

In 1989, Manhattan Borough President David Dinkins defeated Mayor Koch in the Democratic primary and Republican Rudolph Giuliani in the general election to become mayor of New York. To a great extent, Koch lost the election because of social disorder issues and because he appeared to be too divisive on racial issues. In the campaign, Koch tried to highlight the achievements of his first two terms because his third term was disastrous. In the beginning of the third term, a few of Koch's political allies and appointees were involved in a major scandal, damaging the reputation of a mayor who claimed to know nothing about it; many observers criticized his naïveté. Crime statistics continued to increase during this period and reversed a trend of crime reduction until 1985. The homeless population not only increased but also displayed a high degree of defiance as the city tried to remove them from transportation facilities, public parks, and other public spaces. There were a number of incidents that showed that the mayor had lost control. As already mentioned in the last chapter, a gang of whites attacked three African American men whose car had broken down in the Howard Beach section of Queens in 1986. The mayor was blamed from all sides for his role in the incident, with minority populations lamenting his divisive rhetoric and whites arguing that he did not care about crime. In the Tompkins Square Park riot of 1988, the police initially prevailed, but after the riot the homeless and other activists reclaimed the park. In April of 1989, a white female investment banker jogging in Central Park was raped and severely beaten, allegedly by a gang of African American youths on a "wilding" excursion. Koch approached the attack from a tough law-and-order perspective while Dinkins spoke of racial rapprochement. In August of 1989, sixteen-year-old Yusuf Hawkins was attacked and killed by a group of baseball bat wielding youths in Bensonhurst, Brooklyn, where he had gone to inspect a used car. Koch refused to admit that the killing had racial overtones and verbally attacked Blacks who protested the killing. Dinkins was once again conciliatory, though he also blamed Koch for the antagonistic climate that he had cultivated among racial groups with his rhetoric. In the primary campaign, Dinkins presented himself as someone who would heal racial divisions and lead the city down a more harmonious road. He described the city as a gorgeous mosaic of racial and ethnic groups and promised to make relations among these groups more congenial. He defeated Koch because of an alliance of liberal whites and minority voters who turned out in the Democratic primary. In the general election campaign, Giuliani tried to portray Dinkins as unprepared to take care of the city's finances because of previous IRS problems. He also argued that Dinkins would be soft on crime. This led Dinkins to proclaim that he would be the toughest-on-crime mayor that the city had ever seen. In the end, Dinkins defeated Giuliani by 47,080 votes, which represented the smallest margin in about eighty years.[39]

MAYOR DINKINS AS ANTICRIME CRUSADER

In many respects, Dinkins was elected during one of the worst times in the city's history. On top of enormous budgetary shortfalls, David Dinkins inherited a host of infrastructural and social problems that were difficult to manage. The problems associated with drugs and crime persisted. The city was experiencing an AIDS epidemic and the homeless population continued to increase even though the city was producing more than five thousand homes a year for low- and moderate-income people through renovation or new construction. Better solutions for the homeless were never really implemented because the city had no money. The school system was in shambles with buildings falling apart, high dropout rates, and neglected teachers. Finally, many of the city's bridges were crumbling, and there were problems with the condition of roadways and the water system.[40]

Despite these issues, the crime problem turned out to be the most challenging. Nine months into his term, a number of terrible crimes receiving continuous media coverage began to undermine the mayor and his ability to govern. Nineteen cab drivers had been murdered that year. Brian Watkins, a tourist from Utah, was stabbed to death in the subway in his effort to protect his family from robbers. Six children were killed by random gunfire in a period of nine days. Two more children were killed in the following week. There was a rise in muggings and drive-by shootings. In response, the *Daily News* ran a series of articles under the heading "City Under Siege," while the *New York Post* published an issue with a large headline saying "Dave, Do Something!" Felix Rohatyn, a Dinkins advisor and an investment banker who was credited with New York's fiscal bailout in the 1970s, said that "I've never lived through anything like this. This is a lot worse than the '70s. People seem to have given up. There's a sense that we're prisoners of something that's beyond our control." Jerry Nachman of the *New York Post* was more proactive in his writings. Having characterized Dinkins's governance style as "measured and managerial," he argued that New Yorkers wanted something like a superman. He suggested that New Yorkers wanted "Gen. George Patton or U.S. Marshall Dillon leading the charge" so that the city could move beyond its "Mad Max" nihilism. During the same period, Ed Koch criticized Dinkins in his column for the *New York Post* and in a weekly television show; City Council President Andrew Stein requested that the governor deploy the National Guard; and Governor Mario Cuomo called for a sizable enlargement of the city police. Originally, Dinkins replied to his critics by stating on a radio show whose listeners were primarily Black: "You are aware the problems of crime and violence in our community are not new. We've had this problem, and now I guess it has gone beyond our borders and others have become concerned. Fact of the matter is, we have been concerned since day one." The point that Dinkins was making was that whites and the mass media became concerned about crime only because it had reached their neighborhoods. Dinkins also tried to say that he only had seven months on the job while others like Koch had as many as twelve years and failed to fight crime. Despite all these points, Dinkins concluded that he had to enlarge the police department and make crime fighting his main priority.[41]

The pressure from the mass media and other political entities transformed David Dinkins into a crusader against crime. After the city council and Governor Cuomo tried to preempt the mayor by proposing increases in police department personnel, Dinkins, true to his cautious and managerial style, released a comprehensive study of the police force and its needs. The proposal, entitled "Safe Streets, Safe City," recommended the deployment of the largest street patrol force in history, which meant that New York City would have the largest police department in the world with 42,405 members that would include 10,500 civilian employees that would free police officers for street duty. The plan promoted community policing (or problem-solving policing), which would seek to transform the police from an agency that mostly responded to emergencies to an agency that deployed officers in neighborhood beat. These officers would have the freedom to establish partnerships with neighborhood merchants and residents in an effort to tackle recurring crime problems endemic to that neighborhood and in an effort to prevent future crime. Community policing officers would also be able to cooperate with other city agencies whenever necessary. Dinkins's program covered all kinds of policing aspects besides neighborhood policing. For example, it would increase the number of transit police officers so that every subway train would have one officer on board between 8 p.m. and 4 a.m. In addition, the program would provide funding for 2,950 more jail beds at Rikers Island and would also increase funding for the offices of district attorneys, the special narcotics prosecutor, the Legal Aid Society, the Criminal Justice Agency, and the Department of Juvenile Justice. "Safe Streets, Safe City" even included youth programs with recreation, employment, and educational opportunities so that many young people in low-income neighborhoods would not involve themselves in criminal activities. The entire anticrime undertaking would cost $1.8 billion over a period of four years. Dinkins's anticrime program was approved with minor modifications by the city council and the state legislature. Increased property taxes, a four-year extension of a city personal income tax surcharge, and a new lottery game funded the plan.[42]

In the 1990s, the term "community policing" began to mean all kinds of things to all kinds of people; however, when the Dinkins plan combined community policing with other crime-fighting and -prevention programs, a serious but not extreme vision of spatial regulation was created. The idea of deploying neighborhood street patrol officers who would cooperate with local residents and businesses was nothing different than order-maintenance policing as articulated by "broken windows" proponents. Operation Pressure Point under Koch was similar to Dinkins's community policing. However, there were many fundamental differences. Dinkins and his police chief, Lee P. Brown, wanted police officers to go beyond strict order maintenance and use their discretion to determine if the behavior of disorderly people in public space was criminal. This meant that police officers would have to contact homeless services agencies if homeless people did certain things that neighborhood residents found objectionable rather than roust them out of the area or arrest them. Youth programs would seek to divert the energies of young people from crime and public misbehavior. The increase of the number of public defenders would provide arrested people with a fairer chance in the courts. Dinkins's plan was tough on crime, but it included many benevolent elements. In the words of police commissioner Brown, "every neighborhood in the city will have one or more police officers assigned who know about that neighborhood, its people, their concerns, the crime problem, the make-up of the blocks, the crises of daily living and the support systems available to help people live better." The idea behind Dinkins's plan was to solve many problems that communities were experiencing without the indiscriminate banishment of people considered disorderly.[43]

In 1993, a second volume of "Safe Streets, Safe City" was released and reported on the relative success of a program that was still underway with plans for the future. By then, over 6,000 police officers had been added to the city's three police forces, another 1,400 were slated to be added by February of 1994; the total uniformed headcount would grow to 38,310. Moreover, because of redeployment and civilianization initiatives, precinct staffing was increasing by 50%. The report also showed how FBI-indexed crime had decreased by 15% between the fiscal year of 1990 and the fiscal year of 1992, subway crime by 31%, and public housing crime by 18%. "Safe Streets, Safe City II" emphasized how 200,000 youth of the city were participating in educational, recreational, and vocational activities sponsored by the Department of Youth Services and described programs that served senior citizens. The report proposed a merger of the city's three police forces into one, an increased use of technology and computers that linked different agencies, a reform of the juvenile justice system and adult probation system, the establishment of community-based courts that would deal with low-level offenders, and the assignment of police officers in public schools. Overall, the report showed that the goals of "Safe Streets, Safe City" were within reach.[44]

Despite notable decreases in crime and improved police deployment during the Dinkins mayoralty, the implementation of "Safe Streets, Safe City" was not what its designers had in mind. The success of the program depended on the cooperation of police rank and file, which never really happened. Many existing police officers distrusted the Dinkins Administration and disliked its vision of community policing. This was because police officers suddenly had to work more, participate in foot patrol, cooperate with the community, and perform many social service functions. In 1992, Police Commissioner Ray Kelly launched a Community Assessment Unit headed by Assistant Chief Aaron Rosenthal to report on the implementation of community policing. A series of reports revealed that the prevailing situation was disastrous. The problem started with training, which was characterized as a "dismal failure, due to an overall blasé attitude on the part of management, which was filtered down to the attendees." At the precinct level, training logs were badly maintained, attendance was poor, and training was conducted in a "haphazard and perfunctory manner." The training officer of one precinct told attendees that foot patrol was burdensome and that if they took better care of radio cars, they would not break down as much, and they would not have to be on the beat as much. In addition, many police officers faked reports on how often they walked their beats, did not cooperate with auxiliary police or with detectives, ignored the community and its requests, and worked only during the daytime on the weekdays. Usually, prostitution and drug dealing occurred at nighttime and during the weekend, something that became even more of a routine once offenders realized that the police walked the beat during bank hours. In general, police officers and sergeants did not believe in community policing; the program had a 40% turnover rate.[45]

Though the city police would have never developed cordial relations with the Dinkins Administration, a number of racial incidents and efforts at police reform made for a climate of intense antagonism between the two entities. In some respects, the police department attempted to destabilize the Dinkins Administration, and no mayor in recent history had ever been able to effectively govern the city without a degree of cooperation from the police. During crucial situations, the city administration experienced lack of cooperation by the police, and eventually there was an open revolt. This allowed the city government to strike back and launch a major investigation of the department once complaints of serious and systematic police misconduct emerged. However, the conflict between the administration and the police undermined the crime-fighting and community-policing effort of the Dinkins Administration from a public relations point of view. Moreover, Dinkins's attempts to mediate conflicts behind the scenes offered credence to the claims of some of his political opponents that he restrained the police department from intervening in situations where African Americans were involved.

Shortly after Dinkins's inauguration, Black residents of Flatbush in Brooklyn started to boycott a Korean produce store because of allegations that its owners had assaulted a Haitian immigrant for purportedly stealing. The boycott and picketing began to include other Korean-owned grocery stores. At first the *New York Post,* and eventually the entire local media, covered the event and criticized Dinkins for failing to end the boycott. The media also focused on the leader of the protesters, Sonny Carson, a convicted kidnapper, and a campaign worker who had once been dismissed by the Dinkins campaign. Carson was quoted as saying that he was "antiwhite" and that in the future there would be no boycotts, only funerals. City Hall attempted to quietly mediate the conflict but failed. Dinkins denounced the protesters and even symbolically bought some fruit from the stores. Eventually, the boycott faded away as the police began to enforce protest limits ruled by the courts. However, the damage had been done. One of the store owners announced plans to sell his store. The mass media,

The Declining Appearance of Order, 1978–1993 143

courts, and federal government blamed Dinkins for not forcefully intervening. Some police officers argued that the administration was reluctant to allow the police department to enforce the law because the protesters were Black. Eventually, the city administration improved communication between Blacks and Koreans and instituted several outreach programs. For Dinkins's image, this was too late.[46]

In August of 1991, disturbances in the Crown Heights section of Brooklyn not only damaged Dinkins's image as conciliator even more but also made Dinkins appear indecisive in matters of social order. Rioting in Crown Heights occurred after two Guyanese children were hit by a car driven by a Hasidic man. In this accident, the girl was injured but the boy was killed. Three hours later, someone in a group of angry Black youths stabbed a Jewish rabbinical student. Rumors about the incidents caused the escalation of disturbances. Mayor Dinkins and other City Hall officials went to Crown Heights, pleaded for peace with Black and Hasidic groups, and met with community leaders from both sides in efforts to conciliate tense relations that existed long before the incidents that sparked the disturbances. Dinkins also stated that the attacks of Black youths against Jewish people were unacceptable and visited the injured parties in the hospital. Still, some of the media blamed Dinkins for not doing enough and the police for failing to respond. Some police officers blamed Dinkins for restraining them. Two years later, a state report on the Crown Heights events condemned the leadership of the police during the incidents and discovered a breakdown in the chain of command. The state report rejected the notion that the mayor or any other top official restrained the police from efficiently intervening. However, the report claimed that although the mayor and top officials knew that the police were not acting effectively and that the disturbances were out of control, they did not question the police department's assurances that police were handling the situation. Ultimately the report implied that there was a leadership vacuum and that Dinkins and his police commissioner were at fault. The *New York Times* ran an article with a front-page headline saying: "Crown Heights Study Finds Dinkins and Police at Fault in Letting Unrest Escalate." This state report and the media coverage that followed came a few months before Dinkins ran for reelection in 1993. Dinkins was portrayed as someone who had lost control of his police department and as someone unable to confront social disorder.[47]

The conflict between the PBA and the Dinkins Administration also escalated. In October of 1991, in its effort to win a pay raise for its members, the PBA went to arbitration and filed papers against the city. These papers characterized welfare recipients as "lazy and shiftless" and not deserving of the city's budgetary allocations. One of the attorneys who wrote the arbitration papers claimed that these words reflected the sentiment of PBA president Phil Caruso and that many police officers felt that welfare recipients strained the budget and as a result there was no money for pay raises for the police. The rhetoric used by the PBA at the time included many concealed racial stereotypes, and its message was that the mayor, an African American, preferred to provide public assistance to minority welfare recipients rather than pay increases to white police officers.[48]

If anyone doubted that the PBA and police rank and file viewed Dinkins's mayoralty in racial terms, their riot outside City Hall in 1992 confirmed all these views. In September, police officers demonstrating against city administration initiatives to make the NYPD less corrupt and more accountable rioted outside City Hall. After many incidents indicating police corruption, in the summer of 1992 Dinkins appointed a commission to investigate alleged gross misconduct by police officers and began to push for a stronger police Civilian Complaint Review Board run by civilians. The PBA opposed these actions and organized a large, raucous protest outside City Hall. About four thousand of the demonstrators stormed the barricades and swarmed City Hall, blocking all entrances. Afterward, they went onto the Brooklyn Bridge and blocked traffic for an hour. During the protest, many of the off-duty officers were seen drinking alcohol, damaging automobiles, and attacking reporters. Some of them carried signs that mocked the mayor's Blackness and yelled racial slurs. A beer-drinking officer prevented Una Clarke, a Black City Council member, from entering City Hall and told his friend, "this nigger says she's a member of the City Council." About 300 on-duty officers did little to stop this unruly display, generating outrage among elected officials, the mass media, and the public. In the aftermath of this event, the mass media once again wondered whether the mayor was in charge of the police. Despite disciplining of officers, the passage of legislation allowing for a new Civilian Complaint Review Board by the city council, and the continuation of the investigation of police corruption, Dinkins came out of the event looking like a bad manager once again. After these events, it was difficult to convince many New Yorkers that Dinkins was completely in charge of the police department.[49]

Rudolph Giuliani gave a speech during the police demonstration at City Hall denouncing Dinkins and began to use the relationship of the mayor and the police as a way to promote his own candidacy in the following year's election. In the aftermath of the police protest action, Giuliani said that "at some point people are going to say, how can you have a Mayor who has a Police Department where the overwhelming majority of officers think he's putting their lives at risk." Giuliani calculated that he had the potential to attract many white voters to support his candidacy if he emphasized how the police rank and file distrusted Dinkins. Giuliani also needed to neutralize Dinkins's crime-reduction techniques and the results of "Safe Streets, Safe City." When asked whether the public believed that Dinkins was soft on crime or that an unruly mob of white police officers was calling the mayor racial epithets, Giuliani replied that this depended on "the predisposition people have in the first place." Clearly, Giuliani counted on such predispositions, thinking that whites were not convinced that Dinkins had reduced crime or that police officers were at fault.[50]

In the 1993 general mayoral election, Giuliani portrayed Dinkins as a mayor who allowed New Yorkers' quality of life to decline. He ran television and radio commercials that targeted squeegee men, drug dealers, panhandlers, and the homeless as people who contributed to the "disorder that is driving the city down." He frequently conflated social disorder with serious crime and promised to use the power of government to marginalize these offenders. In a policy paper, Giuliani promised to halve the number of people in homeless shelters, to institute a 90-day maximum shelter stay, and to eliminate the provision of permanent housing for homeless families. Giuliani counted on many New Yorkers being tired of the homeless problem and becoming intolerant of poor people in the city. Dinkins defended himself by pointing at statistics showing substantial reductions in crime and by faulting Giuliani's proposals for dealing with the homeless.[51]

In October and November of 1993, Dinkins also moved against squeegee men, who had become poster boys of social disorder, in an effort to preempt Giuliani's charges that he was not tough on quality-of-life offenders. This patrol offensive decreased by two-thirds the number of people at the entrances of bridges and tunnels waiting to clean car windshields. Most of the arrests were for disorderly conduct. After this campaign, police officials and their consultants concluded that it would not be very difficult to displace squeegee men from many parts of the city. Besides displacement, there was little that the city government was planning on doing; many of the squeegee men had alcohol and drug abuse problems and lived at the margins of mainstream society. Their window-cleaning behavior represented a last-ditch effort to be productive and generate some income. Eventually, Giuliani's first police commissioner, William Bratton, admitted that Dinkins dealt with the squeegee men but that Giuliani got the credit.[52]

In the end, Giuliani defeated David Dinkins by a very small margin of votes that was similar to Dinkins's victory over Giuliani four years before. As J. Phillip Thompson has written, Giuliani did an excellent job of mobilizing the conservative white electoral base of New York while Dinkins disappointed many of his liberal supporters, who preferred funding for social programs rather than an enlargement of the police. In addition, many white New Yorkers did not believe Dinkins's crime-fighting plans and chose Giuliani, who promised to be a tougher mayor. The events in Crown Heights, the demonstrations by the police, and the commercials by the PBA did not help; they translated into an image of a mayor embattled with his own police department, making many wonder how the city government could fight crime if its officers openly revolted against it. Charges that Dinkins restrained the police also had some resonance among whites who distrusted an African American mayor. In the election of 1993, New Yorkers chose a tougher approach toward low-income people and their proliferation in public space. What they did not know was how far the Giuliani Administration would go on matters of spatial regulation.[53]

7 The Radicalization of Spatial Regulation, 1994–2001

On a policy level, the "Broken Windows" theory implies that police can restore a sense of order and civility to the city, can restore the quality of life experienced by citizens, and can reduce crime and fear of crime by attending to the relatively minor but seemingly ubiquitous annoyances of urban life—for example, aggressive panhandling, squeegee cleaners, public drunkenness, and graffiti.[1]
—Police Commissioner William J. Bratton

They should get off the booze, get off drugs and get off their asses.[2]
—Police Commissioner William J. Bratton

What they said to me I'll never forget. In public, one says, "You niggers have to learn how to respect police officers."[3]
—Abner Louima

On his 40th birthday on July 25, 1996, at 6:45 a.m., Harold Dusenbury was walking to a construction site where he was working in Greenwich Village. An electrician who lived in Willingboro, New Jersey, Dusenbury had just arrived from his long commute to the city; he was wearing a t-shirt and jeans and was carrying a plastic bag containing his tools and work clothes. Suddenly, a police car racing the wrong way on a one-way street jumped the curb. Without saying anything, a police officer exited the car, knocked Dusenbury's head against a metal shutter, and threw him on the street, trying to handcuff him. Other police officers arrived on the scene and began to kick Dusenbury in the head, use racial slurs, and call him a drug dealer. The police officers attacked Dusenbury because they had heard on their radios that a Black man wearing a t-shirt and jeans had just fled Washington Square Park after brandishing a knife. Dusenbury, who was wrongly identified as the suspect by the police, suffered permanent physical damage, including brain injuries. After this incident he was unable to work. The Manhattan District Attorney and the NYPD exonerated the police officers, claiming that it was a "tragic mistake" and that the police officers had not done anything out of the ordinary. However, the city settled a civil case in 1999 without admitting wrongdoing and paid Dusenbury $2.7 million.[4]

The Dusenbury case was one of many questionable and brutal police actions in the age of zero tolerance that spanned 1994 to 2001. During this period, Mayor Rudy Giuliani made order maintenance and crime fighting his main priorities of government and presided over a radical version of spatial regulation. Just like Koch, Giuliani cultivated a culture of intolerance against racial minorities by using similar rhetoric and promising to be tough on criminals and welfare recipients. The main difference was that the Giuliani Administration could now also deploy the police in order to accompany the rhetoric with actions. These actions, which were promoted as necessary in order to make the city orderly and enhance the quality of life of its residents, included continuous and comprehensive police attacks against people who made urban space seem disorderly because of their presence, not because they committed any violations. However, it is difficult to have such a radical vision of regulating public space in a crowded and diverse city without routinely violating the civil and human rights of ordinary people. The Giuliani Administration did not mind that the police department sometimes abused its power in its efforts to regulate ordinary people who were mostly nonwhites and did not mind that the rights of free speech and assembly of social-movement organizations were being restricted. After all, since the 1960s, law and order strategies had targeted "undesirables" and protesters because of assumptions that both groups disrespected authority and made cities disorderly. People who made high-profile public spaces "unfriendly" to affluent tourists and residents were chased away, arrested, brutalized, and castigated as disposable people with no place in the city. Social-movement organizations that tried to gather supporters in public space also became the object of extreme regulation because they were viewed as threats to the administration and its policies. Gradually, these policies were applied citywide, with the city administration assuming that it was not possible to efficiently regulate high-profile public spaces without also instilling a degree of order in low-income neighborhoods where most of the "disorderly" people lived.

Unlike Koch and Dinkins, Giuliani was determined not to allow the spatial effects of neoliberal economic reforms to derail his administration and refashioned the city government from a neoliberal to a neoconservative entity. Initially, the city government focused on matters of spatial regulation but gradually expanded its exercise of power in matters that went beyond urban space. Mayor Giuliani made it clear that he and his administration were in charge of the city, not the corporations or their advocacy organizations. Instead of deferring to corporations, under Giuliani, the city government became an autocratic entity that did not permit competing centers of power to interfere in matters of governance.

Figure 7.1 Mural criticizing Giuliani's spatial policies in Williamsburg, Brooklyn. (Photograph by Themis Chronopoulos, 1997.)

THE ESTABLISHMENT OF QUALITY-OF-LIFE POLICING

A few days after his inauguration, Mayor Giuliani announced that the city's community policing would be redefined and simplified. This announcement came the day that the NYPD released a series of memoranda that discussed problems with community policing the previous year. Giuliani argued that community policing should be redirected toward fighting crime and away from social service tasks that were added during the Dinkins Administration. He agreed with police officers who complained that New York community policing had become too confusing and that it was not the responsibility of the police to put neighborhoods in touch with social services. Giuliani's vision of community policing included a more aggressive policing practice that would strictly focus on law and order.[5]

Giuliani hired as his police commissioner William J. Bratton, who set out to reform the way that the NYPD operated. Bratton was chief of the New York City Transit Police between 1990 and 1992 and had been credited with making the subways more orderly. He was assisted by George

Kelling, co-author of the "broken windows" article, who had been hired by the MTA as a consultant for ways to police the subway system. One of Bratton's first acts as Transit Police chief was to instruct transit officers to eject panhandlers from the subway system on their first encounter instead of giving them warnings. The goal was to make the system panhandler free at all costs. Under Bratton, the transit police combated fare evaders, displaced homeless people, deterred graffiti writers, and arrested people for minor violations including disorderly conduct. Bratton subscribed to the philosophy that serious criminals also committed minor offenses and credited his methods for a decrease in subway crime. Giuliani hired Bratton in the hope that his subway system methods could be applied citywide. Almost immediately, Bratton shook up the NYPD from top to bottom in ways that went beyond his Transit Police reforms. He replaced deputy commissioners, bureau chiefs, borough commanders, and precinct commanders with ranking police officers who had aggressive reputations. Bratton also criticized some officers for "looking bored to tears" while on beats and promised to make patrol officers more responsive and responsible. Bratton decentralized many police functions, making borough and precinct commanders accountable for many tasks that were previously assigned to police headquarters. For example, the Organized Crime Bureau, which dealt with drug enforcement, public morals, and auto theft, was assigned to borough commanders, and the Detectives Bureau was assigned to precinct commanders. In his first year, Bratton insisted that the city was continuing to practice community policing in a redefined fashion. However, the term began to be used less frequently; what replaced it was "quality-of-life policing" along with "zero-tolerance policing."[6]

Since his days as chief of the Transit Police, Bratton had become an admirer of the "broken windows" theory and its possible applications. Throughout his tenure as police commissioner, he cited this theory as a guiding force:

> The strategies and policies outlined in *Reclaiming the Public Spaces of New York* are predicated upon the observations and postulates subsumed by the "Broken Windows" theory. This theory was first articulated by James Q. Wilson and George Kelling of Harvard University in 1982, and it maintains that unattended public disorder conditions are ultimately criminogenic, because they suggest to the public that traditional social controls have been eroded, that society has lost some of its civility, and that crime and disorder are both widespread and tolerated within our society. These disorderly conditions, as well as the sense of fear they elicit, create a vicious cycle in which citizens curtail their activities, lock themselves behind closed doors, and refrain from engaging in routine activities within their neighborhoods, parks, and other public places. When the law-abiding members of society curtail their activities in this way, their acquiescence is a signal to the criminal

element that disorder is tolerated, and is taken as invitation to engage in additional disorderly conduct and crime.[7]

Though disorderly people and criminals were not the same groups, Bratton usually referred to them interchangeably, since the "broken windows" theory argued that disorderly conditions encouraged crime. This belief was shared by Mayor Giuliani, many of his administration officials, and private holders of power, who equated the proliferation of homeless people in public space with the proliferation of murderers. This ideological stance perhaps explains more fully the way that spatial regulation proceeded during the Giuliani mayoralty.

One of Bratton's first initiatives concerned the implementation of tougher surveillance and sanctions toward youths. Given that this program targeted public schools, it brought the city government closer to its dream of being able to efficiently control young people of color. Under operation Safe Corridor, precinct officers began to monitor the areas around schools, and narcotics officers intensified Buy and Bust activities. Truancy units were established in all seven patrol boroughs, quality-of-life violations were strictly enforced around schools, and in the summer months police officers were assigned to public pools, parks, and playgrounds. The NYPD created a number of juvenile databases kept within the Youth Services Division so that repeat offenders could be identified. Bratton argued that a tougher approach toward school-age youths was necessary because youth crime and violence were increasing at a rate greater than that of the youth population.[8]

On March 12, 1994, the NYPD announced a crackdown on quality-of-life offenses. Encouraged by the positive results of quality-of-life policing in Greenwich Village, the NYPD decided to apply this program in most of the city. The announcement formalized the Giuliani Administration's theme of improving the quality of life in the city by moving against practices such as public urination, public consumption of alcohol, marijuana possession, aggressive car-window cleaning, and open-air drug dealing. As professed by police officials, the main goal of the program was to reduce disorderly behavior in public space.[9]

In the following months, the NYPD expanded the quality-of-life program and found ways to make it more efficient. Toward those goals, the police department decided to overhaul the way it treated criminal court summonses. A major change involved taking offenders without a government-issued picture identification card to the police station for interrogation and possible booking. The NYPD also created a computerized database that contained the information of individuals receiving summonses and their court appearances so that people who failed to appear in court could be arrested. Other initiatives already in place such as the surveillance of the areas around public schools and the rounding up of truant teenagers became part of this quality-of-life program. The NYPD also declared a war against open-air drug dealing, and a couple of months later the NYPD expanded the definition of quality-of-life offenders to include people playing portable radios or car stereos loudly, unlicensed street vendors, graffiti writers, illegal dumpers, reckless bicyclers, and prostitutes. Mayor Giuliani said that the city's 75 precinct commanders should focus on fighting "visible signs of a city out of control." In their frequent press conferences, Giuliani and Bratton cited recommendations of the "broken windows" theory as a guide for their actions. Over the course of time, crackdowns on quality-of-life offenses were applied in more parts of the city and targeted an increasing number of violations.[10]

The decentralization of the NYPD continued in the summer of 1994, making precinct commanders responsible for fighting most violations. For the first time in decades, local police officers were able to address street prostitution and underage drinking. In the early 1970s, in an effort to fight widespread local precinct corruption, the city government removed enforcement for alcohol- and prostitution-related offenses from local police officers. Instead, it formed specialized police units that reported to police headquarters to investigate the sale of alcohol to minors by liquor stores and bars, as well as all forms of prostitution. Now local precincts would be able to perform their own investigations and decoy operations. The Giuliani Administration argued that the changes were worthwhile despite the possibility of increased corruption. Under these changes, local precinct commanders would bear the complete responsibility for any violations occurring in their areas and they were replaced whenever they failed to reduce crime and social disorder. Bratton's decentralization of police functions did not mean the elimination of roaming police squads with citywide authority. It meant that patrol officers would no longer just respond to emergencies and pretend to patrol neighborhoods; they would actually have to patrol. Besides Bratton's corporate management techniques, the NYPD began to use computerized statistics of crime organized by area. Known as Comp Stat (computer-generated comparative statistics), this new method allowed police headquarters to immediately identify areas with high crime rates. In frequent meetings, precinct commanders were expected to explain why certain types of crime had risen in their areas and the steps that they were planning to take in order to deal with the problem. If these commanders did not know why crime had increased in their areas or had no plans in place to tackle this criminal activity, they were in trouble. In 1994, this practice made for the weeding out of many precinct commanders and their replacement with new Bratton appointees. Gradually, Comp Stat allowed precincts to target certain types of crime and social disorder, focus on problem areas, and request additional assistance from headquarters if the crime-fighting task at hand appeared to persist.[11]

The following year, the merger of the city's three police forces—transit, public housing, and the NYPD—into one further strengthened the ability of the police commissioner to mobilize law enforcement resources.

Though the merger resembled a centralization move, it actually enhanced the NYPD's decentralization process by making precincts responsible for local public housing and subway stations. It was Giuliani who pressured the state, the Metropolitan Transportation Authority, and other entities to allow this merger, which would have been unconstitutional without the approval of the state government. The city administration argued that a merger would allow the city to save money and become more effective in policing its citizens. Moreover, city and police officials claimed that the quality of policing in public housing projects and in the transportation system would not decline because of this police merger. The merger allowed the city government to directly police the subways and public housing projects and increase or decrease policing according to needs. Funds appropriated for policing needs in the New York City Housing Authority and the New York City Transit Authority were transferred to the NYPD. This police merger was in many respects a gift from Giuliani to Bratton, who now had more flexibility in deploying a larger and better-funded police force.[12]

At a time when many people were arrested because of comprehensive order-maintenance applications, funding for the representation of the indigent declined to unacceptable levels. In 1994, the Legal Aid Society, which was once the principal indigent defense organization of New York City, cited impossible working conditions and demanded a 15% reduction in individual caseloads and an increase in wages. Mayor Giuliani responded by threatening to terminate the city's contract with the Society; he also demanded a $16 million retroactive budget cut. After an unsuccessful lawyer strike, the Legal Aid Society settled for the budget cuts and promised to represent the same number of cases as before. Giuliani, incensed by the Legal Aid Society's antagonism, continued to cut its budget and divert funding to newly founded contract law firms that would represent poor people. Funding for indigent defense declined substantially during this period, making for a decline in the quality of representation for people without money. Many lawyers who represented the indigent complained that they were overworked and underpaid and that they were a small part of a criminal justice system designed to generate a high volume of guilty pleas. Without efficient representation, conviction rates were higher because defendants were not adequately informed of their rights and because lawyers did not perform the investigative work required. Many public defenders outside of the Legal Aid Society wanted to represent as many cases as possible because this was how their pay increased; they did not care much about winning those cases. Even the quality of defense in murder cases became compromised.[13]

During this period, the relationship between crime fighting and order maintenance became more obvious. Both practices required sustained police efforts with enough officers deployed efficiently in strategic parts of the city. Beyond that, order-maintenance policing without reductions in crime would be problematic for the police and the city administration because many citizens would begin to question the rationale of going after neighborhood kids and letting serious criminals get away. A successful war against social disorder could only occur if serious crime decreased. To that end, the NYPD engaged in crime fighting alongside order maintenance. For example, the war against public drug dealing was an extension of order maintenance with many crime-fighting components. Once the police flooded the streets and started to arrest sellers, the drug trade went underground, with steerers discreetly directing people to apartments that functioned as sales centers. However, this enforcement also eliminated open drug wars and competition among drug dealers that could be deadly to members of gangs involved in the drug trade as well as to bystanders. Suddenly, many communities became more peaceful, not only because sellers were not on every street corner but also because shootouts and other street violence became rare. A similar strategy involved the police trying to catch people with illegal guns. Since there were more police officers stopping and searching people, the risk of getting caught with a firearm increased substantially. Again, police harassment rose but public gunfights decreased.

While fighting quality-of-life offenses and crime, the Giuliani Administration also discovered the power of publicity and tried to use it for political gains. Every few weeks, the mayor, administration officials, or police officials would announce a new public-space offender that needed to behave or face arrest, even if the NYPD had already moved against that offender. These offenders included licensed street vendors operating in congested areas of Midtown and on small sidewalks, prostitutes and their clients, liquor stores selling alcohol to minors, X-rated shops, graffiti writers, taxi drivers, newsstand operators, and many others. These announcements sought to make New Yorkers believe that the city government was active and on top of things. By carefully singling out groups that some people in the city considered disorderly, the city government sought to capitalize on the dissatisfaction of certain groups of people against others. One week the government went after squeegee men, the following week graffiti writers, the week after taxi drivers or newsstand operators, and so on. All of the groups targeted were at the margins of society from a mainstream capitalist perspective and were also highly visible in public space; the people appeased were from more affluent backgrounds with some kind of a grievance against these other populations and their activities.

The problem with this publicity was that police commissioner Bratton received most of the credit and Mayor Giuliani was obscured; this was the subtext of a clash between Giuliani and Bratton. The problems began in late 1994 when the *Daily News* ran a front-page story entitled "Bratton's Juggernaut," featuring a sizable photo of Bratton. The story referred to Operation Juggernaut, an antidrug initiative that Jack Maple, deputy commissioner for crime-control strategies, had devised and the mayor had endorsed. Having determined that a high percentage of criminal activity occurred because of the drug trade, the NYPD would deploy 5,000 police officers in an antidrug squad that would target areas with the most drug operations. Operation Juggernaut had not been officially announced and it was obvious that someone from the NYPD brass had leaked it to the press. The beneficiary of this publicity was Bratton. Furious from the publicity that Bratton received, Giuliani delayed the plan for fifteen months until Bratton was no longer the police commissioner and blamed John Miller, who was in charge of NYPD's public relations, for the leak to the press. On February 10, 1995, Miller resigned after he refused to follow City Hall's orders to shrink his staff. Miller, who had been one of Bratton's closest aides, was blamed by administration officials for giving Bratton too much credit for reductions in crime and social disorder and for shunning the mayor's efforts. In an angry speech, Giuliani claimed that he wanted police officers to work on fighting crime and not on public relations and that Miller resigned because he refused to shrink his office staff. Miller accused Giuliani of trying to politicize and control police department information. Regardless, Bratton continued to receive national and international attention throughout 1995 and became somewhat of a celebrity; the narrative that emerged was that Bratton was the architect of the dramatic decreases in crime in New York City and that his methods should be emulated in other cities around the world. In January of 1996, *Time* magazine put Bratton on its cover. Giuliani continued to announce new quality-of-life initiatives while trying to take credit for successes; however, his commissioner had upstaged him.[14]

On March 26, 1996, Bratton announced his resignation after twenty-seven months on the job. It was clearly the outcome of friction between the commissioner and the mayor. In 1995, the Giuliani Administration began to investigate some of the commissioner's out-of-town trips, thinking that they were improper; the investigation included a vacation trip of Bratton to the Bahamas as a guest of the financier Henry Kravitz. Giuliani was also irked when he found out that Bratton had signed a $350,000 book contract with Random House. He began to investigate the contract terms. Bratton secretly told Giuliani not to worry about having to reappoint him because he was going to resign. However, Bratton delayed in announcing his resignation, and this forced an annoyed city administration to announce that the police commissioner was seeking a private job. With Bratton's resignation, the Giuliani Administration would be able to show that its own management techniques were behind crime reduction and that the mayor as chief executive deserved the credit.[15]

The methods that Bratton used to fight crime and to reduce social disorder were successful, though they also opened the door for many systematic police abuses that went unchecked. The great majority of the people disciplined because of their activities in public space were low-income Blacks and Latinos. The great majority of the city administration's and NYPD's cheerleaders were middle- and upper-income whites.

But as long as the NYPD's spatial regulation focused on the most marginalized groups of people such as the homeless, young minority males, and panhandlers, many entities that should have questioned some of the methods the NYPD employed were slow to react. This changed in subsequent years as the targets of order maintenance increased and the process became more brutal and unconstitutional. Many observers have argued that the high-profile police abuses of the post-Bratton era (as well as lesser police abuses) would have never happened had Bratton remained in his post. Even the Reverend Al Sharpton, who did not always get along with Bratton, stated that the "tone Bratton set was that the police community is not going to get away with barbaric and over-the-line actions."[16]

Giuliani replaced Bratton with Howard Safir. Safir was the city's fire commissioner and a friend of Giuliani's. The two had worked together in the Justice Department in the 1980s, where Safir was in charge of a witness protection program for the U.S. Marshals. Once Safir became police commissioner, Giuliani became so involved in the operations of the NYPD that in 1999 a poll revealed that many people considered Safir to be a figurehead. Most respondents thought that it was Giuliani who really ran the NYPD and not the police commissioner. According to Wayne Barrett, Giuliani was so prepared to take over the NYPD that he took charge of the seating chart at Safir's inauguration. Moreover, many people inside the police department considered Safir to be a "lightweight." Whether Safir was just a figurehead is subject to debate. However, it was clear that Giuliani had a strong hand in police matters, regularly taking credit for police initiatives and successes and making sure that the Bratton publicity problem did not reemerge. Safir rarely gave press conferences by himself; he usually gave them together with the mayor. This strategy was risky because any spike in crime statistics would be blamed on Giuliani. The mass media could then claim that it was Bratton who really made a difference. The Giuliani Administration intensified its regulation of public space, making sure that this did not happen. Once Safir was in office, the Giuliani Administration facilitated the redeployment of hundreds of uniformed police officers performing administrative duties to the streets so that the numbers of police officers engaging in law enforcement would increase. In the summer of 1996, Safir issued guidelines that listed violations that could be used against the homeless. Then he launched an offensive against the homeless in Manhattan south of 110th Street. During this offensive, police officers swept specific areas, trashed the belongings of homeless people around the street, and arrested those who refused to move away. After the police action, sanitation workers collected the belongings of the homeless spread around the sidewalks and the streets and placed them in garbage trucks. Safir also adopted many of Bratton's antidrug strategies, some of which were implemented for the first time because of the Operation Juggernaut delay. Safir embraced Bratton's policies in public space and redoubled many of them.[17]

"THIS IS GIULIANI TIME"

In August of 1999, Abner Louima, a thirty-year-old Haitian immigrant, was arrested and sodomized with a broomstick inside a restroom in the 70th Precinct station house in Brooklyn. The assault on Louima received national attention and deepened perceptions that New York police officers were routinely brutalizing Blacks and Latinos in their effort to carry out mayor Giuliani's zero-tolerance policy. What happened after 4 a.m. on August 9, 1997, in the streets of Brooklyn is instructive. NYPD officers were summoned to Club Rendez-Vous located on Flatbush Avenue in Brooklyn to disperse a large crowd of people who had gathered outside to watch the fight of two patrons. The police officers tried to force the crowd to disperse, and in the process, some bystanders became unruly and started to yell and throw bottles. During the commotion, police officer Justin Volpe attacked an intoxicated patron by the name of John Rejouis and threw him to the ground. Rejouis, a corrections officer, tried to show Volpe his badge; instead, Volpe slapped Rejouis's hand and knocked the badge to the ground. Abner Louima began to yell at Volpe about his treatment of Rejouis. Louima also refused to move after Volpe attempted to push him away. As officers Charles Schwarz, Thomas Wiese, and others approached and tried to handcuff Louima, Volpe was struck on the head and fell to the ground. Volpe thought that Louima had hit him, even though it was Jay Nicholas, Louima's cousin, who had hit him. Police officers began to chase Nicholas, who ran away down Flatbush Avenue. Volpe joined the chase, thinking that he was chasing Louima. At some point, Volpe encountered Patrick Antoine, who was walking home and had not been in the club or anywhere near it. Volpe beat Antoine in the head and face using a flashlight. Antoine suffered bruises and contusions on his head and a laceration over his right eye that required seven stitches. He was arrested by other officers who arrived on the scene. In the meantime, officers Schwarz and Wiese had arrested Louima and were driving him to the 70th Precinct in their patrol car. While driving, Sergeant Michael Bellomo radioed a description of the man who had assaulted Volpe; his description matched that of Louima. At that point, Schwartz and Wiese stopped the patrol car near Nostrand Avenue and Glenwood Road, got out of the car, opened the rear door and began to beat the handcuffed Louima. Afterward, Schwarz and Wiese drove to Glenwood Road and Bedford Avenue and notified Bellomo by radio that they had arrested the man who assaulted Volpe. Officers Thomas Bruder and Volpe heard this message and drove to the scene, where they met Schwarz and Wiese. After consulting with the other police officers,

Volpe taunted Louima and beat him with a radio and his fist. Louima was still handcuffed.[18]

In the police precinct, the atrocities continued. Louima's pants and underwear fell to his ankles while he was being processed; he continued to remain handcuffed. Upon arriving at the precinct, Volpe saw Louima being processed at the front desk. He then grabbed a wooden broomstick, broke it over his knee, and placed the one section of the stick in the bathroom. Shortly thereafter, Volpe borrowed a pair of leather gloves from officer Mark Schofield. Once Louima's processing ended, the driver of the patrol car took him to the bathroom; Volpe followed. In the bathroom, Volpe picked up the stick and told Louima, "I'm going to do something to you. If you yell or make any noise, I'll kill you." Volpe pushed Louima to the ground, hit him in the groin, and put his foot over Louima's mouth because he began to scream. Volpe and the other officer began to punch Louima. Then the other officer lifted Louima from the ground. Volpe then used the stick to sodomize Louima. Afterwards, Volpe held the stick, covered with Louima's feces, in front of Louima's mouth and taunted him. Before confining Louima to a cell, Volpe told him that he would kill him if he revealed the night's incidents to anybody. Volpe finally returned the leather gloves, now covered with blood, to Schofield. Though Louima had suffered life-threatening injuries, the police did not care. For an hour and a half, the precinct would not provide a police escort to the ambulance that had arrived to take Louima to the hospital. When he finally arrived at the hospital, Louima was handcuffed to his bed and placed under guard; relatives were not allowed to see him. Police officers claimed that Louima had sustained his injuries during a homosexual encounter. When his relatives went to the precinct to file a complaint, they were told to go home. Meanwhile, the Internal Affairs Bureau covered up a complaint by a hospital worker that Louima had sustained extensive injuries; there was no log of the complaint or a follow-up.[19]

Volpe considered his behavior to have been nothing out of the ordinary. The following morning, he bragged about his actions to several officers. In the New York Community Hospital where he and other officers were being treated for minor injuries incurred outside the nightclub, Volpe was overhead saying, "I broke a man down." When Volpe returned to the 70th Precinct, he told Sergeant Kenneth Wernick what he had done to Louima, and added, "I took a man down tonight." Volpe even showed Wernick the stick he had used in the sexual assault. Afterward, Volpe showed the stick to officer Michael Schoer, who smelled Louima's feces on the stick and asked, "What is that, dog shit?" Volpe replied, "No, human shit."[20]

Later, Volpe provided false information to Assistant Kings County District Attorney Sheila O'Rourke about his assault on Antoine. Volpe told O'Rourke that Antoine punched and pushed him while he was trying to handcuff Louima. Volpe swore over his version of the story, which amounted to criminal charges against Antoine. Those included a felony assault, disorderly conduct, and obstructing government administration. One or more of these charges have always been used by police officers to cover up misconduct.[21]

Louima and Antoine were treated at Coney Island Hospital in Brooklyn. Antoine received seven stitches to close a laceration on his head and was discharged the same day. Louima was not as lucky. Initially he was diagnosed with swelling in his head and a laceration over his eye, but shortly thereafter the doctors discovered internal injuries to his bladder and rectum. That night, the doctors surgically repaired a three-centimeter perforation to his bladder and a two-centimeter perforation to his rectum; they also performed a colostomy and cystostomy. Louima remained hospitalized for more than a month. At some point he suffered intestinal blockage, which required emergency surgery and the implantation of a colostomy bag. In February of 1998, Louima underwent surgery again to remove the colostomy bag. Louima continued to suffer from abdominal pain, strong headaches, and frequent insomnia.[22]

In the aftermath of the Louima incident, lots of attention was given to the phrase "Giuliani Time" and its meaning. Immediately after his assault, Louima said that during the beating, Volpe had told him, "This is Giuliani time, not Dinkins time." He later recanted this statement, saying that he began to use it after an auxiliary police officer told him he had heard police officers making similar statements. The phrase "Giuliani Time" had potency among minority populations of the city during that period. There were also other alleged cases during which bystanders claimed to have overheard a version of the phrase. However, Sasha Torres argued that "Giuliani Time" went beyond police brutality: "Giuliani time is a fantastical temporality, energized by a vision of the city with a Starbucks on every corner, Gapified, Disneyfied, and washed clean of undesirable elements like public sex and poor people." The Louima incident reflected the violence necessary for such changes to occur in the city. There were police brutality cases before the Louima incident that should have warned the Giuliani Administration about police excesses; however, it appears that the mayor and his aides did not care. The mayor believed that he could rally public opinion in support of his administration and the police as long as crime and social disorder were under control. In this way, the use of force would somehow be justified. For a period of time this strategy worked, with Giuliani quick to exonerate police officers involved in questionable cases while characterizing people attacked by police officers as irresponsible.[23]

After Giuliani took over as mayor, police brutality incidents rose. The descriptions of a few of these cases show that all was not well with the NYPD at that time. For example, in January of 1994, an unarmed seventeen-year-old Black Brooklyn resident by the name of Shu'aib Abdul Latif was shot by the police during a drug raid at a residential building. The reason for Latif's death was unclear; though a Brooklyn Grand Jury decided against bringing charges against the officers, the city eventually settled a civil case. In

February of 1994, Victor Rosado was beaten and robbed by three off-duty police officers at a convenience store in Queens. Rosado, who pulled out money to pay for cigarettes, was asked by the police officers where he found the money before he was beaten and robbed. In April of 1994, Ki Tae Kim, a Korean grocer, was subjected to racial slurs by a police officer and beaten after a dispute that Kim had with a customer who accused him of trying to pass him a counterfeit bill. During the same month, Ernest Sanyon, an African American, died during his arrest by Staten Island police officers. Sanyon was a bystander when the police were arresting another man, but police officers accosted Sanyon after a firecracker exploded nearby. The police claimed that Sanyon ran away and resisted arrest. However, witnesses said that a police officer hit him with a gun on the head and that other officers continued the beating. Sanyon suffocated because of pressure to his chest, neck, and back while he was handcuffed. In July of 1994, Oliver Jones, an African American, was beaten repeatedly with flashlights by police officers. He was standing outside his apartment in the Bronx and was among a crowd of people watching another man being arrested. The beating occurred when someone yelled "police brutality." Police officers tried to falsely charge Jones with stealing a police radio, but their attempts failed. In August of 1994, an off-duty NYPD officer shot Desmond Robinson in the back. Robinson, an African American undercover Transit Police officer, was pursuing two youths; the NYPD officer continued to shoot after Robinson was lying on the ground, violating NYPD training procedures. There were many other incidents that should have caused alarm to the police commissioner, but the fact that almost all of these questionable police actions did not get much media attention allowed Bratton and Giuliani to continue as if nothing had happened.[24]

The most troubling incident of police brutality in 1994 was the death of Anthony Baez; this death showed how the NYPD did not take complaints against its officers seriously. In December of 1994, Puerto Rican Anthony Baez died in the hands of police officer Francis Livoti because of an illegal chokehold. Baez's crime was to complain to a police officer who had just arrested his brother for playing football in the street outside their family's house. Livoti, who was accused of Baez's death, was already under scrutiny in the NYPD because of eleven complaints of being unnecessarily rough in his eleven years of service. One of those complaints occurred in 1990 in the Bronx and involved the arrest of Manuel Bordoy and Ivan Cruz. Bordoy approached Livoti while he was twisting Cruz's arm behind his back and told him that he was using excessive force. In response, Livoti punched Bordoy twice in the face and broke his jaw in three places. Another of those complaints involved the arrest of sixteen-year-old Steven Resto in 1993, also in the Bronx. Livoti slapped Resto in the face for illegally driving a go-cart prior to arresting him. Then he drove Resto to the 45th Precinct station house, removed him from the police car, and pushed him up against the patrol car while grabbing his throat. Resto gasped for air and became dizzy. The Civilian Complaint Review Board substantiated the Resto complaints in March of 1995 after Livoti was indicted for the Baez case. Eventually, Livoti was convicted and served a prison term. The indifference of the NYPD toward these complaints was staggering.[25]

The way that the Livoti case was handled showed how many of the actions of the Giuliani Administration regarding the NYPD were political. Before the Baez killing, Livoti had been placed under the NYPD's special monitoring program because of alleged brutality. His precinct commander requested that Livoti be moved to a desk job or transferred out of the precinct; this precinct commander distrusted Livoti's temper because of numerous reports. Chief of Department Lou Anemone refused to transfer Livoti because of his PBA status as a delegate. Livoti was apparently close to Phil Caruso, who was the head of the PBA and a supporter of Giuliani. Weeks after Baez's death, Anemone praised Livoti for his service. Livoti chose a nonjury trial for the Baez case. Caruso made several appearances during the trial and publicly hugged and kissed Livoti. Judge Gerald Sheindlin acquitted Livoti in 1996. Giuliani commented on the decision, stating that it was a "careful, well-thought-out, legally reasoned opinion." At that point, U.S. Attorney Mary Jo White opened her own civil rights investigation. Mayoral candidate Fernando Ferrer began to use Livoti's favorable treatment by the NYPD as a campaign issue. In the beginning of 1997, Commissioner Safir dismissed Livoti from the NYPD. That October in a mayoral political debate, Giuliani reversed his statement and characterized the "not guilty" Livoti verdict as a "failure of the criminal justice system." Eventually, Livoti was convicted twice. The federal judge who sentenced him was disturbed by the facts of the case and publicly condemned the NYPD for allowing Livoti to patrol the streets after numerous complaints. The state judge also made public statements calling the testimonies of police officers who worked with Livoti during the Baez incident a "nest of perjury."[26]

In 1995, although police brutality cases continued, the police misconduct story that received the most press concerned NYPD officers on a drunken spree while off duty. In this case, dozens of NYPD officers visiting Washington, D.C., to attend a Fraternal Order of Police event went on a drunken rampage through several downtown hotels. Their actions included firing automatic weapons into the air, stealing license plates and car headlights, groping women, spraying fire extinguishers, and pulling fire alarms. These police officers were disciplined. The NYPD insisted that incidents like these represented a rare exception and that there should be no cause for alarm.[27]

In his effort to insulate the NYPD from outside review, Giuliani moved against the Civilian Complaint Review Board (CCRB), something that eventually proved catastrophic when it came to human rights. In 1993, while Dinkins was still mayor, the CCRB became an organization fully controlled by civilians. That year, Giuliani spoke out against the civilianization of the CCRB in the raucous demonstration of police officers outside City Hall. Under the old system, the mayor appointed six board members of the CCRB and the police commissioner appointed another six. Under the new system, the mayor appointed all board members of the CCRB. The investigators were all civilian. During the first year of the Giuliani Administration, members of the city council accused the mayor of attempting to cripple the CCRB by leaving staff positions unfilled. By March of 1994, one third of CCRB investigators had not been hired, even though those positions had been budgeted the year before. This occurred at a time when complaints against the police increased by 46%. The majority of these complaints came from low-income neighborhoods and were made by minority residents. In February of 1995, a CCRB official speaking on the condition of anonymity said that police misconduct incidents in the central Bronx were "random and senseless acts of viciousness." He added that this included the "use of physical force to control people." Allegations in this sizable and low-income portion of the Bronx included beatings by police officers using walkie-talkies and flashlights. One pregnant woman complained that she was slammed against a car after she asked why she was receiving a ticket. A man alleged that he was punched, struck with a nightstick, and told "Nigger, does not belong in this country." In most of the cases, the police officers were white while the people abused were Black or Latino. By April of 1995, because of staffing shortages, the CCRB had fallen so far behind in handling complaints that the majority of them would never be addressed; in addition, state law dictated that the city could discipline a public employee only within eighteen months of a complaint filed. At that rate, the CCRB would be unable to substantiate most complaints. During the same period, Giuliani ignored reports by the CCRB that recommended changes in police behavior and increased funding, viewing them as challenges to his power. The NYPD, which traditionally opposed the CCRB, also undermined its operations by refusing to provide information regarding civilian complaints. Even if the CCRB was able to substantiate a police misconduct complaint, it was still up to the police commissioner to discipline the police officers who were involved. In the three-and-a-half-year period ending in June of 1999, Police Commissioner Safir disciplined only one in four police officers found by the CCRB to have engaged in misconduct. Between January 1998 and June 1999, Safir dismissed half of the substantiated police misconduct complaints. In 1997, Public Advocate Mark Green requested access to NYPD files in order to investigate the reasons behind refusals to discipline police officers. The NYPD argued that Green should apply to a City Council Committee for a subpoena to obtain the records. Green sued and won in state courts in 1997, 1998, and 1999. The Giuliani Administration kept stalling. After July of 1999, Safir began to discipline more police officers because the federal government began to investigate police misconduct. Even so, this discipline usually amounted to a couple of lost vacation days or a lecture.[28]

After the Louima incident, the Giuliani Administration made efforts to address the problem of police brutality, though in the end these efforts amounted to very little. After severe criticism from many sectors of the city, a march of thousands of people from Grand Army Plaza in Brooklyn to City Hall, and many political overtones during the 30th Annual West Indian American Day Parade, Giuliani formed a Task Force on Police Brutality that even included some of his political opponents such as Norman Siegel, executive director of the New York Civil Liberties Union. A year later and in the midst of his campaign for reelection, Giuliani agreed to increase the funding of the CCRB by $1.5 million and to increase its staff by 20%. The Giuliani Administration and the NYPD also claimed that police misconduct complaints were down. As it turned out, most of these actions were taken so that Giuliani could neutralize a potentially explosive issue in the mayoral election of 1997. After the election, Giuliani characterized some of his appointees to the Task Force as "silly," "small-minded," and "cop bashers." Moreover, claims about the decrease in misconduct complaints were inaccurate because the administration underreported the numbers and withheld actual figures until after the election. In the first two months of 1998, complaints against police officers rose by 36%, while Giuliani was considering cutting the budget of the CCRB. The mayor also continued to appoint members to the task force so that the majority of its members would not criticize him and the NYPD. He eventually broke promises to fund it and did not provide any cooperation from the city's agencies, including the NYPD. In principle, the mayor was still not comfortable with a civilian CCRB investigating the police and wanted to control the actions of the task force, whose utility was eventually completely compromised. Once released, the city administration ignored the entire report of the task force.[29]

On February 12, 1999, at approximately 12:35 a.m., members of NYPD's Street Crime Unit approached Amadou Diallo outside of his Soundview, Bronx, apartment building and fired forty-one shots, nineteen of which struck and killed Diallo. Four white officers were in plain clothes and claimed that they were looking for an alleged rapist. They thought Diallo matched the composite sketch. Diallo, a twenty-two-year-old immigrant from Guinea, was unarmed and had nothing to do with the rape. He allegedly reached toward his pocket for his wallet when the police officers shot him, thinking that he was reaching for a gun. What we know about this case came from the four officers who provided a well-rehearsed testimony at their trial. Sidney Harring has suggested that there is an alternative explanation of what happened that night:

> "Tactical" squads, like the one that killed Diallo, operate very aggressively, basically "rousting" a series of likely offenders in the hope of turning up a gun or contraband drugs that would justify a "bust." ... These "rousts" are mostly illegal, since they violate Americans'

Fourth Amendment protections against unreasonable searches and seizures.... Most often, tactical squads don't even attempt to meet the legal standard. Having stopped and searched young men on the barest of hunches, they simply fail to fill out the required "incident reports," knowing that almost none of these encounters will ever come to official notice.... If a search is productive, that is, produces a gun or drugs, then the police must fabricate a story to cover that search. Officers think one up, agree on it, and simply tell and retell that story as long as they need to. The Diallo killing resulted from one of these routine unconstitutional searches; the Diallo story, as related in the Albany trial, was simply another story constructed to cover that search.[30]

Since this illegal stop and search resulted in death, the police officers involved had more of a reason to fabricate a credible story. What is also telling is that after Diallo's death, the NYPD ransacked his apartment looking for something illegal. Eventually, the City of New York admitted that Diallo was wrongfully killed and settled with Diallo's family for $3 million. The four police officers were acquitted after a change of venue to Albany, New York, in February of 2000.[31]

In the aftermath of the Diallo shooting, there were massive political mobilizations against police brutality and racial profiling. On March 9, 1999, Reverend Al Sharpton's National Action Network began to organize

Figure 7.2 Memorial mural of Amadou Diallo in Soundview, Bronx. (Photograph by Themis Chronopoulos, 2007.)

daily civil disobedience actions outside police headquarters in lower Manhattan. Thousands of people were arrested, including former mayor David Dinkins, Congressman Charles Rangel, Congressman Gregory Meeks, President of Local 1199 Dennis Rivera, Reverend Floyd Flake, State Comptroller H. Carl McCall, and Revered Jesse Jackson. Even former mayor Ed Koch planned to go to police headquarters but felt weak and lightheaded the morning before his appearance and was taken to the hospital. At first Giuliani called the political mobilizations "silly" and "publicity stunts." Giuliani and NYPD officials also claimed that these civil disobedience actions were divisive and lacked diversity because most of the protesters were Black. The problem with this argument was that the protest actions continued for weeks and grew increasingly diverse. For example, claims that Jewish groups had refused to participate in the movement because of rhetoric used against the police were not true. On March 24, 1999, 126 out of 212 people arrested were members of Jews for Racial and Economic Justice. This number included several rabbis. The crowd had signs that said, "Stop the Death Squads" and "Arrest Giuliani" and sang psalms in Hebrew before the arrests started. At some point, even Governor George E. Pataki suggested that Mayor Giuliani lacked tolerance in his responses: "I think the city is doing very well, but part of governing is being tolerant and listening to criticism and responding appropriately to criticism." Police Commissioner Safir came under fire because he skipped a city council hearing on the Diallo case and went to Los Angeles to attend the Oscars. Giuliani struggled to manage the crisis, though the actions of his administration were confusing and at times contradictory. Although he said that the charges against the demonstrators outside One Police Plaza should be dropped, in the midst of these peaceful civil disobedience actions, the NYPD changed its detention policy. Instead of releasing protesters after a desk appearance ticket, the NYPD began to hold them in jail for arraignment, usually overnight. Although Giuliani worked hard to reach some compromise, three months after the death of Diallo, he criticized the parents of a sixteen-year-old who was shot by the police while running away for allowing their child to be outside at 12:30 a.m. The mayor's standing in polls began to drop precipitously. This was the largest crisis that his administration had ever faced.[32]

In the summer of 1999, the U.S. Attorney in Brooklyn, Zachary W. Carter, completed a two-year investigation into the way that the NYPD handled police misconduct cases. The investigation concluded that there was a pattern of unreasonable leniency toward police officers involved in misconduct. Carter sought a settlement with the Giuliani Administration under the threat that the U.S. Justice Department would seek a court-ordered overhaul of the NYPD or oversight by a federal monitor. While the negotiations were taking place, Mayor Giuliani vowed no concession and argued that the department had been unfairly bashed for a number of months. Carter, who at the time was leaving his position as U.S. Attorney, would need the approval of Attorney General Janet Reno in order to sue the Giuliani Administration. This would create a political problem, with the Clinton Justice Department attacking the Giuliani Administration at a time when Hillary Clinton was going to run against Giuliani for the U.S. Senate. As a result, a Justice Department legal action was deferred.[33]

In the years that followed, the constitutionality of stop-and-frisk practices of the NYPD became a central issue. This is because Diallo was the target of such a practice when he was gunned down. In December of 1999, New York State Attorney General Eliot Spitzer released a report that found racial bias in stop-and-frisk incidents. After the numbers were adjusted to reflect higher crime rates in low-income minority neighborhoods, Blacks and Latinos were found to be more likely to be stopped than whites. The study reviewed incidents from 175,000 cases that happened between January 1998 and March 1999. Some of the most frequent conclusions by people who were stopped and frisked were that the police officers abused their authority, targeted minorities, and did not care about citizens and their rights. Some of the descriptions of people who were stopped and frisked included Jean Davis, a fifty-four-year-old African American woman who worked as a home health aide for elderly persons. Two blocks from her home one night, she noticed a white man following her. She quickened her pace, fearing that he was going to rob her. The man grabbed her around the neck and made her walk down the street. He told her that he was a police officer but showed no identification. He took her to a car where he and another man forced her to put her hands on the hood of the car, patted her down, and removed all of the contents from her pockets. She was allowed to go when nothing illegal was found. Davis was terrified, at first because she thought that she was being abducted by a stranger and eventually because the police officers were acting in an abusive manner. Another person who was stopped and frisked was Edward Stevens, a fifty-year-old teacher from the Bronx who was originally from the Virgin Islands. Stevens left his school at lunchtime and drove his Mercedes Benz to a pharmacy to pick up medication for his daughter. A police officer in a police cruiser pulled him over for unknown reasons. The police officer asked Stevens for his license and registration and also asked him who owned the car. After a few minutes, Stevens asked the police officer what was happening. The police officer told him to stop rushing him. Twenty minutes later, Stevens asked again because his lunch break had ended. The police officer was visibly agitated and asked Stevens to get out of his car and place his hands on the hood. The police officer proceeded to frisk him. The officer told Stevens that he did not have the right to question a police officer. Then the officer handcuffed him, brought him to the police station, and placed him in a cell. At 3:30 p.m., the police officer told him that he could leave. When Stevens asked for proof that he had been stopped so that he could show it to his employer, the police officer wrote him a desk appearance ticket for resisting arrest, disorderly conduct, and other minor violations. The Board of

Education inquired, and eventually all of the charges against Stevens were dropped. In 2001, the CCRB released its own report for stop-and-frisk practices that occurred between January of 1997 and March of 1999. The study discovered that African Americans filed twice as many complaints as Latinos and six times as many as whites. African Americans and Latinos were more likely to experience violence at the hands of the police, and African Americans were more likely to have had gun drawn in them by the police. Although police officers were required to file a form whenever they stopped and frisked someone, these forms were missing in most of the cases the CCRB reviewed. Stop and frisk, which had become one of the most prevalent police activities in the police force's war against crime, had many legally questionable aspects.[34]

The NYPD's stop-and-frisk policy represented a legally sophisticated, spatially wider and more constant version of the dragnet operations in Times Square during the late 1960s and early 1970s. These old-style dragnet operations had failed because the courts struck down antiloitering and other constitutionally dubious ordinances and because the police could not round people up on a daily basis. Stop-and frisk policies were more sophisticated than the old-style roundups in the sense that they continuously targeted individuals or small groups of people mostly in low-income neighborhoods under the legal excuse that the police officers were responding to a complaint. However, they were not any more efficient than dragnet operations, since the great majority of people who were stopped and frisked were never arrested. These procedures worked as devices of intimidation, since a large number of officers prepared to use excessive force flooded public spaces. In the 1990s, the practices against "undesirables" were expanded and included many parts of the city other than Times Square.

In March of 2000, there was another high-profile killing of an unarmed civilian by the NYPD. Patrick Dorismond, a twenty-six-year-old security guard from Haiti, was killed by an undercover narcotics detective in the vicinity of Times Square. The slaying occurred after an undercover detective pretending to be a crack cocaine buyer approached Dorismond while he was looking for a cab. Dorismond was angered by the solicitation. An altercation ensued when the detective and two other detectives rushed toward Dorismond and one of them shot him. The NYPD admitted that the original detective never identified himself as a police officer. However, Mayor Giuliani, then running for the U.S. Senate, began to assault Dorismond's character almost daily. Giuliani ordered Safir to release a sealed juvenile record, which stated that when he was thirteen years old, Dorismond was arrested for robbery. In the days that followed, Giuliani also claimed that Dorismond was a criminal and that his record included attempted robbery, assault, gun possession, and domestic violence. As it turned out, the juvenile robbery case was dismissed before reaching a court, the assault had become a charge of disorderly conduct when Dorismond punched another teenager over a dispute involving marijuana, the gun possession claim was false, and the domestic violence case had been withdrawn by the girlfriend; the officer who wrote the domestic violence report stated that there had been no physical injuries. Giuliani's announcements were controversial because he unsealed the juvenile and adult records of Dorismond, which was illegal given that Dorismond was never convicted of any crime as an adult. Giuliani justified the unsealing of these records by arguing that Dorismond was dead and that he no longer had any privacy rights. Criticism against the mayor's actions continued, and Giuliani's approval rating sank to 32%. In one of the Dorismond press conferences David Diaz, a WCBS-TV reporter, said: "Mister Mayor, how would you respond to the people who feel that not only is the Police Department out of control, you're out of control, that you're the lawless one in the city? You set the tone. You disregard court opinions when you don't like them. What is your answer to those who say that Giuliani is out of control? Giuliani is the chief lawless one?" Giuliani replied, "Oh come on," and added, "let's move on to a serious question."[35]

While the debate over Dorismond was taking place, the Civil Rights Commission of the U.S. Justice Department released a report of its investigation on the NYPD and civil rights. The Civil Rights Commission widened the investigation that had been undertaken by U.S. Attorney Zachary Taylor and attempted to determine whether aggressive policing in New York had violated the civil rights of minority New Yorkers. The report concluded that according to NYPD's own data, its police officers engaged in racial profiling. For example, data from 1998 showed that 51% of the people stopped and frisked in Staten Island were Black even though Staten Island's population was only 9%Black. The Commission recommended the creation of a law enforcement mechanism that would investigate allegations of police brutality and an NYPD outreach program geared toward minority residents. The U.S. Justice Department considered the appointment of a federal official to monitor the NYPD but moved slowly. In 2001, the Justice Department of newly elected President George W. Bush chose not to seek NYPD reforms.[36]

Racial profiling by the NYPD even affected two of Giuliani's closest African American supporters, Queens Congressman Reverend Floyd Flake and Deputy Mayor Rudy Washington. Flake, who had endorsed Giuliani in his 1997 re-election campaign, met with Giuliani in the aftermath of the Diallo killing to complain about the racial profiling of the middle-class children who attended his church. When Giuliani responded with vague statistics, Flake told Giuliani about a white police officer who stopped and abused him when he was driving with his wife to his church. The police officer yelled at Flake, "Nigger, didn't I tell you to stop that car?" After realizing that Flake was a member of the U.S. Congress, the officer let him go. After the Diallo killing, Rudy Washington was also stopped twice by the police and treated badly. In the second instance, a police officer almost arrested him because he thought that his MTA board member identification was fake. A lieutenant who happened to be passing by recognized Washington as deputy mayor and ordered the police officers, who were ready to put him in a squad car, to let him go. In response, Giuliani asked the NYPD to issue Washington a special police identification badge with his name on it. At the same time, Giuliani continued to deny that racial profiling existed.[37]

Despite the numerous investigations and efforts by several federal, state, and local agencies to reform the NYPD, the Giuliani Administration refused to consider any of the recommendations. Led by the mayor, the city government maintained that there was nothing wrong with the NYPD and that it did not violate people's rights. Although the federal government came close to imposing a federal monitor, this did not happen, probably because the Giuliani Administration would find ways to get around this monitor in the same way that it had marginalized the CCRB. That being the case, radical spatial regulation continued.

FROM NEOLIBERALISM TO NEOCONSERVATISM

While comprehensive spatial regulation proved beneficial to the neoliberal political–economic structure during the 1990s, it also required the formation and maintenance of a sizable, efficient, and autocratic government, which was antithetical to neoliberal ideals. A big and powerful government is dangerous to corporate interests because it is unlikely to always defer to the wishes of corporate elites. What happened in New York during this period is that the mayor and his administration became increasingly intolerant of competing centers of power and expanded their attitude toward spatial regulation into other spheres of governance.

In its early years, the Giuliani Administration appeared to be staunchly neoliberal. Neoliberals were at ease with most of the policies and the rhetoric coming from City Hall. The city administration went out of its way to accommodate corporate and real estate interests, sought to privatize some government functions such as the sheltering of the homeless, and tried to cut the number of public employees. There are many reasons why this happened. When Giuliani took over City Hall, the biggest problem was a large shortfall in the budget. Giuliani felt that he needed the support of the business sector in order to weather the fiscal storm. In 1994, the Giuliani Administration was saved from fiscal default by Governor Mario Cuomo and his son, Undersecretary of Housing and Urban Development Andrew Cuomo. Mario Cuomo amended his executive budget and funded the city with an extra $130 million in Medicaid assistance. He also convinced the Municipal Assistance Corporation to provide $200 million to finance a crucial severance program for public employees willing to retire. Andrew Cuomo provided the city with an additional $73 million in housing aid for the homeless. Mario Cuomo, who had not been as helpful to Dinkins, was running for a fourth term as governor in 1994 and had no interest in punishing New York City with huge budget cuts during an election year. Republican Giuliani was grateful for the assistance that he received, because it allowed him to fund tens of millions of dollars in overtime, most of which went to the fire and the police departments. As a result, he endorsed Democrat Cuomo in the 1994 gubernatorial election. Nonetheless, Cuomo lost to Republican George Pataki that fall.[38]

In the years that followed, the Giuliani Administration grew increasingly neoconservative and drifted away from orthodox neoliberalism. The shift from neoliberalism to neoconservatism occurred in an organic way pushed by the administration's needs and wants. This shift represented the political maturity of this administration, the eagerness of the mayor to have his government in charge of everything including the economy, the need to position Giuliani as a candidate for higher office, and the impossibility of having a strong, autocratic government that was content with other entities that pursued public policy. Moreover, during this period, the city's economy improved substantially, meaning that Giuliani no longer depended on the assistance of the business sector when it came to state financing decisions.

Neoconservatism did not translate into a hostile environment toward corporations. Neoconservatism meant that the mayor and the city government were in charge of economic development and in turn took credit for that development. It also implied that the city, not corporations and their associations, was in charge of spatial regulation and services. Corporations that conformed to this vision of city affairs benefitted. For example, at the end of 1998, the Giuliani Administration announced a $900 million subsidy for the New York Stock Exchange because of the possibility of it relocating to New Jersey. The relocation threat was never credible and the NYSE never really needed the money since it was running large surpluses. The subsidy was granted because Giuliani had developed cordial relationships with the people in charge of the exchange. On the other hand, business improvement districts suffered because they grew too powerful and competed with the mayor for power.[39]

Business improvement districts (BIDs) represent comprehensive examples of neoliberal urban governance. BIDs usually form in commercial areas and exist as territorial subdivisions inside cities. BIDs provide services in addition to those of the city government and represent an effort to make an area attractive to tourists, shoppers, and businesses. The businesses and landowners within the BID district pay a tax surcharge, which the municipality returns to the BID so that it can fund its operations. Though most BIDs focus on sanitation, security, and infrastructural maintenance, some of them also devise strategies to attract and retain businesses, provide services to the homeless, create public amenities, and landscape streets, parks, and sidewalks. Since they work closely with the city government, BIDs have the ability to lobby on behalf of their members and even to obtain public funding. Unlike other types of community associations that seek to empower the resident, BIDs seek to empower the property owners and businesses.[40]

When Giuliani became mayor of New York in 1994, there were thirty-one BIDs in the city collecting about $32 million from their members. Fifteen more considered forming. The largest BID was the Grand Central Partnership, which was created in the mid-1980s when Mobil Corporation and Philip Morris Incorporated threatened to move their offices away from the area because of disorderly conditions. The Grand Central Partnership was credited with illuminating the area at night, maintaining the streetlights, replacing missing street signs, removing graffiti, cleaning the sidewalks, installing wheelchair ramps, planting flowers, assisting tourists, and providing security from 8 a.m. to 11 p.m. Besides tax assessments to businesses, the Partnership financed its operations by selling $32 million in bonds. In the first few years of his administration, Giuliani was a strong supporter of the BID system. In a speech that he gave in 1994 in front of more than 200 BID directors, staff, and members, Giuliani said that BIDs "are filling in for government," reflecting his support of privatizing many public functions. John S. Dyson, Deputy Mayor for Economic Development and Finance, argued that BIDs had "reinvented government."[41]

In the early years of his mayoralty, Giuliani accommodated many of the requests made by BIDs regarding spatial matters, and some of the most important issues concerned the existence and operation of street vendors. The city administration began to enforce an obscure regulation that banned street vendors with food carts from more than 300 blocks that were supposedly congested in Manhattan and Brooklyn. Daniel Biederman, president of the city's three largest BIDs including Grand Central Partnership, explained that the BIDs did not care about congestion as much as appearance. They found the food carts to be ugly and wanted them to look more like food carts one might find in Disneyland. He argued that "We've got to compete with Disneyland, if we want to attract tourists." The city government also began to target artists selling their work in the streets after BIDs requested their removal. Many artists were threatened or arrested by the police and their art was damaged or confiscated. In 1996, the U.S. Court of Appeals ruled that artistic expression was a form of protected speech and that the city violated the First Amendment and the Equal Protection Clause by arresting unlicensed visual artists. After that decision, the city government continued to harass artists in certain public areas, though on most occasions they would not arrest them in order to avoid potential legal actions.[42]

The Grand Central Partnership turned out to be the most controversial BID, especially in its relations with homeless people. Homeless people had been frequenting the Grand Central area throughout the 1980s, and many business owners wanted their removal. In 1989, the Grand Central Partnership came up with a plan to get the district's homeless people off the streets. At the urging of its members, the Grand Central Partnership created a separate entity whose board consisted of director Biederman and two Partnership employees. This entity created a job-training program that hired homeless people to remove other homeless people from bank machine vestibules. The Grand Central Partnership contracted with the banks to create this "homeless outreach program" and received $1.6 million in return for keeping their ATM areas free of homeless persons. Those who worked as outreach workers were paid $1.16 an hour. The Partnership argued that $1.16 per hour was not a wage but a training stipend. Eventually, more than a hundred program participants sued the Grand Central Partnership for violation of minimum wage laws and won. But the problem was larger. Homeless people frequently complained that they had been brutalized by Grand Central Partnership outreach workers, though no one paid much attention. In April of 1995, four former workers of the Partnership claimed that with the encouragement of their supervisors, they had beaten homeless people to make them leave the area. The employees added that the Partnership's associate director of social services had formed what he termed "goon squads" comprising tough men who had criminal records and knew how to fight. In return, members of the goon squads received food, clothing, subway tokens, and cash. According to Heather Barr:

> The four ex-Partnership workers described throwing the belongings of homeless people into gutters, tearing up cardboard shelters, shoving, punching and kicking homeless people, and bludgeoning them with the walkie-talkies that the workers carried. Sometimes after beating a homeless person, they said, they would call 911 and tell police that the homeless person had attacked them. They also explained that they intentionally chased homeless people from areas which the Partnership had contracted with other sites not under contract. This, in turn, helped generate new contracts.[43]

As these accounts surfaced, homeless advocates and other Partnership employees also said that they were aware of these violent tactics. The Grand Central Partnership denied the charges, claiming that these were disgruntled ex-employees and that the entire story had been fabricated by homeless advocates. However, public agencies began to investigate the Grand Central Partnership and its activities. Several witnesses came forward and provided accounts of violence against homeless people by Partnership goon squads. City inspectors also began to investigate allegations of sexual activity, drugs, and violence at St. Agnes, a homeless center operated by the Partnership. The Department of Housing and Urban Development (HUD), which had given the Partnership a $547,000 grant, also investigated and found that the social service outreach work of the BID was incompatible with serving the needs of its business members. HUD took most of the grant money back. The city council discovered managerial irregularities and a lack of accountability. Finally, City Hall began to audit the Partnership's books because of questionable accounting practices, including the setting aside of money to use for the creation of a BID in Jersey City, New Jersey.[44]

Gradually, the city government became less enthusiastic about BIDs and the controversies surrounding their operations. In 1995 and 1997, the city council released reports whose findings were damning for BIDs: the investigations found that many business owners were not well informed about BID operations and that they were paying too much money for additional services. About one-third of landlords and property managers considered BIDs a bad investment. An additional quarter of landlords were uncertain of the utility of BIDs. BID leaders had also manipulated member votes and even dropped from the district large businesses that opposed their plans; in general, they abused their power. In response to these findings, the city council presented the city administration with eleven legislative proposals to improve BID performance and accountability. The Department of Business Services imposed performance evaluations and required evidence of support of a majority of constituents before renewing contracts with BIDs but rejected the city council's legislative proposals as "burdensome, time consuming, costly and intrusive." Still, the city administration had already become concerned with the ability of BIDs to sell bonds, because in case of default, the municipal government would be held responsible. In September of 1996, the Department of Business Services denied a request by the Grand Central Partnership to borrow $10.7 million. The following year, the Department of Business Services decided to issue a moratorium on amending BID plans or allowing the creation of new ones.[45]

After Mayor Giuliani won re-election, his administration moved against BIDs. The event that triggered this was a deal that Police Commissioner Safir made with the Alliance for Downtown, the BID of the Wall Street area, in February 1998. Under the terms of the deal, the NYPD would open a new police substation with two hundred police officers in the Wall Street area. The Alliance for Downtown would help maintain this police substation and would also fund a new police museum that Carol Safir, the wife of the commissioner, would head. Elected officials and representatives of community organizations began to criticize the deal, claiming that a private entity was buying off public services that would be unavailable in other areas with higher crime rates. Giuliani angrily brushed the critics aside, rejecting their "overzealous, out-of-control populist reaction." However, days later, Giuliani grew uncomfortable over details of the deal that Safir had devised without his input and ordered a complete review of the operations of all BIDs. Two months after the police substation debacle, the Giuliani Administration announced new rules that would require the city's thirty-nine BIDs to clear every major undertaking with the Department of Business Services. Under the new rules, the city administration shortened the BID contracts to two years from five and required a survey of BID constituents to determine the level of satisfaction and support prior to contract renewals. It also established term limits for BID board members and officers, required them to abide by conflict-of-interest and financial-disclosure rules, and mandated that BID boards and not chairpersons make committee assignments. BIDs would be unable to interact with city agencies without the coordination of the Department of Business Services and would be unable to develop procurement, personnel, outreach, and complaint procedures without the approval of the Department of Business Services. Finally, the city administration made a new rule that barred individuals from serving as presidents for more than one BID. This rule targeted Dan Biederman, who headed three BIDs.[46]

The fallout of the administration's hostility against BIDs was almost immediate. Gretchen Dykstra, who was president of the Times Square Business Improvement District for six years and was credited with using paratrooper tactics in her efforts to get rid of sex-related businesses and gay bars in Times Square, resigned. In July of 1998, the city government refused to renew the contract of the Grand Central Partnership, claiming that Dan Biederman and his staff were not cooperating with the Department of Business Services. In a press release, the city administration argued that Biederman, who earned $120,000 a year as the president of the Grand Central Partnership, $115,000 as the president of the 34th Street BID, and $100,000 as the president of the Bryant Park BID, was violating the new rules that prohibited multiple positions in BIDs. The city government also threatened the 34th Street BID with contract termination if the 34th Street BID did not stop commingling assessment funds with the Grand Central Partnership and the Bryant Park BIDs and if the 34th Street BID did not stop sharing management with other BIDs. When the Grand Central Partnership resisted the efforts by the city government to change it, the Giuliani Administration considered the formation of a new BID in the area. In September of 1998, Biederman resigned but remained a consultant of the Grand Central Partnership; when the Department of Business Services found this unacceptable, Biederman dissociated himself from the Partnership completely. In the end, the Grand Central Partnership survived but only after board members opposing the Giuliani Administration resigned and Giuliani's Finance Commissioner Alfred C. Cerullo III became its president.[47]

BIDs attempted to smooth relations with the city administration but failed. In 1999, the Department of Business Services turned down several BIDs' requests to increase their funding through tax assessments and strict oversight. In the beginning of 2001, Giuliani proposed to charge BIDs a fee for municipal services. The existence of BIDs became difficult between 1998 and 2001.[48]

The move of the Giuliani Administration against BIDs happened because of practical governance concerns. BID actions interfered with governmental actions, and the BID publicity machine tried to improve its image at the expense of the city administration. By 1998, city officials realized that BIDs represented competing centers of power that were frequently antithetical to the interests of the city administration and definitely incompatible with the direction that New York City governance had taken in the late 1990s. Rudy Washington, who was Giuliani's Deputy Mayor for Community Development and Business Services, summarized the friction of the city administration and BIDs as one of governance. He argued that BIDs did not complement the work of city agencies; they just duplicated it. He said that BIDs came into play in the 1980s when the city government was inefficient and dysfunctional. At that time, providing sanitation and security in high-profile business districts was necessary because the city government was unable to do it. Washington's take was that by the mid-1990s, the city administration was providing adequate sanitation and policing services. BIDs used their tax assessments to furnish services that the government was already providing. In some ways, BIDs had become obsolete. This argument was important for the Giuliani Administration, which had made the provision of municipal services such as policing and sanitation its cornerstone of governance. If BIDs were indispensable, then the city government was not doing its job very well.[49]

The neoconservative transformation of the Giuliani Administration affected the relations of the mayor with all kinds of organizations, including those exhibiting art. Toward the end of September 1999, Mayor Giuliani began to attack a number of works in the Brooklyn Museum's upcoming temporary exhibit "Sensation: Young British Artists from the Saatchi Collection" as "sick" and "disgusting." In his attacks, Giuliani singled out one painting in particular entitled "The Holy Virgin Mary" by Chris Ofili and argued that it was offensive to Catholics. Giuliani demanded that the Brooklyn Museum cancel the exhibition and threatened to withdraw city funding for the museum. Despite the threats, the Brooklyn Museum went on with the exhibition. Given the controversial nature of a few of the works appearing in "Sensation," the Brooklyn Museum decided not to admit minors under the age of 17 unless they were accompanied by adults. The Giuliani Administration argued that taxpayer money should not be used to support the desecration of religious and national symbols and that the Brooklyn Museum violated its contract with the city in restricting the free admittance policy for schoolchildren. As the exhibit continued, the city government began to withhold funds already appropriated to the Brooklyn Museum for operating expenses, maintenance, and capital construction. The city government also began eviction proceedings in state court against the museum, arguing that although the collections of the museum had been in their current location for more than a hundred years, the city owned the land and the building.[50]

The struggle of Mayor Giuliani with the Brooklyn Museum was another signal that the city administration was becoming increasingly neoconservative. This conflict resembled the antipathy that neoconservatives have frequently held against certain artistic representations and their opposition of public subsidies for the arts. In this case, Mayor Giuliani wanted to fortify his conservative credentials as he prepared to run for the U.S. Senate. Giuliani and his advisers hoped that his strongly worded objections over the exhibition and his determined actions against the museum would appeal

176 *Spatial Regulation in New York City*

to conservative suburban and upstate New York voters. Giuliani's actions against the museum also reflected how the city administration was becoming as unforgiving in its disagreements with businesses and organizations as it had been with "disorderly" people in public space. By 1999, builders, developers, real estate agents, directors of nonprofit organizations, and business leaders carefully avoided doing or saying anything against the mayor and his administration because they feared governmental retaliation.[51]

In the end, a federal district court ordered the Giuliani Administration to reinstate funds for the Brooklyn Museum. Federal Judge Nina Gershon ruled that the mayor violated the First Amendment when he cut city funding for the museum and initiated eviction proceedings. In her decision, Gershon ordered the city to restore funding and terminate eviction proceedings. She also prohibited the city from taking any other adverse actions such as future reductions of the museum's budget or changes in the composition of its Board of Trustees. After the decision, Giuliani verbally attacked Gershon for rushing her ruling.[52]

THE CRUSHING OF POLITICAL DISSENT

During Giuliani's second term, the city administration extended its zero-tolerance philosophy of order maintenance so that it could include protest actions, political rallies, and marches. The police mobilization for the Million Youth March event that took place in Harlem on September 5, 1998, illustrated this case. It resembled a comprehensive neighborhood invasion. Bob Herbert argued that the police who showed up in Harlem during that holiday weekend were ready for war:

> Residents who emerged from their apartments and brownstones at the start of a beautiful holiday weekend were greeted by an army of police officers who had arrived with helicopters, horses, tractor-trailer trucks, buses, cars, vans and motorcycles. Police barricades seemed to go up everywhere. Subway stations were shut down, their entrances blocked by yellow tape that read: "'Police line—do not cross."[53]

Residents found it virtually impossible to move around their neighborhood because many streets were closed for "security" purposes. People attempting to reach the rally were told to take different blocks, only to find out that those blocks were also closed off. Bus and subway service all but disappeared for a few hours while helicopters kept on hovering above the area. Some building rooftops were taken over by police snipers while undercover police cars roamed in blocks near the event with undercover police officers occasionally coming out of them in order to stop and frisk groups of Black people. Before and during the Million Youth March, the city administration displayed a hostile attitude toward the organizers. The Million Youth March was organized

The Radicalization of Spatial Regulation, 1994–2001 177

by Khalid Muhammad, a former Nation of Islam spokesperson and a controversial figure because of his statements about race. He had applied for permits for many months for this event in New York without much success. On August 26, 1998, a federal district court issued a preliminary injunction against the NYPD for the rally that would take place on September 5 and required the issuance of a permit. The city administration immediately appealed, and the U.S. Court of Appeals ruled on September 1 that the event could take place but in six instead of twenty-nine blocks and for four instead of twelve hours. Meanwhile, Muhammad and Giuliani engaged in a war of words, with Giuliani characterizing the event as a "hate march" and Muhammad calling Giuliani a "cracker." The actual march was not well organized and only 6,000 people attended; 3,000 police officers provided security. The event was supposed to end at 4 p.m., but at 3:55 p.m., hundreds of police officers in riot gear surrounded the stage where Muhammad was giving the final speech. At 4:03 p.m., a helicopter hovered above the area of the march; this was a signal for the police to storm the stage and shut down the sound system. For about fifteen minutes there were clashes between police officers, organizers, and attendees. The events of the Million Youth March showed how the city administration could use heavy-handed methods in order restrict protest actions and public gatherings. This police behavior occurred because Mayor Giuliani and the NYPD began to view violations of free speech and assembly rights as necessary components of order maintenance.[54]

The NYPD used various tactics in its attempts to delay and compromise public gatherings and most of them involved the issuance of permits. According to New York City Administrative Code §10–110, the NYPD was responsible for issuing permits for marches, demonstrations, commemorations, and rallies to take place in public space. However, this ordinance did not make the NYPD respond to requests in a timely fashion. In 1998, police officials claimed that applicants were usually informed by the NYPD five to six weeks before an event. The problem was that certain requests were considered immediately while others were significantly delayed.[55]

One of the tactics used by the NYPD was to delay and reject permission for a public event. Since the NYPD would reject the permit application only a few days before the public gathering, the social-movement organization would have to rapidly deploy competent legal resources to the courts in order to force permission. This happened in the case of the Million Youth March when it was denied a permit to hold its original event in 1998 and a second event in 1999. In both cases, the courts forced the NYPD to issue a permit, but only a few days before the actual event.[56]

Another NYPD tactic was to delay and permit the public event. The delayed permission meant that the public event remained in limbo and that social-movement organizations did not have adequate time to mobilize their supporters. In 1998, a federal district court found that some organizations applied for a permit months in advance only to be notified a few days before the event that their request was granted. The request of the Federation of

178 *Spatial Regulation in New York City*

Figure 7.3 The electrocution of free speech in Williamsburg, Brooklyn. (Photograph by Themis Chronopoulos, 1997.)

Hellenic Societies of Greater New York that applied for a permit on August 6, 1997, for an event that would take place on March 29, 1998, was not formally approved until March 17, 1998; the permit letter was mailed on March 23. The United States Veterans applied for a permit on February 20, 1998, for an event taking place on May 25, 1998; the NYPD did not approve the request until May 18 and did not send the permit letter until May 19. There were many instances when this delay occurred, though the most troublesome involved demonstrations against police brutality. The Coalition Against Police Brutality applied for a permit on March 12, 1998, for a march that would take place on March 31 and was not granted a permit until the day before. There were eleven cases during this period where the NYPD notified applicants three days before the activity, meaning that the organizers did not have ample time to make arrangements or publicize the event. Some of the marches that began to receive delayed permission were annual events that used to receive approval routinely and well in advance; their organizers were surprised and not prepared for the delays.[57]

Another NYPD tactic was to delay and permit the public event but with modifications. In 1998, when taxi drivers wanted to demonstrate the change of rules governing them by driving a large procession of taxis through Queensborough Bridge and Midtown Manhattan to City Hall, the Giuliani Administration attempted to limit the procession to twenty taxicabs. A federal court decided that the demonstration could proceed with up to 250 taxicabs and argued that more limits would violate the First Amendment. The Million Marijuana March Organization was not as fortunate. When the organization requested permission to march on Fifth Avenue between Washington Square Park and 96th Street in Central Park, a march had previously occurred each year for decades, the NYPD denied the request and offered an alternative site at Battery Square Park. The organization contended that the power of the police commissioner to deny a permit based on his own assessment that a rally might be "disorderly in character" violated free speech. Eventually, the U.S. Court of Appeals sided with the police commissioner for procedural reasons. In many cases, last-minute approvals that included a change of route put the event into limbo, because organizers were unable to inform potential participants of any changes. Even if the social-movement organization could go to court and obtain permission to use its original route, valuable publicity time was lost. In the end, this unpredictable behavior of the NYPD worsened in 1998 and raised questions as to whether permits were delayed because the NYPD or city administration disagreed with the content of these events, which was illegal. However, the NYPD and the city government were well versed in these legal matters and avoided the rejection of public gatherings because of their content. They could always object to something else.[58]

There were numerous other restrictive actions taken by the city government against social-movement organizations and public gatherings. For example, in 1998, the City of New York decided to limit the size of expressive activities at City Hall or bar them completely. Events sponsored by the mayor were exempted. When Housing Works—an organization that advocates for the rights of persons with HIV and AIDS—attempted to hold a press conference on the steps of City Hall, many of the participants who suffered from AIDS were shunted away while police snipers aimed at them from the roof of City Hall. In 2000, a federal court permanently enjoined the city from limiting the number of people assembling on the steps of City Hall to fifty and the number of people conducting demonstrations on the adjacent plaza to 150. The city did not appeal. In another case, the International Action Center—a group opposing corporate and military imperialism—challenged efforts by the Giuliani Administration to force the group from Times Square and prevent it from using amplified sound during its events. The city ended these efforts after a lawsuit and agreed to continue issuing sound permits for events happening all over the city. In another case, the NYPD also revoked sound permits from Hebrew Israelites (Black Israelites) and threatened to arrest them if they continued to preach in the Times Square area. In 1999, the city settled the case, paid the group a sizable sum, and agreed not to take any further actions against them without first consulting with the NYCLU. In yet another case, participants in a rally/vigil protesting antigay violence and honoring the memory of Matthew Shepard, a gay college student who had been murdered in Wyoming, were arrested and charged with disorderly conduct when they walked through the street and failed to return to the sidewalk when ordered by the police. The demonstrators claimed that there was no room to stand on the sidewalk because it was full of people. They sued the city because after being arrested they were kept in custody instead of being issued a desk appearance ticket and released. The courts decided that the refusal of the NYPD to issue desk appearance tickets in this case was not unreasonable because of fear that the protesters were unruly.[59]

Although many social-movement organizations were surprised by this heightened regulation of public gatherings, it reflected a natural development of government focusing on spatial regulation. Demonstrations, marches, and protest actions are extreme public events by nature, with groups of people gathering supporters in order to voice grievances. The city government could not engage in a radical version of spatial regulation against "undesirables" while tolerating the public gatherings of dissenters. Radical spatial regulation has many antidemocratic elements, and in New York City, most of these elements came together after 1997.

The radicalization of spatial regulation during the Giuliani Administration represented the first comprehensive urban disorder eradication project since urban renewal. It was different from urban renewal because it focused on social and not physical disorder and because it sought to banish disorderly groups and individuals rather than produce orderly ones. It was similar to urban renewal in the sense that the civil and human rights of many people were violated. Grand-scale disorder-eradication projects have a tendency to violate people's rights. They seek to marginalize the behavior of portions of the population by using the authority of the government to employ violence. Atrocities against low-income people are committed on behalf of the affluent, regardless of whether the affluent approve of these methods.

In the end, the dramatic reduction of crime that occurred in the 1990s could have happened without many of the heavy-handed methods of the city government. By the time Bratton left office, most of the original goals of reducing crime and disorder had been achieved. Although Bratton took credit for these successes, the city administration would be able to highlight its law-and-order credentials by 1997, when the mayor stood for reelection. The problem was that it was difficult to mobilize the disciplinary functions of government and then demobilize them. Police brutality, disrespect, and misconduct became routine repertoires of spatial regulation; a fear existed within the city administration that order maintenance without the abuses would not be as efficient.

This radical version of spatial regulation began to show its antidemocratic elements after 1997, when the Giuliani Administration became more neoconservative. Protest actions and public gatherings were limited because they were also viewed as sources of social disorder. The constitutional rights of protesters and social-movement organizations were routinely violated. Neoconservative governance meant that the government was not merely interested in neutralizing democratic tendencies by delegating power to nongovernmental entities as in the case of neoliberal governance; the neoconservative government became interested in neutralizing democracy more directly by attacking dissenters in the streets and in the courts.

Epilogue
The Legacy of Displacement and Exclusion

This book demonstrates how spatial regulation became one of the most important ways to reverse the decline of New York City in the post–World War II period. As New York began to lose its status as a leading global city, the perception of urban disorder, whether that disorder was physical (e.g., slums, shabby streets, crumbling infrastructure) or social (e.g., homeless people, hustlers, rowdy teenagers), represented a threat to the middle class and investors and thus to the financial and political viability of the city government. Consequently, mayors and other elected and nonelected leaders mounted initiatives such as urban renewal, exclusionary zoning, antivagrancy laws, and order-maintenance policing to control, if not erase, disorder. These initiatives were part of a class project that deflected attention from the underlying causes of poverty, eroded civil rights, and sought to enable real estate investment, high-end consumption, mainstream tourism, and corporate success. The various strategies of spatial ordering that were employed corresponded to shifts in political ideology. Liberals who dominated New York City politics between the 1940s and the early 1970s emphasized physical solutions against disorder such as urban renewal and the elimination of slums. However, as urban renewal became discredited and crime increased dramatically, neoconservatives denounced postwar liberalism as the source of the city's decline. After the fiscal crisis of 1975, brands of neoliberalism and neoconservatism merged and articulated a new vision of spatial regulation based on aggressive policing. Instead of redeveloping low-income African American and Latino neighborhoods, the authorities targeted people who committed minor infractions in public space. By the 1990s, these efforts to regulate urban space were promoted under the banners of "broken windows" and "zero-tolerance policing."

In 1991, Charles Murray, in an essay about the American future, wrote that the most worrisome trend in the United States was the formation of a caste society. Murray predicted that the wealthy would increase to between 10 and 20% of the population and that they would seek to circumvent public institutions in a way that only the top 1% of the population previously could. Murray's prediction was accurate. The upward redistribution of wealth, coupled with a significant reduction of taxes for the affluent, has resulted in the creation of a wealthier and more sizable upper class in the United States. David Harvey views this restoration of class power as neoliberalism's main project. By the first decade of the twenty-first century, New York City was the place where this upper-class power became profoundly obvious. New York City became known as the "luxury city" with many of the nation's new rich relocating there. This kind of luxury city would not have been possible unless it was preceded by the orderly city.[1]

The quest to transform New York City into an orderly city recommenced in the mid-1970s after physical solutions to urban disorder had been discredited. New York was the first political subdivision in the United States to implement neoliberal reforms. In the aftermath of the fiscal crisis, the city's elites took a more active role in the management of the economy and the marketing of the city's image. Mayor Koch, who was the city's first neoliberal mayor, shrank the city government, antagonized municipal unions, and declared that his business-friendly policies would benefit New York's middle classes. Perhaps most importantly, he launched continuous attacks against African Americans and Latinos, who comprised the largest segment of the city's low-income population, and after the uprising of 1977 emerged as the most potent challengers of fiscal retrenchment. The city governance that emerged during the Koch Administration (1978–1989) can best be defined as neoliberal in policy and neoconservative in discourse. The middle- and working-class whites of the outer boroughs were appeased because the mayor appeared to be articulating their views on race and class. At the same time, Koch's neoliberal policies handsomely benefitted the city's elites, which grew in size mainly because of newcomers who were attracted by the corporate sector.

The problem with Koch's shrinkage of the city government is that crime and social disorder also increased in New York. In the 1980s, the city administration started to enlarge some government functions, but by then it was too late. The city's elites equated New York's recovery with the reduction of crime and social disorder, not because this was the only way to rebuild the city, but because they viewed a safe city as a way to a more prosperous future. For example, New York City could have taken the road of São Paulo, which is a successful corporate and financial center despite high crime rates. Affluent people who live and work in São Paulo have chosen a lifestyle of spatial fortification under which public space is surrendered to low-income people, who constitute more than half of the population. New York's corporate and real estate sectors had a different vision for New York. They wanted affluent residents and visitors to frequent public parks, walk the city's sidewalks, use public transportation, and visit high-profile commercial and entertainment areas without interference from low-income people. Although Koch failed to deliver this vision, the hope that it was possible remained.[2]

The irony is that David Dinkins, a liberal mayor, made the city safer for affluent people to operate within. Dinkins enlarged the police force and deployed it more efficiently. However, Dinkins and his police commissioners championed a liberal version of community policing, which separated social disorder from serious crime, required police officers to respect civil rights, and ordered law enforcement personnel to refer "disorderly" people to the appropriate social service agencies. The NYPD resisted community policing and attempted to destabilize the Dinkins Administration. Although crime declined in 1992 and 1993, Dinkins was defeated in his re-election bid against Giuliani because his mayoralty was framed as being tolerant of criminals and "disorderly" people.

The Giuliani Administration designed a radical version of spatial regulation based on neoconservative principles of governance. Giuliani and his police commissioners equated "disorderly" people with serious criminals and viewed the disrespect of civil rights as a way to make the police force more effective. Moreover, the Giuliani Administration used government agencies in order to antagonize social-movement organizations so that their members would be dissuaded from demonstrating in public. Protesters were branded as "disorderly" people as well. This continuous war against social disorder was justified as a crime-fighting strategy, and, since serious crime actually declined, many of the constitutional abuses by the city government went overlooked. As the city's economy recovered after the mid-1990s, critics of zero-tolerance policing were dismissed as people who did not understand public policies that facilitated economic growth.

Many observers would argue that the regulatory policies described in this book were successful and that New York City saw its fortunes rise from the depths of the mid-1970s crisis to renewed economic and demographic growth. After all, physical and social solutions to urban disorder were designed to save Columbia University, revive flagging portions of the Upper West Side, make Times Square more appealing to tourists, and generally make the city more attractive to the middle and upper classes. There is, however, something unsettling in the methods employed to achieve urban order and engender city rebuilding. Spatial policies that sought to displace African Americans and Latinos from certain public spaces or their neighborhoods, at a time when these populations were comprising the majority of New York City, are problematic. The city decided to rebuild itself by excluding and displacing large portions of its population. This legacy of rebuilding through exclusion and displacement meant that the city government would continue these practices in order to maintain its orderly and successful status.

As it turned out, the orderly city represented a major precondition of the luxury city. The term "luxury city" originated in 2003, when multimillionaire Michael Bloomberg—who succeeded Giuliani as mayor—declared that "if New York City is a business, it isn't Wal-Mart—it isn't trying to be the lowest-priced product in the market . . . It's a high-end product, maybe even a luxury product."[3] Since his election in 2001, Bloomberg ran the city government as a corporation with himself as its chief executive officer.

His administration favored big businesses and developers, sought to attract large corporations from around the world, and marked the return of neo-liberal governance in New York City. Bloomberg and his Deputy Mayor for Economic Development, Daniel L. Doctoroff, have been described as the architects of this new luxury city, which included the rezoning of thousands of city blocks so that private developers could build luxury condominiums, boutique hotels, high-end shops, and corporate offices. Doctoroff was hailed as the new Robert Moses of New York, since his developer-friendly policies engendered physical development not seen since the 1950s. There is, however, an underside of this luxury city.[4]

The luxury city was possible because zero-tolerance policing purportedly tamed the city's lower classes during the 1990s and because the Bloomberg Administration continued to use the NYPD as a force of intimidation. Although Mayor Bloomberg showed no interest in employing the neoconservative rhetoric of Koch and Giuliani against African Americans and Latinos, the NYPD continued many of the questionable policies of the Giuliani era that included stop-and-frisk practices, the abuse of power, and public intimidation. Complaints about police misconduct rose even more during the first decade of the twenty-first century, and this with a smaller police force. Poor people continued to be excluded and displaced by the police as well as by the market. Homelessness reached record levels in Bloomberg's New York, though the appearance of homeless people in high-profile spaces has not been as widespread.[5]

As has been made clear in this book, a government that excludes and displaces a large portion of its population in the name of urban order will not easily discontinue these policies. Displacement and exclusion of one group usually means the attraction and inclusion of another. As low-income people were displaced and excluded, affluent people poured into the city. The luxury city was constructed so that the lifestyle demands of these newcomers could be fulfilled. However, the market forces of the luxury city also began to displace and exclude middle-class New Yorkers. In each of the years between 2002 and 2006, more people left New York for other locations than in 1993, when the city was still suffering from an economic downturn. Most of these New York residents relocated because the city was becoming too expensive for them. Although some middle-class people tried to weather the high cost of New York by moving to cheaper neighborhoods in Brooklyn and Queens, the luxury city followed them there. Excluded from the public policies that enable the creation of a luxury city, middle-class residents are slowly being displaced from it. The fight against urban disorder may have succeeded, but for the majority of the population, this does not make for a livable city.[6]

Notes

NOTES TO THE INTRODUCTION

1. James Q. Wilson and George L. Kelling, "The Police and Neighborhood Safety," *The Atlantic* (March 1982): 29–38.
2. For glimpses of New York's changing urban fortunes in the postwar period see George J. Lankevich, *New York City: A Short History* (New York: New York University Press, 2002); E. B. White, *Here is New York* (New York: Little Bookroom, 2000); Jon C. Teaford, *The Rough Road to Renaissance: Urban Revitalization in America, 1940–1985* (Baltimore: The Johns Hopkins University Press, 1990); Robert A. Beauregard, *Voices of Decline: The Postwar Fate of US Cities* (Oxford: Blackwell, 1993); Joshua B. Freeman, *Working Class New York: Life and Labor since World War II* (New York: The New Press, 2000); William Sites, *Remaking New York: Primitive Globalization and the Politics of Urban Community* (Minneapolis: University of Minnesota Press, 2003); Marshall Berman and Brian Berger, *New York Calling: From Blackout to Bloomberg* (London: Reaktion Books, 2007); Kim Moody, *From Welfare State to Real Estate: Regime Change in New York City, 1974 to the Present* (New York: TheNew Press, 2007).
3. Diane E. Davis, "El factor Giuliani: delincuencia, la 'cero tolerancia' en el trabajo policiaco y la transformación de la esfera pública en el centro de la ciudad de México," *Estudios Sociológicos* XXV (septiembre–diciembre 2007): 639–681; Jordi Pius Llopart, "Robocop in Mexico City," *NACLA: Report on the Americas* XXXVII (September/October 2003): 22–23.
4. Robert Sampson and Stephen Raudenbush, "Systematic Social Observation of Public Spaces: A New Look at Disorder in Urban Neighborhoods," *American Journal of Sociology* 105 (November 1999): 603–651; Erving Goffman, *Behavior in Public Places: Notes on the Social Organization of Gatherings* (New York: Free Press, 1963); Lyn H. Lofland, *A World of Strangers: Order and Action in Urban Public Space* (New York: Basic Books, 1973); Wesley G. Skogan, *Disorder and Decline: Crime and the Spiral of Decay in American Neighborhoods* (New York: Free Press, 1990); Frank Hearn, *Moral Order and Social Disorder: The American Search for Civil Society* (New York: Aldyne de Gruyter, 1997).

NOTES TO CHAPTER 1

1. Susan Sontag, *Illness as Metaphor* (New York: Farrar, Straus and Giroux, 1978), 74.

2. Jacob A. Riis, *How the Other Half Lives: Studies among the Tenements of New York* (New York: Charles Scribner's Sons, 1890), 135–175; Jacob A. Riis, *The Children of the Poor* (New York: Charles Scribner's Sons, 1892), 1–8; Roy Lubove, *The Professional Altruist: The Emergence of Social Work as a Career, 1880–1930* (Cambridge: Harvard University Press, 1965); Amos G. Warner, Stuart A. Queen, and Ernest B. Harper, *American Charities and Social Work* (New York: Thomas Y. Crowell Co., 1930); Stanley Wenocur and Michael Reisch, *From Charity to Enterprise: The Development of American Social Work in a Market Economy* (Urbana: University of Illinois Press, 1989).
3. Roy Lubove, *The Progressive and the Slums: Tenement House Reform in New York City, 1890–1917* (Pittsburgh: University of Pittsburgh Press, 1962), 49–80; A. Scott Henderson, *Housing and the Democratic Ideal: The Life and Thought of Charles Abrams* (New York: Columbia University Press, 2000), 45–82; Nicolas Dagen Bloom, *Public Housing That Worked: New York in the Twentieth Century* (Philadelphia: University of Pennsylvania Press, 2008), 13–44; Alexander von Hoffman, "A Study in Contradictions: The Origins and Legacy of the Housing Act of 1949," *Housing Policy Debate* 11 (2000): 300–302.
4. Alison Isenberg, *Downtown America: A History of the Place and the People Who Made It* (Chicago: University of Chicago Press, 2004), 166–202; von Hoffman, "A Study of Contradictions," 305–309.
5. von Hoffman, "A Study of Contradictions," 299–326.
6. Robert Caro, *The Power Broker: Robert Moses and the Fall of New York* (New York: Random House, 1974); Joel Schwartz, *The New York Approach: Robert Moses, Urban Liberals, and Redevelopment of the Inner City* (Columbus: Ohio State University Press, 1993).
7. Caro, *The Power Broker*, 1974; Schwartz, *The New York Approach*, 1993.
8. Andrew S. Dolkart, *Morningside Heights: A History of its Architecture and Development* (New York: Columbia University Press, 1998), 1–2.
9. Andrew Alpern, *Apartments for the Affluent: A Historical Survey of Buildings in New York* (New York: McGraw-Hill, 1975); Elizabeth C. Cromley, *Alone Together: A History of New York's Early Apartments* (Ithaca: Cornell University Press, 1990); Dolkart, *Morningside Heights*, 276–323; Clifton Hood, *722 Miles: The Building of the Subways and How They Transformed New York* (New York: Simon and Schuster, 1993); Richard Plunz, *A History of Housing in New York City: Dwelling Type and Social Change in the American Metropolis* (New York: Columbia University Press, 1990); *The New York Times*, "Columbia Extends Housing Program," November 23, 1919, sec. 2, p. 1.
10. Jeffrey S. Gurock, *When Harlem Was Jewish, 1870–1930* (New York: Columbia University Press, 1930); Gilbert Osofsky, *Harlem: The Making of a Ghetto: Negro New York, 1890–1930* (New York: Harper & Row, 1966); Felix Riesenberg and Alexander Allard, *Portrait of New York* (New York: MacMillan, 1939), 131–132; E. Franklin Frazier, "Negro Harlem: An Ecological Study," *American Journal of Sociology* 43 (July 1937): 72–88; Michael Drosnin, "Ten 'Residence Hotels' Center of Most Area Crime," *Columbia Spectator*, October 18, 1964, 1; Center for New York City Affairs, *A Program for Tenants in Single Room Occupancy <SRO> & for their New York City Neighbors* (New York: New School for Social Research, 1969), 3–5; Kaminsky and Shiffer Architects AIA, *Model SRO: Single Room Occupancy Housing* (New York: The Architects, 1970), 3–5; Nicholas Pileggi, "Renaissance of the Upper West Side," *New York*, June 30, 1969, 28–39.
11. E. Virginia Massimine, *Challenges of a Changing Population: A Study of the Integration of the Puerto Ricans in a West Side Community in Manhattan*

(New York: Center for Human Relations Studies, New York University, 1953), 20–24; Caro, *The Power Broker*, 964.
12. Confidential Memorandum by Nicholas Murray Butler to the Board of Trustees, Columbia University, January 7, 1946, Marcellus Hartley Dodge File, Nicholas Murray Butler Papers, Rare Book and Manuscript Library, Columbia University Library.
13. Committee on Research in Urban Land Use and Housing, Columbia University, "Memorandum on Redevelopment of Morningside Heights," January 17, 1947, p. 1, Box 46, William Russel Papers, Teachers College Archives.
14. For a more comprehensive account of the early debates and redevelopment actions that Morningside Heights institutional officials were involved in during the postwar period, see Joel Schwartz, *The New York Approach* (1993), 151–159 and 185–189, and Martha Biondi, *To Stand and Fight: The Struggle for Civil Rights in Postwar New York City* (Cambridge: Harvard University Press, 2003), 113–114.
15. Schwartz, *The New York Approach*, 152.
16. Schwartz, *The New York Approach*, 151–159; Shelley v. Kraemer, 72, 334 U.S. 1; 68 S. Ct. 836; 92 L. Ed. 1161; 1948 U.S. (1948).
17. Schwartz, *The New York Approach*, 151–159; Shelley v. Kraemer (1948).
18. Gertrude L. Samuels, "A Community at Work: A Lesson for Others," *The New York Times Magazine*, August 6, 1950, 18.
19. Minutes of the Executive Committee, MHI, June 16, 1949, p. 3, Box 46, William Russel Papers, Teachers College Archives; Minutes of the Executive Committee, MHI, 7 March 1949, p. 1, Box 584, MHI Subseries, Columbia University Central Files; Minutes of the Executive Committee, MHI, 19 December 1949, Box 584, MHI Subseries, Columbia University Central Files; David Rockefeller to Dwight D. Eisenhower, January 5, 1950, Box 584, MHI Subseries, Columbia University Central Files, 2; Minutes of the Board of Directors, MHI, 16 November 1950, Box 584, MHI Subseries, Columbia University Central Files, 2; David Rockefeller to Henry P. Van Dusen, 27 November 1950, Box 584, MHI Subseries, Columbia University Central Files.
20. Elizabeth Hepner, *Morningside-Manhattanville Rebuilds* . . . (New York: MHI, 1955), 8; John G. Van Dusen, "Morningside Heights, Inc.," (B.A. thesis, Princeton University, 1954), 86–88; David Snell, "Reds Try to Junk 2 Columbia Area Housing Projects," *New York World-Telegram and The Sun*, March 20, 1952; Gertrude Samuels, "Rebirth of a Community," *The New York Times Magazine*, September 25, 1955, 37; Martin Shefter, "Political Incorporation and the Extrusion of the Left: Party Politics and Social Forces in New York City," *Studies in American Political Development* I (1986): 59–79; Caro, *The Power Broker*, 1974.
21. Schwartz, *The New York Approach*, 196–197 and 203; New York City Committee on Slum Clearance, *Title I Slum Clearance Progress* (New York: The Committee, 1958).
22. "New Faculty Housing Planned by University," *Columbia Daily Spectator*, December 14, 1961, 1; Donald H. Shapiro, "Plan New Housing Facilities for Columbia Faculty Members," *Columbia Daily Spectator*, May 1, 1963, 1; "Columbia Faculty Gets New Housing," *The New York Times*, October 22, 1967, 76. Proposals for construction in the northern boundary of Morningside Heights had proliferated in the early 1950s, though at the time, Columbia's President Dwight D. Eisenhower wanted to build an engineering building there.
23. "Institutional Development Plans," Report to the MHI Annual Meeting of the Board of Directors, April 19, 1956, Box 585, MHI Subseries, Columbia

University Central Files; "Columbia Plans Public Play Area," *The New York Times,* December 30, 1955; Report by Stanley Salmen, MHI Executive Director, "Public Safety on Morningside Heights," January 6, 1960, p. 1–2, Box 585, MHI Subseries, Columbia University Central Files; Report by Stanley Salmen, MHI Executive Director, 17 April 1961, p. 3, Box 585, MHI Subseries, Columbia University Central Files; Marie M. Runyon, "Morningside Park School Site," Letter to the Editor, *The New York Times,* July 19, 1965, 26; New York City Planning Commission, *Report Recommending Against the Demapping of a Section of Morningside Park* (New York: The Commission, 1964), Box 2, Christiane Collins Collection, Manuscripts, Archives, and Rare Books Collection, Schomburg Center for Research in Black Culture.
24. Clarence G. Michalis, J. Stewart Baker, and George E. Warren to Robert Moses, 17 November 1955, Box 585, MHI Subseries, Columbia University Central Files; MHI, Columbia University, and Teachers College, "Some Facts About the Population of Morningside Heights," December, 1948, p. 27, Box 584, MHI Subseries, Columbia University Central Files; Minutes of the Board of Directors, MHI, 23 November 1948, p. 3, Box 584, MHI Subseries, Columbia University Central Files; Report by Lawrence M. Orton, MHI Executive Director, to the MHI Board of Directors, 18 November 1954, p. 2, Box 585, MHI Subseries, Columbia University Central Files; Report by Lawrence M. Orton to the MHI Executive Committee, September 15, 1955, p. 7, Box 585, MHI Subseries, Columbia University Central Files; MHI, "Sketch Plan for Morningside Heights," March 20, 1958, p. 7, Box 585, MHI Subseries, Columbia University Central Files. These grants aided the reconversion of existing structures rather than their clearing.
25. MHI, "Proposal to the Honorable Robert F. Wagner, Mayor of the City of New York and the Honorable Hulan F. Jack, Borough President of Manhattan" (New York: MHI, 1959); Charles Grutzner, "Slum Clearance Asked in Big Area Around Columbia," *The New York Times,* October 15, 1959, 1; City of New York Housing and Redevelopment Board, "Summary Statement in Support of Map Entitled 'Proposed General Land Use, Showing Major Street Changes and Community Facilities' from the Morningside General Neighborhood Renewal Plan Area," January 11, 1963, p. 5, Box 586, Morningside Renewal Council Subseries, Columbia University Central Files.
26. Emily Goldblat, "Image and Reality in Patterns of Change on Manhattan's Upper West Side" (master's thesis, Columbia University, 1969); Robert E. Selsam, "The Upper West Side Urban Renewal Area: An Evaluation with Special Emphasis on Implications for New York City and the Urban Renewal Program" (master's thesis, Columbia University, 1970).
27. Robert A. M. Stern, Thomas Mellins, and David Fishman, *New York 1960: Architecture and Urbanism Between the Second World War and the Bicentennial* (New York: Monacelli Press, 1995), 665.
28. Committee on Slum Clearance, *Manhattantown: Slum Clearance Plan Under Title I of the Housing Act of 1949* (New York: The Committee, 1951).
29. Ibid.
30. Ibid., 6–8 and 33–46.
31. Caro, *The Power Broker,* 964.
32. Ibid.
33. Ibid., 963–964.
34. Marya Mannes, *The New York I Know* (Philadelphia: J. B. Lippincott Company, 1961), 18–20 and 35.
35. Ibid.
36. United States Senate, Committee on Banking and Currency, Subcommittee on Housing and Urban Affairs, *FHA Investigation: Hearings Before the*

Committee on Banking and Currency (Washington, DC: U.S. Government Printing Office, 1954); Women's City Club of New York, *Tenant Relocation at West Park: A Report Based on Field Interviews* (New York: The Club, 1954); Women's City Club of New York, *Manhattantown Two Years Later: A Second Look at Tenant Relocation* (New York: The Club, 1956); Caro, *The Power Broker*, 961–983.
37. Women's City Club of New York, *Tenant Relocation at West Park*, 3, 4, 8.
38. Ibid.
39. Stern et al., *New York 1960*, 726.
40. *Kaskel v. Impellitteri*, 306 N.Y. 73; 115 N.E.2d 659; 1953 N.Y. (1953).
41. Ibid.
42. Ibid.
43. Mr. Harper, "After Hours," *Harper's* 213 (July 1953): 85.
44. Stern et al., *New York 1960*, 667–673.
45. Schwartz, *The New York Approach*, 276–279, 175; Stern et al., *New York 1960*, 677–680.
46. City Planning Commission of the City of New York, *Report on Lincoln Square Urban Renewal Plan and Project* (New York: The Commission, 1957), 10; Committee on Slum Clearance, *Lincoln Square: Slum Clearance Plan Under Title I of the Housing Act of 1949* (New York: The Committee, 1956), 37–45.
47. Frederick Gutheim, "Athens on the Subway," *Harper's Magazine* 217 (October 1958): 66–67.
48. Russell Bourne, "Building's Two-Star General," *Architectural Forum* (June 1958): 118–119.
49. Editorial, "Lincoln Center Is Born," *New York Herald Tribune*, May 14, 1959, 18.
50. Caro, *The Power Broker*, 1040–1116; J. Clarence Davies III, *Neighborhood Groups and Urban Renewal* (New York: Columbia University Press, 1966); J. Anthony Panuch, *Building a Better New York: Final Report to Mayor Robert F. Wagner* (New York: The City, 1960); School of Architecture, Columbia University, *Urban Renewal Study: West Side Project* (New York: Columbia University, 1960); Don Ross, "Upper West Side—Squalor, Culture Side by Side," *The New York Herald Tribune*, June 25, 1961, 1 and 17.

NOTES TO CHAPTER 2

1. Jane Jacobs, *The Death and Life of Great American Cities* (New York: Random House, 1961), 375–376.
2. James C. Scott, *Seeing Like a State: How Certain Schemes to Improve the Human Condition Have Failed* (New Haven: Yale University Press, 1998), 6.
3. Jacobs, *The Death and Life of Great American Cities*, 21–24.
4. Adrian Forty, *Words and Buildings: A Vocabulary of Modern Architecture* (New York: Thames & Hudson, 2000), 240–248; David P. Jordan, *Transforming Paris: The Life and Labors of Baron Haussmann* (Chicago: University of Chicago Press, 1996); Robin Evans, *The Fabrication of Virtue: English Prison Architecture, 1750–1840* (Cambridge: Cambridge University Press, 1982); Nathan Glazer, *From a Cause to a Style: Modernist Architecture's Encounter with the American City* (Princeton: Princeton University Press, 2007).
5. Nicholas Fox Weber, *Le Corbusier* (London: Weidenfeld & Nicolson, 2006); Le Corbusier, *Essential Le Corbusier: L'Esprit Nouveau Articles* (Oxford: Architectural Press, 1998). Mardges Bacon has found the singling out of Le

Corbusier as responsible for modernist city planning by Jacobs and others to be exaggerated, though not without merit. Bacon argues that by 1935 most of Le Corbusier's principles behind the Radiant City had become elements of New York City housing and planning policy, though many of these principles had probably developed independently; Mardges Bacon, *Le Corbusier in America: Travels in the Land of the Timid* (Cambridge: MIT Press, 2001), 168–169. Eric Mumford has shown that CIAM members had almost no involvement in the towers with gardens built in the United States, though Le Corbusier's ideas influenced many of the manifestos of CIAM; Eric Mumford, *The CIAM Discourse on Urbanism, 1928–1960* (Cambridge: MIT Press, 2000).
6. David Plotke, *Building a Democratic Political Order: Reshaping American Liberalism in the 1930s and 1940s* (New York: Cambridge University Press, 1996).
7. Scott, *Seeing Like a State,* 6 and 114–117.
8. Jacobs, *The Death and Life of Great American Cities,* 222 and 376.
9. Ibid., 34.
10. Ellen Lurie, *A Study of George Washington Houses, A Federally-Aided, Low Cost Housing Project in East Harlem: The Effect of the Project on its Tenants and the Surrounding Community* (New York: Union Settlement Association, 1956), 18–19.
11. Ibid.
12. Ibid.
13. Ellen Lurie, "Community Action in East Harlem," in *The Urban Condition: People and Policy in the Metropolis,* ed. Leonard J. Duhl (New York: Basic Books, 1963), 248.
14. Oscar Newman, *Defensible Space: Crime Prevention though Urban Design* (New York: Macmillan, 1972), 12.
15. Ibid., 12 and 22–39.
16. Jacobs, *The Death and Life of Great American Cities,* 47–50.
17. Bloom, *Public Housing That Worked,* 223–225.
18. Ibid., 220–242.
19. Robert E. Herman, Commissioner and State Rent Administrator, State of New York, Temporary State Housing Rent Commission, "Prospects for Rehabilitation: A Demonstration Study of Housing in Morningside Heights, New York City" (December 1960): 5, 19, 22; Clarence C. Sherwood, "Fourth Report on Building Code Enforcement Program on Morningside Heights, September 1960 to January 1961" (January 1961): 4, Box 585, MHI Subseries, Columbia University Central Files.
20. T. L. Hungate, Chairman of the MHI Subcommittee on Public Safety, "A Report to the Program of the Subcommittee on Public Safety of MHI," p. 1, Box 584, MHI Subseries, Columbia University Central Files.
21. Schwartz, *The New York Approach,* 151.
22. Stanley Salmen, "Public Safety on Morningside Heights," January 9, 1961, p. 2, Box 491, Stanley Salmen Files, Columbia University Central Files.
23. Ibid.
24. Stanley Salmen, "Report of the Executive Director," April 17, 1961, p. 5–6, Box 585, MHI Subseries, Columbia University Central Files; MHI, *Morningside Heights Core Area Study* (New York: MHI, 1968), n. p.
25. Michael Drosnin, "Slum Demolition Leads to Crime Drop," *Columbia Daily Spectator,* October 27, 1964, 1.
26. Stanley Salmen, MHI Executive Director, "Morningside Heights Plan," 16 November 1958, p. 3, Box 585, MHI Subseries, Columbia University Central Files.

27. Minutes of the MHI Board of Directors, 17 November 1955, p. 3, Box 585, MHI Subseries, Columbia University Central Files; Lewis Yablonsky to the Morningside Heights Security Personnel, January 13, 1956, Box 585, MHI Subseries, Columbia University Central Files; David M. Alpern, "Neighborhood Crime Brings Police Action," *Columbia Daily Spectator,* December 8, 1960; James Lynn, "Crime War: One-Block Police Beat," *The Herald Tribune,* December 1, 1964, 1.
28. Clarence C. Sherwood, Director, MHI Crime Prevention Program, "Report on Building Code Enforcement Program on Morningside Heights, December 1958 to March 1959" (March 1959): 6, Box 585, MHI Subseries, Columbia University Central Files; Drosnin, "Ten 'Residence Hotels' Center of Most Area Crime," 3; Clarence C. Sherwood, "Second Report on Building Code Enforcement Program on Morningside Heights, April to November 1959" (November 1959): 4, Box 585, MHI Subseries, Columbia University's Central Files; Clarence C. Sherwood, "Fourth Report on Building Code Enforcement Program on Morningside Heights, September 1960 to January 1961" (January 1961): 4, Box 585, MHI Subseries, Columbia University Central Files.
29. Salmen, "Morningside Heights Plan," 16 and 21; Michael Drosnin, "Agency Tries to Take Over Bryn Mawr," *Columbia Daily Spectator,* November 12, 1964, 1; Roger Kahn, *The Battle for Morningside Heights: Why Students Rebel* (New York: William Morrow and Co., 1970), 86; William D. Schwartz, "CU Purchases Six Buildings in Area Surrounding Campus," *Columbia Daily Spectator,* May 10, 1962, 1; Rust Gilbert, "Yorkshire Relocation Plan Conducted by CU Since July," *Columbia Daily Spectator,* October 2, 1963, 1; Jeffrey Newman, "Columbia to Purchase Local Apartment House," *Columbia Daily Spectator,* February 8, 1965, 1.
30. Greenspan, "The Wider War on Morningside Heights," 32; Frances Bromiley, "Columbia University vs. the People," *Rights and Reviews* (Winter 1995): 10–12; "Columbia Helping Evicted Tenants," *The New York Times,* October 20, 1963, 121; Kahn, *The Battle for Morningside Heights,* 87; Faculty Civil Rights Group at Columbia University, "The Community and the Expansion of Columbia University" (December 1967); "The Case of 609 West 115 Street," *Morningsiders United Newsletter,* May 18, 1967, 3.
31. Faculty Civil Rights Group at Columbia University, "The Community and the Expansion of Columbia University" (December 1967).
32. *Morningsiders United Newsletter,* May 18, 1967, 3.
33. Edward V. Solomon to Dr. John V. Butler, Chairman, MHI Community Programs Committee, 11 October 1965, p. 3, MHI Subject Ephemeral Files, University Archives and Columbiana Library.
34. "Two Columbia U. Profs Victims of Street Attacks," *The Herald Tribune,* May 24, 1964, 22; Michael Drosnin, "Crime Problem: Does It Affect Attraction of Students, Faculty?" *Columbia Daily Spectator,* October 29, 1964, 1; Joel Linsider, "Letters by Kirk, Chamberlain Ask Support to Stop Crime," *Columbia Daily Spectator,* October 1, 1964, 1 and 3; Lawrence H. Chamberlain, Vice President, Columbia University, "Memorandum for Members of the Morningside Heights Community," June 30, 1964, Subject Ephemeral Files, Columbia University Archives and Columbiana Library.
35. *New York State Commission Against Discrimination v. Pelham Hall Apartments,* 10 Misc. 2d 334; 170 N.Y.S.2d 750; 1958 N.Y. (1958); *Martin v. City of New York,* 22 Misc. 2d 389; 201 N.Y.S.2d 111; 1960 N.Y. (1960); Biondi, *To Stand and Fight,* 223–241; Marilynn S. Johnson, *Street Justice: A History of Police Violence in New York City* (Boston: Beacon Press, 2003), 234–241.

36. Michael Drosnin, "Fire Director of Community Services Dept.," *Columbia Daily Spectator,* December 4, 1964, 1.
37. Kahn, *The Battle for Morningside Heights,* 87.
38. Greenspan, "The Wider War on Morningside Heights," 32.
39. Lawrence O'Kane, "Morningside Tenants Protest Renewal at City Hall Hearing," *The New York Times,* March 12, 1965, 17.
40. Samuel Kaplan, "Angry Group of 9 Calls on Barzun," *The New York Times,* May 4, 1965, 45.
41. "Columbia, NYU Face Racial Fight: C.O.R.E. Director Charges Housing Discrimination," *The New York Times,* February 1, 1962, 17; "Columbia Helping Evicted Tenants," 121; "Plan to Picket Columbia," *West Side News and Morningsider,* July 29, 1965, 1; Robert Alden, "Neighbors Assail Columbia Growth," *The New York Times,* January 18, 1964, 25–26; "Columbia Housing Protest," *The New York Times,* August 14, 1965, 9; John Kifner, "50 Picket Kirk Home to Mourn Buildings 'Killed' by Columbia," *The New York Times,* July 9, 1967, 44.
42. Sydney H. Schanberg, "Columbia Named in Rights Inquiry," *The New York Times,* February 28, 1964, 15.
43. "Columbia Urges Community Plan," *The New York Times,* January 12, 1965, 39.
44. "Tenants Accuse Columbia of Bias," *The New York Times,* October 4, 1961, 39; Faculty Civil Rights Group at Columbia University, "The Community and the Expansion of Columbia University" (December 1967): 7–8; "Eviction Hearing in Renovation Case," *The New York Times,* January 24, 1962, 15; "Housing Bias Case Won by Columbia," *The New York Times,* February 7, 1962, 40; Michael Drosnin, "Real Estate Arm of CU Asks City Closing of Hotel," *Columbia Daily Spectator,* October 23, 1964, 1; Michael Drosnin, "Tenants Fight CU Takeover of Bryn Mawr," *Columbia Daily Spectator,* December 3, 1964, 1; Henry Welt, "Bryn Mawr Residents Picket NY County Civil Court Today," *Columbia Daily Spectator,* December 17, 1964, 1; "The Hotel Where Addiction and Violence Thrived is Being Closed," *The New York Times,* November 3, 1965, 26; Emanuel Perlmutter, "Columbia Wins Fight to Close an 'Undesirable' Hotel Nearby," *The New York Times,* February 25, 1965, 20.
45. Edith Penamon, "New Day in Harlem," *Rights and Reviews* (Winter 1965): 13–14; Charles De Laney, "CORE to Organize Tenants in Preparation for Renewal," *Columbia Daily Spectator,* October 5, 1965, 1; Kaplan, "Harlem Residents Ask Columbia's Aid," 41.
46. "Plan to Build New College Gym on Morningside Park Location," *Columbia College Today* 8 (March 1960): 2 and 6; Bernard B. Fishalow, "Columbia Prepares Blueprint for Planned $9 Million Gym," *Columbia Daily Spectator,* March 11, 1965, 5; Ralph Blumenthal, "Gym-In-Park Deal 'Upsets' Hoving," *The New York Times,* January 25, 1966, 38; Kahn, *The Battle for Morningside Heights,* 94; Peter Greene, "CU CORE Pickets Against Park Site for Proposed Gym," *Columbia Daily Spectator,* February 23, 1966, 1.
47. Dwight C. Smith, Chairman, Morningside Renewal Council, to Thomas P. Hoving, Commissioner of Parks, April 29, 1966, Box 2, Christiane Collins Collection, Manuscripts, Archives, and Rare Books Collection, Schomburg Center for Research in Black Culture; Dwight C. Smith to the Editor, *The New York Times,* 9 May 1966, Box 2, Christiane Collins Collection, Manuscripts, Archives, and Rare Books Collection, Schomburg Center for Research in Black Culture; Dwight C. Smith to Hon. John V, Lindsay, Mayor, April 26, 1967, Box 2, Christiane Collins Collection, Manuscripts, Archives, and Rare Books Collection, Schomburg Center for Research in

Black Culture; Dwight C. Smith to Hon. Percy Sutton, Manhattan Borough President, 16 May 1967, Box 2, Christiane Collins Collection, Manuscripts, Archives, and Rare Books Collection, Schomburg Center for Research in Black Culture.
48. George Keller, "Six Weeks That Shook Morningside," *Columbia College Today* (Spring 1968): 45–46; Jerry L. Avorn et al., *Up Against the Ivy Wall: A History of the Columbia Crisis* (New York: Atheneum, 1969); Morris Dickstein, *Gates of Eden: American Culture in the Sixties* (New York: Basic Books, 1977); Robert Stulberg, "Student Demonstrators Take Over Hamilton Hall; Administration Refuses to Talk 'Under Coercion,'" *Columbia Daily Spectator*, April 24, 1968, 1; Arthur Kokot, "Negotiations Over Tri-Partite Body Tenuous; Brown and Carmichael Appear at Hamilton," *Columbia Daily Spectator*, April 27, 1968, 1; Robert B. Stulberg, "600 Policemen Occupy University," *Columbia Daily Spectator*, April 27, 1968, 1; Kenneth Barry, "Residents March in Protest of Gymnasium Construction," *Columbia Daily Spectator*, May 2, 1968, 1; "University Calls in 1,000 Police to End Demonstration as Nearly 700 Are Arrested and 100 Injured; Violent Solution Follows Failure of Negotiations," *Columbia Daily Spectator*, April 30, 1968, 1.
49. Martin Tolchin, "Kirk Retiring at Columbia; Cordier Named," *The New York Times*, August 24, 1968, 1; David K. Shipler, "New Head of Columbia Seeks Campus Harmony," *The New York Times*, August 25, 1968, 88; Peter Kihss, "Columbia Head Assails War, But Hundreds Walk Out," *The New York Times*, June 3, 1970, 48.
50. New York City Planning Commission, *Manhattanville West: Industrial-Commercial Survey Findings* (New York: The Commission, 1968), Box 5, Christiane Collins Collection, Manuscripts, Archives, and Rare Books Collection, Schomburg Center for Research in Black Culture; Joseph P. Fried, "Columbia Softens Role in Huge Harlem Project," *The New York Times*, October 17, 1968, 28; MHI, *Morningside Heights Core Area Study*, n. p.; Architects' Renewal Committee in Harlem, Inc., "Report on the Present and Future Use of the Piers Area (West Harlem Market)" (1968), Box 5, Christiane Collins Collection, Manuscripts, Archives, and Rare Books Collection, Schomburg Center for Research in Black Culture; Walter South, National Director of Housing for the Urban League, "Now Columbia Grabs Harlem Piers Area," (1968), Box 5, Christiane Collins Collection, Manuscripts, Archives, and Rare Books Collection, Schomburg Center for Research in Black Culture.
51. Gerald Fraser, "2 Groups Protest Columbia's Move to Revive Plans for Gym," *The New York Times*, February 26, 1969, 22; Editorial, "Columbia's New Approach, *The New York Times*, February 28, 1969, 38; "Columbia Trustees Scrap the Gym-In-Park Plan," *The New York Times*, March 4, 1969, 28; Sylvan Fox, "Columbia Hires Pei to Project its Growth for Decades Ahead," *The New York Times*, November 8, 1968, 1 and 3; "Columbia Considers Gym Under Campus in Expansion Plan," *The New York Times*, May 8, 1969, 49; Joseph P. Fried, "Columbia Plans Limited Growth," *The New York Times*, May 9, 1969, 27.
52. Emanuel Perlmutter, "Professor Slain in Mugging Here," *The New York Times*, September 21, 1972, 1; Ronald Smothers, "Youth, 16, Is Held in Columbia Death," *The New York Times*, September 22, 1972, 1; Israel Shenker, "Blind Store Owner, 65, Robbed for Sixth Time," *The New York Times*, July 28, 1976, 35; Max H. Seigel, "Safety Promised Morningside Hts.: Lindsay Pledges 'Enormous Efforts' on Tour of Area," *The New York Times*, September 5, 1973, 26; "Patrolling of Morningside Park Increased after Stabbing There," *The New York Times*, September 8, 1973, 35.

53. Judith Cummins, "Columbia Presses for Transfer Signs on IRT Platforms," *The New York Times,* February 8, 1975, 23; "Signs Will Alert Riders on IRT Broadway Line," *The New York Times,* February 25, 1975, 39; Dallas C. Galvin, "Why Should Morningside Park Be Ripped Up for a Lily Pond?" Letter to the Editor, *The New York Times,* March 1, 1989, 24(A); David W. Dunlap, "Pond Springs Where Gym Fouled Out," *The New York Times,* June 5, 1989, 3(B).
54. Sarah Crichton, "A Housing Dream that Failed," *The West Sider,* April 22, 1976, 5.
55. Stanford Colob, "The West Side's Private Police—How and Why," *Manhattan Tribune,* October 2, 1971, 1 and 15; Jacqueline Bernard, "Valley is Down in the Dumps," *The West Sider,* April 3, 1975, 5; "State Has Hope for Manhattan Valley," *The West Sider,* April 17, 1975, 15; Richard Johnson, "$$ Flow for Abandoned Buildings," *The West Sider,* July 22, 1976, 2; John Lewis, "The Brave Still Strive in a Valley of Death," *Daily News,* March 25, 1977, 8; Joan Moulds, "Valley's Decay West Side's Sore Eye," *The West Sider,* March 31, 1977, 7; Sam Campbell, "The Valley's So Low," *The West Sider,* March 16, 1978, 3; Jeff Tamarin, "Still Hope for Manhattan Valley, *The West Sider,* August 3, 1978, 16.
56. "Cause of a Wall Collapse Is Sought," *The New York Times,* May 28, 1979, sec. 2, p. 2; Richard Higgins, "Tragedy Puts Columbia to New Test as Landlord," *The New York Times,* August 5, 1979, sec. 8, p. 1; Edward B. Fiske, "Winds of Change on Morningside Heights," *The New York Times,* September 28, 1980, sec. 6, p. 38; Tom Robbins and Jack Newfield, "Our Annual Roster of New York's 10 Worst Landlords: Columbia Joins the Rolls," *The Village Voice,* August 18, 1987, 12; Morris Dickstein, "Columbia Recovered," *The New York Times,* May 15, 1988, sec. 6, p. 32; Lee A. Daniels, "Some Top Universities in Squeeze Between Research and Academics," *The New York Times,* May 10, 1989, 1(A).
57. Caro, *The Power Broker,* (1974); Stern, *New York 1960,* 133.
58. New York City Planning Commission, *Plan for New York City 1: Critical Issues* (New York: Department of City Planning, 1969).

NOTES TO CHAPTER 3

1. *Manhattan Plaza v. Snyder,* 107 Misc. 2d 470, 435 N.Y.S.2d 449, 1980 N.Y. (1980).
2. "Police Begin Times Sq. Cleanup After Night Workers Complain," *The New York Times,* February 6, 1969, 78.
3. Editorial, "Crime in Times Square," *The New York Times,* February 17, 1969, 34.
4. Frederick L. Strong, Letter to the Editor, "Limits in Courts," *The New York Times,* February 25, 1969, 42.
5. "12 of 292 Arrests in Times Sq. in 6 Days Bring Convictions," *The New York Times,* February 13, 1969, 26; Thomas F. Brady, "Times Square, New York: 'Cesspool of the World,'" *The New York Times,* February 21, 1969, 50; "Smith Scores Mayor on Times Sq. Arrests," *The New York Times,* March 14, 1969, 25; "227 Arrested in Times Sq. in the First Week of June," *The New York Times,* June 13, 1969, 35.
6. "125 Seized in Times Square in a Drive on Undesirables," *The New York Times,* July 31, 1954, 1; "23 More Undesirables Are Seized in Times Square as Round-Up Spreads," *The New York Times,* August 1, 1954, 1; "656 More

Notes 195

in Police Net," *The New York Times,* September 5, 1954, 53; "Night Court Swamped by Street Round-Up," *The New York Times,* April 11, 1955, 25; "Undesirables Seized," *The New York Times,* June 10, 1956, 88; "City Police Step Up Mass Arrest Drive," *The New York Times,* June 17, 1966, 66; David Shulman, "Hoodlums in Times Square," Letter to the Editor, *The New York Times,* May 22, 1961, 30; Eric Pace, "New Police Drive Waged in 'Village' and Times Sq. Area," *The New York Times,* March 16, 1966, 16 and 31; McCandlish Phillips, "Policemen Added at Bus Terminal," *The New York Times,* January 10, 1967, 39; *Shuttlesworth v. Birmingham,* 382 U.S. 87; 86 S. Ct. 211; 15 L. Ed. 2d 176; 1965 U.S. (1965); *Terry v. Ohio,* 67, 392 U.S. 1; 88 S. Ct. 1868; 20 L. Ed. 2d 889; 1968 U.S. (1968); *Wainwright v. New Orleans,* 13, 392 U.S. 598; 88 S. Ct. 2243; 20 L. Ed. 2d 1322; 1968 U.S. (1968); *Coates v. Cincinnati,* 117, 402 U.S. 611; 91 S. Ct. 1686; 29 L. Ed. 2d 214; 1971 U.S. (1971); *Papachristou v. Jacksonville,* 70–5030, 405 U.S. 156; 92 S. Ct. 839; 31 L. Ed. 2d 110; 1972 U.S. (1972); *State of New York v. Berck,* 32 N.Y.2d 567; 300 N.E.2d 411; 347 N.Y.S.2d 33; 1973 N.Y. (1973).

7. George Chauncey, *Gay New York: Gender, Urban Culture, and the Making of the Gay Male World, 1890–1940* (New York: Basic Books, 1994), 331–354; Robert C. Allen, *Horrible Prettiness: Burlesque and American Culture* (Chapel Hill: University of North Carolina Press, 1991), 252–253; Thomas Kessner, *Fiorello H. La Guardia and the Making of Modern New York* (New York: McGraw-Hill, 1989), 351–353; H. Paul Jeffers, *The Napoleon of New York: Mayor Fiorello La Guardia* (New York: John Wiley & Sons, 2002), 191–196; Brooks McNamara, "The Entertainment District at the End of the 1930s," in *Inventing Times Square: Commerce and Culture at the Crossroads of the World,* ed. William R. Taylor (New York: Russell Sage Foundation, 1991), 179–181.
8. Bernard J. Frieden and Lynne B. Sagalyn, *Downtown Inc.: How America Rebuilds Cities* (Cambridge: MIT Press, 1989); Teaford, *The Rough Road to Renaissance,* 145–162.
9. Joel Schwartz, *The New York Approach,* 276–287.
10. Mayor's Committee for World Fashion Center, *The World Fashion Center, New York's Post War Business Project No. 1: A Report by the Mayor's Committee for World Fashion Center* (New York: The Committee, 1944); Stern et al., *New York 1960,* 432–436.
11. Stern et al., *New York 1960,* 432–441.
12. John F. Kasson, *Amusing the Million: Coney Island at the Turn of the Century* (New York: Hill & Wang, 1978), 87–112; "Re-zoning of Times Sq. Area Proposed; Keeping it Gay, but Less Like a 'Carnival,'" *The New York Times,* March 11, 1948, 40.
13. Edgar Van, "Policing of Times Square," Letter to the Editor, *The New York Times,* December 13, 1952, 20.
14. Editorial, "Times Square," *The New York Times,* December 15, 1952, 24.
15. "Business Group Asks Times Square 'Purge,'" *The New York Times,* November 25, 1952, 31; T. J. McInerney, Managing Director, Broadway Association, "Deterioration of Times Square," Letter to the Editor, *The New York Times,* December 18, 1952, 28; Lawrence M. Orton, Commissioner, "New Zoning Advocated," Letter to the Editor, *The New York Times,* December 20, 1952, 16.
16. "For a Better Square," Editorial, *The New York Times,* January 23, 1954, 12.
17. Harrison, Ballard & Allen, *Plan for the Rezoning of New York City: Proposed Zoning Resolution* (New York: Ballard & Allen, 1950); Harrison, Ballard & Allen, *Plan for Rezoning the City of New York: A Report Submitted to the*

City Planning Commission (New York: Harrison, Ballard & Allen, 1950); "'Honky-Tonks' Hit as Times Sq. Blot," *The New York Times,* January 13, 1953, 29; "Broadway Blues," Editorial, *The New York Times,* July 30, 1953, 22; "3 Candidates Urge Times Sq. Clean-Up," *The New York Times,* October 20, 1953, 34; "Cleaning Up Times Square," Editorial, *The New York Times,* November 14, 1953, 16; "Curb on Arcades in Times Sq. Voted," *The New York Times,* December 24, 1953, 17; City Planning Commission, *Amendments to the Zoning Resolution* (New York: City Planning Commission, 1954); "Upgrading Times Square," Editorial, *The New York Times,* January 4, 1954, 18; "Times Sq. Clean-Up Believed Assured," *The New York Times,* January 12, 1954, 20; Charles, G. Bennett, "New Honky-Tonks in Times Sq. Barred by Estimate Board Vote," *The New York Times,* January 15, 1954, 1; William M. Farrell, "Honky-Tonks Due for a Slow Death," *The New York Times,* January 22, 1954, 29.

18. Lynne B. Sagalyn, *Times Square Roulette: Remaking the City Icon* (Cambridge: MIT Press, 2001), 45–48; Laurence Selenick, "Private Parts in Public Places," in *Inventing Times Square,* 340–353; William Kornblum and Vernon Boggs, *West 42nd Street: "The Bright Light Zone"* (New York: Graduate School and University Center of New York, 1978), 76; Gail Sheehy, "Cleaning Up Hell's Bedroom," *New York* 5 (November 13, 1972): 55–59; Gail Sheehy, "The Landlords of Hell's Bedroom," *New York* 5 (November 20, 1973): 67–80.
19. David Allen Karp, "Public Sexuality and Hiding Behavior: A Study of Times Square Sexual Community" (PhD diss., New York University, 1971); *State of New York v. Williams,* 55 Misc. 2d 774; 286 N.Y.S.2d 575; 1967 N.Y. (1967); Emanuel Perlmutter, "IRT to Abandon 42nd Street Arcade, Called Breeding Place of Crime," *The New York Times,* January 22, 1964, 39; "City Moves in Fast on IRT Arcade Job," *The New York Times,* January 23, 1964, 33; Sidney E. Zion, "2,300 Seized in Prostitution Drive Here," *The New York Times,* September 26, 1967, 62; Sidney E. Zion, "Loitering Cases Dismissed Here," *The New York Times,* September 27, 1967, 48.
20. *Dominguez v. Beame,* 76 Civ. 1117 (CMM), 1978 U.S. Dist. (1978); *Dominguez v. Beame,* 460, 78-7353, 603 F.2d 337; 1979 U.S. App. (1979); Murray Schumach, "New Police Policy Frees Prostitutes of Roundup Fears," *The New York Times,* April 4, 1976, 1. In 1976, the New York Civil Liberties Union and the Legal Action Center filed a lawsuit in federal court against this practice, but by the time the decisions came out, the city administration had stopped such arrests.
21. John Schlesinger, *Midnight Cowboy* (1969).
22. Kevin Floyd, "Closing the (Heterosexual) Frontier: *Midnight Cowboy* as National Allegory," *Science & Society* 65 (Spring 2001): 99–130.
23. Alan Chartock and Richard Kent, *The Midtown Project: Report Submitted to the New York Police Department, Office of Programs and Policies—Funding, Research and Development Section* (New York: Times Square Law Enforcement Coordinating Committee, May 1974); Charles Grutzner, "Prostitute Pressed by Police," *The New York Times,* March 17, 1971, 51; David A. Adelman, "Some New Tricks for the Oldest Profession," *The New York Times,* March 28, 1971, 3(E).
24. Chartock and Kent, *The Midtown Project,* 14–28; Norman Redlich and Steven L. Isenberg, *First Annual Report, Times Square Law Enforcement Coordinating Committee* (New York: The Committee, 1973), 3–5 and 31; *City of New York v. Goldman,* 78 Misc. 2d 693; 356 N.Y.S.2d 754; 1974 N.Y. (1974).
25. Johnson, *Street Justice* (2003); Commission to Investigate Allegations of Police Corruption and the City's Anti-Corruption Procedures, *Commission Report*

(New York: The Commission, 1972); Vincent J. Cannato, *The Ungovernable City: John Lindsay and His Struggle to Save New York* (New York: Basic Books, 2001); S. James Press, *Some Effects of an Increase in Police Manpower in the 20th Precinct of New York City* (New York: New York City Rand Institute, 1971).
26. *1487 Amusement Corporation v. Redlich*, 72 Civ. 4292, 72 Civ. 4311, 350 F. Supp. 822; 1972 U.S. Dist. (1972); *414 Theatre Corp v. Murphy*, 73 Civ. 22, 360 F. Supp. 34; 1973 U.S. Dist. (1973); *State of New York v. Mitchell*, 74 Misc. 2d 1053; 346 N.Y.S.2d 495; 1973 N.Y. (1973).
27. *Miller v. California*, 70–73, 413 U.S. 15; 93 S. Ct. 2607; 37 L. Ed. 2d 419; 1973 U.S. (1973).
28. Tom Goldstein, "City is Moving with Difficulty to End Times Sq. Pornography," *The New York Times*, November 2, 1975, 46; *New York v. Mature Enterprises*, 76 Misc. 2d 660; 352 N.Y.S.2d 346 (1974); *State of New York v. Mature Enterprises*, 35 N.Y.2d 520; 323 N.E.2d 704; 364 N.Y.S.2d 170; 1974 N.Y. (1974).
29. *Young v. American Mini Theatres*, 75–312, 427 U.S. 50; 96 S. Ct. 2440; 49 L. Ed. 2d 310; 1976 U.S. (1976).
30. "Ripley's Wax Museum Here Closes," *The New York Times*, January 9, 1972, 51.
31. Isadore Barmash, "Manhattan Retailing Vibrant Despite Loss of Stern's," *The New York Times*, April 3, 1969, 59; Jill Gerston, "Woolworth Leaving Times Square Area," *The New York Times*, December 7, 1974, 33.
32. "Politicians and Porn," *Economist*, April 2, 1977, 59.
33. *State of New York v. Smith*, 88 Misc. 2d 590; 388 N.Y.S.2d 221; 1976 N.Y. (1976); *State of New York v. Smith*, 44 N.Y.2d 613; 378 N.E.2d 1032; 407 N.Y.S.2d 462; 1978 N.Y. (1978); Murray Schumach, "Major Drive on Illicit Sex Is Being Drafted by City," *The New York Times*, September 1, 1975, 1; Nathaniel Sheppard, Jr., "Beame and Broadway Cast Call for Eradication of 'Porno Plague,'" *The New York Times*, April 29, 1976, 43; Steven R. Weisman, "Senate in Albany Votes a Loitering Bill Aimed at Curbing Rise in Prostitution," *The New York Times*, May 20, 1976, 40; Ronald Smothers, "Prostitution Loitering Bill Passes Albany Legislature," *The New York Times*, June 11, 1976, 24; Selenick, "Private Parts," 329–353; Office of the Mayor, *Midtown Enforcement Project: Report of Operations, January 19, 1976 through December 8, 1976* (New York: The Office, 1976).
34. Alexander Reichl, *Reconstructing Times Square: Politics and Culture in Urban Development* (Lawrence: University Press of Kansas, 1999), 59.
35. Paul Goldberger, "Manhattan Plaza: Quality Housing to Upgrade 42d St.," *The New York Times*, August 19, 1974, 27.
36. Joseph P. Fried, "Manhattan Plaza is Focus of Dispute for High Stakes," *The New York Times*, August 20, 1975, 41; Robert Schur, "Manhattan Plaza: Old Style Ripoffs Are Alive and Well," in *Critical Perspectives on Housing*, eds. Rachel G. Bratt, Chester Hartman, and Ann Meyerson (Philadelphia: Temple University Press, 1986), 277–291; Joseph P. Fried, "Manhattan Plaza Wins Approval As Housing for Performing Artists," *The New York Times*, February 4, 1977, 37; Joseph P. Fried, "Deficiencies at Manhattan Plaza in Choice of Tenants is Charged," *The New York Times*, July 5, 1978, 6(B); Irvin Molotsky, "Manhattan Plaza is Criticized by U.S.," *The New York Times*, August 31, 1980, 30.
37. Lou Stoumen, *Times Square: 45 Years of Photography* (New York: Aperture, 1985), 15.
38. *Lloyd v. Tanner*, 71–492, 407 U.S. 551; 92 S. Ct. 2219; 33 L. Ed. 2d 131; 1972 U.S. (1972); Stern at al., *New York 1960*, 448–451; John Portman and

Jonathan Barnett, *The Architect as Developer* (New York: McGraw-Hill, 1976); Open Space Institute, *Times Square South: Pre-Development Analysis* (New York: KBS Associates, 1981).
39. John Portman and Scott Gilchrist, *Marriott Marquis Hotel* (Toronto: Archivision, 1994); Gregory F. Gilmartin, *Shaping the City: New York and the Municipal Art Society* (New York: Clarkson Potter, 1995), 446–449.
40. The City at 42nd Street, Inc., *The City at 42nd Street: A Proposal for the Restoration and Redevelopment of 42nd Street* (New York: The City at 42nd Street, Inc., 1980); Paul Goldberger, "A New Plan for West 42nd Street," *The New York Times,* January 31, 1979, 1(B); Department of City Planning, *42nd Street Development Project: A Discussion Document* (New York: Department of City Planning, 1981); Reichl, *Reconstructing Times Square,* 77–113.
41. New York State Urban Development Corporation, *42nd Street Development Project: Draft Environmental Impact Statement* (New York: The Corporation, 1984), 8.
42. Ibid., 92.
43. Ibid.
44. Jim Sleeper, "Boom and Bust with Ed Koch," *Dissent* 34 (Fall 1987): 441.
45. Herbert J. Gans, "The 42nd Street Development Project Draft EIS: An Assessment," Report prepared for the New York City Board of Estimate (1984).
46. Ibid.
47. Brendan Gill, "Disneyitis," *The New Yorker,* April 29, 1991, 97; Sharon Zukin, *The Culture of Cities* (Cambridge: Blackwell, 1995), 222; Michael Sorkin, ed., *Variations on a Theme Park: The New American City and the End of Public Space* (New York: Hill & Wang, 1992).
48. Reichl, *Reconstructing Times Square,* 98–103; *Rosenthal & Rosenthal Inc. v. The New York State Urban Development Corporation,* 605 F. Supp. 612; 1985 U.S. Dist. (1985); *Rosenthal & Rosenthal Inc. v. The New York State Urban Development Corporation,* 771 F.2d 44; 1985 U.S. App. (1985).
49. Task Force on the Regulation of Sex-Related Businesses, *Sex-Related Businesses in Manhattan: A Report to Manhattan Borough President Ruth W. Messinger* (New York: The Task Force, August 1994); Herald Price Fahringer, "Zoning Out Free Expression: An Analysis of New York City's Adult Zoning Resolution," *Buffalo Law Review* 46 (Spring 1998): 403–431.

NOTES TO CHAPTER 4

1. David Harvey, *A Brief History of Neoliberalism* (New York: Oxford University Press, 2005); Anne Norton, *Leo Strauss and the Politics of American Empire* (New Haven: Yale University Press, 2004); Wendy Brown, "American Nightmare: Neoliberalism, Neoconservatism, and De-Democratization," *Political Theory* 34 (December 2006): 690–714; Jason Hackworth, *The Neoliberal City: Governance, Ideology, and Development in American Urbanism* (Ithaca: Cornell University Press, 2007).
2. David Plotke, *Building a Democratic Political Order* (1996); Robert O. Self, *American Babylon, Race and Struggle for Postwar Oakland* (Princeton: Princeton University Press, 2003); Lankevich, *New York City,* 181–204.
3. Michael W. Flamm, *Law and Order: Street Crime, Civil Unrest, and the Crisis of Liberalism in the 1960s* (New York: Columbia University Press, 2005).
4. Milton Friedman and Rose Friedman, *Free to Choose: A Personal Statement* (San Diego: Harcourt Brace Jovanovich, 1979), 28–30.
5. Harvey, *A Brief History of Neoliberalism,* 31.

6. F. A. Hayek, *The Road to Serfdom* (Chicago: University of Chicago Press, 1944); F. A. Hayek, *The Constitution of Liberty* (Chicago: University of Chicago Press, 1960); Milton Friedman, *Capitalism and Freedom* (Chicago: University of Chicago Press, 1962), 2; John Gerard Ruggie, "International Regimes, Transactions, and Change: Embedded Liberalism in the Postwar Economic Order," *International Organization* 36 (1982): 379–415; Gérard Duménil and Dominique Lévy, *Capital Resurgent: Roots of the Neoliberal Revolution*, trans. by Derek Jeffers (Cambridge: Harvard University Press, 2004); Paul Krugman, "Gilded Once More," *The New York Times*, April 27, 2007, 27; Louis Uchitelle, "The Richest of the Rich, Proud of a New Gilded Age, *The New York Times*, July 15, 2007.
7. Freeman, *Working-Class New York*, 258.
8. Freeman, *Working-Class New York*, 2000; William K. Tabb, *The Long Default: New York City and the Urban Fiscal Crisis* (New York: Monthly Review Press, 1982); Martin Shefter, *Political Crisis/Fiscal Crisis: The Collapse and Revival of New York City* (New York: Columbia University Press, 1992).
9. Glenn Flower, "Koch Favors Test of Trash Pickups by Private Carter," *The New York Times*, March 4, 1978, 46.
10. Charles Brecher and Raymond D. Horton, eds., *Setting Municipal Priorities, 1981* (Montclair, NJ: Allanheld, Osmun, 1980); Citizens Budget Commission, *The State of Municipal Services, 1983* (New York: Citizens Budget Commission, 1984); John H. Mollenkopf, *A Phoenix in the Ashes: The Rise and Fall of the Koch Coalition in New York City Politics* (Princeton: Princeton University Press, 1994).
11. Brecher and Horton, *Setting Municipal Priorities, 1981*, 2.
12. Terry Jean Rosenberg, Community Service Society of New York, *Poverty in New York City 1980–1985* (New York: The Society, 1987); John H. Mollenkopf and Manuel Castells, *Dual City: Restructuring New York* (New York: Russell Sage Foundation, 1991), 11; Roger Sanjek, *The Future of Us All: Race and Neighborhood Politics in New York City* (Ithaca: Cornell University Press, 1998), 119–184.
13. Partnership for New York City, "History," Partnership for New York City, http://www.nycp.org/history.html (accessed May 31, 2010).
14. Miriam Greenberg, *Branding New York: How a City in Crisis Was Sold to the World* (New York: Routledge, 1998).
15. Sanjek, *The Future of Us All*, 119–184; J. Phillip Thompson III, *Double Trouble: Black Mayors, Black Communities, and the Call for a Deep Democracy* (New York: Oxford University Press, 2006), 198–202.
16. Fiscal Policy Institute, *The State of Working New York 2003: Unbalanced Regional Economies through Expansion and Recession* (New York: The Institute, 2003); Sam Roberts, "In Manhattan, Poor Make 2¢ for Each Dollar to the Rich," *The New York Times*, September 4, 2005, 33; Sanjek, *The Future of Us All*, 176–180.
17. Irving Kristol, "The Neoconservative Persuasion," *The Weekly Standard*, August 25, 2003.
18. Edward C. Banfield, *The Unheavenly City Revisited* (New York: Little, Brown & Company, 1974), 25–51.
19. Banfield, *The Unheavenly City Revisited*, 53.
20. Oscar Lewis, "The Culture of Poverty," *Scientific American* 215 (October 1966): 19–25; Oscar Lewis, *The Children of Sanchez: Autobiography of a Mexican Family* (New York: Random House, 1961); Oscar Lewis, *La Vida: A Puerto Rican Family in the Culture of Poverty—San Juan and New York* (New York: Secker and Warburg, 1965).

21. Banfield, *The Unheavenly City Revisited*, 72.
22. James Q. Wilson, "What Makes a Better Policeman," *The Atlantic* (March 1969): 129–135.
23. Flamm, *Law and Order*, 46 and 51–66; James Q. Wilson, *Thinking About Crime* (New York: Basic Books, 1975); James Q. Wilson and Barbara Boland, "The Effect of the Police on Crime," *Law and Society Review* 12 (1978): 367–390; James Q. Wilson and Barbara Boland, "The Effect of the Police on Crime: A Response to Jacob and Rich," *Law and Society Review* 16 (1981): 163–169.
24. "The American Underclass," *Time*, August 29, 1977, 14 and 15; Ken Auletta, *The Underclass* (New York: Random House, 1982); June Axinn and Marc J. Stern, *Dependency and Poverty: Old Problems in a New World* (Lexington, MA: Lexington Books, 1988); William Julius Wilson, *The Declining Significance of Race: Blacks and Changing American Institutions* (Chicago: University of Chicago Press, 1978); Ken Auletta, "Saving the Underclass," *Washington Monthly* 17 (September 1985): 12; Nicholas Lemman, "The Origins of the Underclass," *The Atlantic* 258 (July 1986): 54; William Julius Wilson, *The Truly Disadvantaged: The Inner City, the Underclass, and Public Policy* (Chicago: University of Chicago Press, 1987); Mortimer B. Zuckerman, "The Black Underclass," *US News & World Report*, April 14, 1986, 78; Stephen Steinberg, *Turning Back: The Retreat from Racial Justice in American Thought and Policy* (Boston: Beacon Press, 1995).
25. Wilson and Kelling, "The Police and Neighborhood Safety," 29–37 and 33.

NOTES TO CHAPTER 5

1. Beatriz Colomina, "The Split Wall: Domestic Voyeurism," in *Sexuality and Space*, ed. Beatriz Colomina (New York: Princeton Architectural Press, 1992), 75n.
2. Jilian Mincer. "Is the Transit Authority Winning the War on Grime?" *The New York Times*, November 24, 1985, sec. 4, p. 24.
3. William E. Geist, "In Bronx, Commuters Learn ABC's of IRT," *The New York Times*, March 9, 1983, 1(A).
4. Editorial, "Clean and Green: Monumental Signs," *The New York Times*, October 20, 1984, sec. 1, p. 22.
5. Editorial, "The Writing on the Walls," *Chicago Tribune*, March 29, 1985, 22C.
6. "Under the Apple," *Time*, April 8, 1985, 38.
7. Philip Lentz, "Graffiti Cleanup a Shiny Symbol of Subway System's Turnaround," *Chicago Tribune*, May 18, 1989, 6(C); "Underground: Not-So-Stainless Steel," *The New York Times*, June 15, 1985, sec. 1, p. 22; Jilian Mincer, "Is the Transit Authority Winning the War on Grime?" *The New York Times*, November 24, 1985, sec. 4, p. 24; "Paved/Scrubbed: Campaigning on Graffiti," *The New York Times*, October 23, 1986, 26(A); Constance L. Hays, "Transit Agency Says New York Subways are Free of Graffiti," *The New York Times*, May 10, 1989, 1(A); "Free at Last," *The Record*, May 12, 1989, 10(B); Martha A. Miles, "In the Subway, a Measure of Control is Up," *The New York Times*, May 14, 1989, sec. 4, p. 24.
8. Paul Goldberger, "Ode on the R-62A: Subway Car or a Whispering Silver Mirage?" *The New York Times*, July 27, 1985, sec. 1, p. 25.
9. "Cracking Down, Catching Up: Trashed Trucks," *The New York Times*, November 28, 1986, 30(A).
10. Nathan Glazer, "Dying Cultural Outposts," *The New York Times*, February 11, 1989, sec. 1, p. 27.

11. Steven Hager, *The Illustrated History of Breakdancing, Rap Music, and Graffiti* (New York: St. Martin's Press, 1984); Herbert Kohl and James Hinton, *Golden Boy as Anthony Cool: A Photo Essay on Naming and Graffiti* (New York: Dial Press, 1972), 125–168; David Ley and Roman Cybriwsky, "Urban Graffiti as Territorial Markers," *Annals of the Association of American Geographers* 64 (December 1974): 491–505.
12. Ley and Cybriwsky, "Urban Graffiti as Territorial Markers," 491–505.
13. Jack Stewart, "Subway Graffiti: An Aesthetic Study of Graffiti on the Subway System in New York City," (PhD diss., New York University, 1989), 148–150, 156–157; Nelson George et al., *Fresh: Hip Hop Don't Stop* (New York: Random House/Sarah Lazin, 1985), 29; Ira Katznelson, *City Trenches: Urban Politics and the Patterning of Class in the United States* (Chicago: University of Chicago Press, 1981), 84–86; Jonathan Rieder, *Canarsie: The Jews and Italians of Brooklyn against Liberalism* (Cambridge: Harvard University Press, 1985), 171–202; Eric C. Schneider, *Vampires, Dragons, and Egyptian Kings: Youth Gangs in Postwar New York* (Princeton: Princeton University Press, 1999), 78–105 and 188–216; Ley, "Urban Graffiti," 492–494, 501; "Philadelphia, Graffiti Capital of the World," *The New York Times*, June 25, 1971, 31.
14. Stewart, "Subway Graffiti," 163–164. Stewart interviewed TAKI 183 on September 9, 1983.
15. Stewart, "Subway Graffiti," 165; "'Taki 183' Spawns Pen Pals," *The New York Times*, July 21, 1971, 37.
16. Joe Austin, *Taking the Train: How Graffiti Art Became an Urban Crisis in New York City* (New York: Columbia University Press, 2001), 39–40. Austin interviewed IZ the WIZ on August 31, 1993.
17. Stewart, "Subway Graffiti," 230 and 234–235.
18. Craig Castleman, *Getting Up: Subway Graffiti in New York* (Cambridge: MIT Press, 1982), 26–40.
19. Ibid., 29–31.
20. George et al., eds., *Fresh* (1985); Robert Farris Thompson, "Hip-Hop 101," *Rolling Stone*, March 27, 1986, 95; Nelson George, *Buppies, B-Boys, Baps and Bohos: Notes on Post-Soul Black Culture* (New York: Harper Collins, 1992); Tricia Rose, *Black Noise: Rap Music and Black Culture in Contemporary America* (Hanover: University Press of New England, 1994); 34–61; Adam Sexton, ed., *Rap on Rap: Straight-Up Talk on Hip-Hop Culture* (New York: Delta, 1995); William Eric Perkins, *Droppin' Science: Critical Essays on Rap Music and Hip Hop Culture* (Philadelphia: Temple University Press, 1996); Nelson George, *Hip Hop America* (New York: Penguin, 1998).
21. Cannato, *The Ungovernable City* (2001).
22. "Garelik Calls for War on Graffiti," *The New York Times*, May 21, 1972, 66.
23. Christopher Jonas and Allan Weintraub, *Cost of Graffiti to the City of New York: Final Draft Report* (New York: Bureau of the Budget, City of New York, 1973).
24. Laurie Johnston, "For Graffiti, DWR Is a Dirty Symbol," *The New York Times*, April 22, 1972, 35; Frank J. Prial, "Subway Graffiti Here Called Epidemic," *The New York Times*, February 11, 1972, 39; David Freeman, "Slop Art," *The New York Times Magazine*, November 26, 1972, 16; Murray Schumach, "At $10-Million, City Calls It a Losing Graffiti Fight," *The New York Times*, March 28, 1973, 51; Paul Chevigny, *Gigs: Jazz and Cabaret Laws in New York City* (New York: Routledge, 1991); Lawrence W. Levine, *Highbrow/Lowbrow: The Emergence of Cultural Hierarchy in America* (Cambridge: Harvard University Press, 1988); Susie J. Tanenbaum,

Underground Harmonies: Music and Politics in the Subways of New York (Ithaca: Cornell University Press, 1995).
25. Frank J. Prial, "Subway Graffiti Here Called Epidemic," *The New York Times*, February 11, 1972, 39.
26. Sheldon Pitterman, "To Clean the Subway Trains," Letter to the Editor, *The New York Times*, April 5, 1973, 44.
27. Edward Ranzal, "Ronan Backs Lindsay Antigraffiti Plan, Including Cleanup Duty," *The New York Times*, August 29, 1972, 66.
28. Bureau of the Budget, City of New York, *Work Plan—Graffiti Prevention Project* (New York: Bureau of the Budget, City of New York, February 26, 1972), 2.
29. Castleman, *Getting Up*, 144.
30. Norman Mailer, *The Faith of Graffiti* (New York: Praeger, 1974), n. p.
31. Ibid.
32. Alfred E. Clark, "Persistent Graffiti Anger Lindsay on Subway Tour," *The New York Times*, October 11, 1973, 47; James Ryan, "The Great Graffiti Plague," *New York Daily News Sunday Magazine*, May 6, 1973, 33; "Lindsay Assails Graffiti Vandals," *The New York Times*, August 25, 1972, 30.
33. Stan Fischler, "Just Call it Scribble City: Defacing New York has Become a Real Art," *Toronto Star*, October 20, 1972, 39.
34. Paul Seligman, Letter to the Editor, *The New York Times*, September 28, 1972, 46.
35. Blandinia B. Ijams, "The Graffiti Nightmare," Letter to the Editor, *The New York Times*, April 3, 1973, 43.
36. Hager, *The Illustrated History*, 1–11; Edward Levitt, "The Rebirth of the Gangs," *New York Sunday News*, August 20, 1972, 11–18; James M. Markham, "Hunts Point Youths Draw Gang Battle Lines," *The New York Times*, September 2, 1971, 1; Edward Kirkman, "Gangs Hold Rap Session on Cops," *Daily News*, December 17, 1971, 5; Gene Weingarten, "East Bronx Story—Return of the Street Gangs," *New York*, March 27, 1972, 31–37; Martin Tolchin, "Gangs Spread Terror in the South Bronx," *The New York Times*, January 16, 1973, 1; Thomas H. McDonald, Douglas J. Besharov, and Alfred A. Delli Bovi, *Armies of the Streets: A Report on the Structure, Membership and Activities of Youth Gangs in the City of New York* (Albany: Subcommittee on the Family Court, New York State Legislature, 1974); Thomas H. McDonald, José D. Alfaro, Douglas J. Besharov, and Alfred A. Delli Bovi, *The Resurgence of Youth Gangs in New York City* (Albany: Subcommittee on the Family Court, New York State Legislature, 1974); Pierce Brian McManus, "Reemergence of the Youth Gangs as an Alternative to the Use of Narcotics," (master's thesis, John Jay College of Criminal Justice, 1974).
37. Stewart, "Subway Graffiti," 175–178; Castleman, *Getting Up*, 95–107.
38. Rieder, *Canarsie*, 60–61.
39. New York Administrative Code, Section 435–13.2 (1972); Editorial, "Scratch the Graffiti," *The New York Times*, September 16, 1972, 28; "1562 Youths Seized in '72 for Their Graffiti Work," *The New York Times*, January 14, 1973, 39; Carter Horsley, "Graffiti's Foes United by Hope," *The New York Times*, November 26, 1972, sec. 8, p. 1; "Fight Against Subway Graffiti Progresses from Frying Pan to Fire," *The New York Times*, January 26, 1973, 39; Michael T. Kaufman, "Boy Scouts Scrub Graffiti Off Walls of Subway Cars," *The New York Times*, February 26, 1973, 35; Schumach, "At $10-Million," 51.
40. Editorial, "Going to the Dogs," *The New York Times*, August 5, 1974, 22.
41. "Subway Graffiti Campaign Given Lower Priority," *The New York Times*, August 7, 1975, 29; New York State Division of Audits and Accounts, *Audit*

Report on the Productivity of Subway Car Cleaners, Car Maintenance Department, New York City Transit Authority (Albany: New York State, 1975).
42. Castleman, *Getting Up*, 161; Gus Dallas, "Critic-Cops Go Underground to Catch a Running Art Show," *Daily News*, November 20, 1977, 10; Castleman, *Getting Up*, 161–174; New York City Transit Authority, *Graffiti and Vandalism on the New York City System* (New York: New York City Transit Authority, November 1980); New York Transportation Authority, *Specifications—Car Maintenance Division—Cleaning Compounds* (New York: The Transportation Authority, April 12, 1976); "Fume Fear Halts Graffiti Work," *The New York Times*, November 1, 1977, 64; Patrick W. Sullivan, "Anti-Graffiti Chemical Called Health Hazard," *New York Post*, November 24, 1977.
43. Joseph B. Treaster, "Blackout Arrests Swamp City's Criminal-Justice System," *The New York Times*, July 15, 1977, 3; Selwyn Raab, "Ravage Continues Far Into Day; Gunfire and Bottles Beset Police," *The New York Times*, July 15, 1977, 42.
44. "The American Underclass," *Time*, August 29, 1977, 14.
45. Ibid., 15.
46. Auletta, *The Underclass*, xvi.
47. Charles Murray, *Losing Ground: American Social Policy, 1950–1980* (New York: Basic Books, 1981); Lawrence Mead, *Beyond Entitlement: The Social Obligations of Citizenship* (New York: Free Press, 1986).
48. Nathan Glazer, "On Subway Graffiti in New York," *The Public Interest* 54 (Winter 1979): 4.
49. Caryl S. Stern and Robert W. Stock, "Graffiti: The Plague Years," *The New York Times*, October 19, 1980, sec. 6, p. 44.
50. Rita Sherman, "Ex-Straphanger," Letter to the Editor, *The New York Times*, October 29, 1980, 30(A).
51. Editorial, "Graffiti: Symbol and Challenge," *New York Post*, October 25, 1980, 8.
52. Ari L. Goldman, "City to use Barbed Wire in Graffiti War," *The New York Times*, December 15, 1981, 1(B).
53. "About New York: Notes from City's Blighted Underground Railway," *The New York Times*, March 11, 1981, 1(B).
54. Joseph P. Fried, "Drive on Subway Vandals is Widened," *The New York Times*, August 13, 1982, 3(B).
55. Ari L. Goldman, "In Spite of Dip, Subway Crime Nears a Record," *The New York Times*, November 20, 1982, 1.
56. "Police Effectiveness: The Three Views of Three Experts," *The New York Times*, December 15, 1982, 1(B).
57. Richard Cohen, "Ivy League Graffiti," *The Washington Post Magazine*, December 13, 1987, 13(W).
58. Atlanta and Alexander, "Wild Style: Graffiti Painting," in *Zoot Suits and Second-Hand Dressers: An Anthology of Fashion and Music*, ed. Angela McRobbie (Boston: Unwin Hyman, 1988), 161.
59. Daniel Seligman, "The Call of the Wild," *Fortune*, October 6, 1980, 37.
60. "City Hoping for Private Operation of Parks," *The New York Times*, October 15, 1980, 5(B).
61. Schneider, *Vampires, Dragons, and Egyptian Kings*, 3–26; "Koch Criticizes Party Policies," *The New York Times*, February 17, 1982, sec. 1, p. 34; Gay Talese, "Ed Koch on His Honor," *The New York Times*, February 12, 1984, sec. 7, p. 1.
62. Miriam Greenberg, *Branding New York: How a City in Crisis Was Sold to the World* (New York: Routledge, 2008), 193–224; Molly Ivins, "John

Dyson, the Gadfly of Carey's Administration," *The New York Times*, April 2, 1977, 24; Consumer Behavior, Inc., *A Study of the New York State Vacation Market. Prepared for the Department of Commerce, State of New York* (New York: Consumer Behavior, 1977); Yankelovich, Skelly and White, Inc., *Research to Support New York State's Economic Development Activities. Prepared for the Department of Commerce, State of New York* (New York: Yankelovich, Skelly and White, 1977–1980). In 1994, Dyson became Rudy Giuliani's Deputy Mayor for Finance and Economic Development.
63. Katznelson, *City Trenches*, 1.
64. These assumptions were premature, given that some graffiti artists, most notably Keith Haring and Jean-Michel Basquiat, entered the mainstream art world in the 1980s and hip-hop became one of the most profitable popular forms of music in the world.
65. Katherine Foran, "TA Tells Disney Clean Up Your Act; A Mickey Mouse Subway Display," *Newsday*, November 24, 1989, 8; "The Worm and the Apple: Transitions; Graffiti Memory," *The New York Times*, November 27, 1989, 18(A); "Gunn Smoke; Flawed Disney Production?" *Newsday*, November 28, 1989, 58. The NYCTA is responsible for public transportation matters within New York City. It is under the Metropolitan Transportation Authority (MTA), which is a state-run agency and is responsible for transportation matters in the entire metropolitan New York region.
66. Glenn Fowler, "Koch Favors Test of Trash Pickups by Private Carter," *The New York Times*, March 4, 1978, 9; United States National Transportation Safety Board, *Special Investigation Report: New York City Transit Authority Subway System Fires* (Washington, DC: National Transportation Safety Board, 1985); Metropolitan Transportation Authority, Office of the Inspector General, *A Review of New York City Transit Authority Efforts to Reduce Subway Car Fires* (New York: MTA, 1987); Metropolitan Transportation Authority, Office of the Inspector General, *Investigation Into the New York City Transit Authority's Management of Unsafe Train Door Openings* (New York: MTA, 1987); Metropolitan Transportation Authority, Office of the Inspector General, *A Review of New York City Transit Authority Subway Service and Performance, 1984–1989* (New York: MTA, 1990).
67. Mollenkopf, *A Phoenix in the Ashes* (1992); Jack Newfield and Wayne Barrett, *City for Sale: Ed Koch and the Betrayal of New York* (New York: Harper & Row, 1989); Arthur Browne, Dan Collins, and Michael Goodwin, *I, Koch: A Decidedly Unauthorized Biography of the Mayor of New York City, Edward I. Koch* (New York: Dodd, 1985); Mollenkopf, *A Phoenix in the Ashes*, 3–22; Paul Peterson, *City Limits* (Chicago: University of Chicago Press, 1981); Charles Morris, *The Cost of Good Intentions* (New York: W. W. Norton, 1980); Murray, *Losing Ground* (1994); Mead, *Beyond Entitlement* (1986); Lawrence M. Mead, *The New Politics of Poverty: The Nonworking Poor in America* (New York: Basic Books, 1992).
68. State of New York, *Division of Criminal Justice Services, Division of Criminal Justice Services Evaluation of the New York City Transit Authority Police* (Albany: Division of Criminal Justice Services, 1979); Wolfgang Saxon, "Use of City Police on Subways Urged," *The New York Times*, January 4, 1982, 1(A); Editorial, "More Transit Police Aren't Enough," *The New York Times*, January 30, 1982, sec. 1, p. 22; Ari L. Goldman, "Police Resume Night Patrols on Subway Trains Tonight," *The New York Times*, April 19, 1982, 1(B).
69. Ari L. Goldman, "Dogs to Patrol Subway Yards," *The New York Times*, September 15, 1981, 1(A); Ari L. Goldman, "City to Use Pits of Barbed Wire in Graffiti War," *The New York Times*, December 15, 1981, 1(B); Leslie Bennetts, "Celebrities Join Mayor in New Battle Against Graffiti Writers,"

The New York Times, April 30, 1982, 1(B); Clyde Haberman, "City to Set Up Island Work Camps to Punish 'Low Level' Offenders," *The New York Times*, May 13, 1982, 1(A); E. R. Shipp, "Koch Says Judges Refuse to Send Minor Criminals to Work Camps," *The New York Times*, October 6, 1982, 1(A); Kevin Flynn, "Writing's on Wall for Graffiti Writers; Koch: I'll Sue their Parents," *Newsday*, August 1, 1989, 6; Rebecca Blumenstein, "LIE Pickets Cry Koch Whitewash," *Newsday*, August 3, 1989, 42.

70. Harrison J. Goldin, *Audit Report on the New York City Transit Authority Police Criminal Background Checks on Persons Apprehended and Issued Notices of Violations* (New York: City of New York, Office of the Comptroller, Bureau of Management Audit, 1987); *Rodriguez v. Morgenthau*, 121 Misc. 2d 694, 468 N.Y.S.2d 833, N.Y. (1983); *In the Matter of a Grand Jury of New York County*, 125 Misc. 2d 918, 480 N.Y.S.2d 998, N.Y. (1984); "$1.7M Deal in Subway Death: TA to Pay Family in Graffiti Artist's Death," *Newsday*, August 29, 1990, 17; Robert D. McFadden, "Black Man Dies After Beating by Whites in Queens," *The New York Times*, December 21, 1986, sec. 1, p. 1; Jane Gross, "A Priest Censures Racism as Sin, Howard Beach Deals with Attack," *The New York Times*, December 22, 1986, 1(A); Margot Hornblower, "N.Y. Marchers Protest Racial Attack: Hundreds Gather in Neighborhood Where Black Died in Chase," *The Washington Post*, December 28, 1986, 1(A); Joyce Purnick, "Ward Declares Goetz Didn't Shoot in Self-Defense," *The New York Times*, February 22, 1985, 1(A); Elizabeth Mehren, "Public's Rage Continues Over Goetz Case," *The New York Times*, September 25, 1986, part 5, p. 1.

71. Metropolitan Transportation Authority, *Strategic Plan, 1985–1989* (New York: MTA, 1984); Constance L. Hays, "Transit Agency Says New York Subways Are Free of Graffiti," *The New York Times*, May 10, 1989, 1(A); Office of the State Comptroller, Division of Audits and Accounts, *New York City Transit Authority: Staffing and Productivity of Subway Station Cleaners* (Albany: Office of the State Comptroller, 1986).

72. Maurice Carroll, "Focus on Quality of City Life," *Newsday*, February 26, 1989, 4.

73. "Koch: Beggars are Bums, So Ignore Them," *The Record*, August 11, 1988, 3(A).

74. Jim Dwyer, "Safety: What Feds Ought to Know," *Newsday*, April 25, 1989, 6.

75. Metropolitan Transportation Authority, Office of the Inspector General, *An Investigation into the History, Usage and Performance of the Coney Island Car Wash* (New York: MTA, 1988); Kirk Johnson, "Report Faults $26 Million Subway Car Wash," *The New York Times*, November 2, 1988, 1(B); Jim Dwyer, "Graffiti-Free Era Comes at a Cost," *Newsday*, May 11, 1989, 6.

76. George L. Kelling, "Reclaiming the Subway," *The City Journal* 1 (Winter 1991): 17–28; George L. Kelling, Robert Wasserman, and Maryalice Sloan-Howitt, *A Strategic Perspective on Policing the New York City Subway* (Boston: St. Germain Group, 1988); George Kelling and Catherine Coles, *Fixing Broken Windows: Restoring Order and Reducing Crime in Our Communities* (New York: Free Press, 1998), 199–256; William J. Bratton with Peter Knobler, *Turnaround: How America's Top Cop Reversed the Crime Epidemic* (New York: Random House, 1998).

77. Stephanie Strom, "Subway Graffiti Back and Bothersome," *The New York Times*, February 11, 1991, 1(B); Dennis Duggan, "A New War on 'Scratchiti,'" *Newsday*, April 6, 1995, 15(A); Lisa Rein, et al., "A Real Pain in the Glass: Vandals Marring Trains' Windows with 'Scratchiti,'" *Daily News*, May 6, 1996, 8.

NOTES TO CHAPTER 6

1. Richard Levine, "Koch Acts Like Himself, and Voters Are Tired of It," *The New York Times,* June 25, 1989, 5(E).
2. Council for Public Safety, *Welcome to Fear City* (New York: The Council, 1975); Glenn Fowler, "Police and Firemen Take Job Campaign to Street," *The New York Times,* June 20, 1975, 43; Charles Brecher and Raymond D. Horton, "Retrenchment and Recovery: American Cities and the New York Experience," *Public Administration Review* 45 (March–April 1985): 267–274.
3. Dennis C. Smith, "Police," in *Setting Municipal Priorities, 1984,* 380–414; Joyce Purnick, "New York Intends to Expand Police to Full Strength," *The New York Times,* April 30, 1987, 1(A); New York City Office of Management of Budget, *Budget, Fiscal Year 1988–1989* (New York: The Office, 1988).
4. Arthur Pawlowski, "New York State Drug Control Policy During the Rockefeller Administration, 1959–1973," (PhD thesis, State University of New York, Albany, 1984).
5. Lynn Zimmer, *Operation Pressure Point: The Disruption of Street-Level Drug Trade on New York's Lower East Side* (New York: Center for Research in Crime and Justice, New York University School of Law, 1987).
6. Maurice Carroll, "Scarcity in Issues Is Found in Poll on the Primary for Mayor," *The New York Times,* August 25, 1977, 1; "Excerpts from the Debate among Democrats Seeking the Nomination for Mayor," *The New York Times,* September 2, 1977, 20; Raymond D. Horton and Mary McCormick, "Services," in *Setting Municipal Priorities, 1981,* 85–112; Brecher and Horton, eds., *Setting Municipal Priorities: American Cities and the New York Experience,* 43–328.
7. Bernadette A. Fiore and Martha F. Schiff, *Operation Pressure Point, 1/19/84–2/18/84: Final Report on Arrest Characteristics and Criminal Court Outcomes* (New York: Criminal Justice Agency, 1984); Zimmer, *Operation Pressure Point,* 6; Jesus Rangel, "Police Laud East Side Drug Drive," *The New York Times,* April 23, 1985, 3(B); Citizens Crime Commission of New York City, *Dealing with the New York Drug Crime Crisis: A Need for a Comprehensive Plan* (New York: The Commission, 1988).
8. Craig Reinarman and Harry G. Levine, "The Crack Attack: Politics and Media in the Crack Scare," in *Crack in America: Demon Drugs and Social Justice* (Berkeley: University of California Press, 1997), 18–20; Peter Kerr, "City is Setting Up New Drug Squad," *The New York Times,* May 22, 1989, 1(A).
9. Steven Belenko and Jeffrey Fagan, *Crack and the Criminal Justice System* (New York: Criminal Justice Agency, 1987); Freda F. Solomon, *1987 Narcotics Division Arrests: Arrestee Characteristics and Criminal Court Case Processing* (New York: Criminal Justice Agency, 1988); Todd S. Purdum, "New York Police Now Seizing Cars in Arrests for Possession of Crack," *The New York Times,* August 5, 1986, 1(A); Todd S. Purdum, "Police Searching for Crack Pipes Raid Hundreds of Stores in City," *The New York Times,* August 22, 1986, 1(A); Peter Kerr, "War on Drugs Shifting Focus to Street Deals," *The New York Times,* April 13, 1987, 1(A); Michel Marriott, "After 3 Years, Crack Plague in New York Only Gets Worse," *The New York Times,* February 20, 1989, 1(A).
10. Henry H. Brownstein, *Drugs and Homicide in New York State* (Albany: New York State Division of Criminal Justice Services, 1988); United States Congress, Committee on Labor and Human Resources, *Children of Substance Abusers: Hearing before the Subcommittee on Children, Families,*

Drugs and Alcoholism of the Committee on Labor and Human Resources (United States Senate, One Hundred First Congress, 1989); Douglas Young, Mark Usdane, Timothy Ireland, and Christopher Gerard, *Alcohol, Drugs and Crime: Vera's Third Interim Report on New York State's Interagency Initiative* (New York: Vera Institute of Justice, 1989); Office of the Mayor, *Annual Management Report on the Quality of City Services* (New York: The Office, 1989); Michel Marriott, "Increase in Drugs Impinges on City Services, Koch Says," *The New York Times,* September 16, 1988, 3(B).

11. Martin Tolchin, "South Bronx: A Jungle Stalked by Fear, Seized by Rage," *The New York Times,* January 15, 1973, 1.
12. Courtland Milloy and Samuel Allis, "In Harlem and South Bronx: Visiting the Oft-Forgotten," *The Washington Post,* October 3, 1979, 1(A).
13. Clyde Haberman, "Japanese Told to Love New York, Cautiously," *The New York Times,* August 27, 1987, 24(B).
14. Bill Moyers, *CBS Reports: The Fire Next Door* (New York: CBS, March 22, 1977); Helen Whitney, *ABC News Close Up. Youth Terror: The View from Behind the Gun* (New York: ABC, June 28, 1978); Ari L. Goldman, "Census-Counters Try Tram Effort in Part of Bronx," *The New York Times,* August 21, 1980, 3(B).
15. City of New York, *Summary: The South Bronx: A Plan for Revitalization* (New York: The City, 1977), 2; Bureau of the Census, *Census of Population and Housing (1980): Census Tracts* (Washington, DC: U.S. Dept. of Commerce, 1983–1984).
16. Robert McFadden, "Derelict Tenements in the Bronx to Get Fake Lived-In Look," *The New York Times,* November 7, 1983, 1(A).
17. "Putting a Happy Face on the Bronx," *The New York Times,* November 13, 1983, sec. 4, p. 6; Jack Eisen, "Plastic Urban Renewal," *The Washington Post,* November 13, 1983, 2(B).
18. William E. Geist, "Residents Give a Bronx Cheer to Decal Plan," *The New York Times,* November 12, 1983, sec. 1, p. 1.
19. Editorial, "Fake Blinds Can't Hide Blight," *The New York Times,* November 14, 1983, 18(A).
20. Eugene Shapiro, "Decals to the Rescue," Letter to the Editor, *The New York Times,* November 14, 1983, 18(A); Ruben Klein, "No More Make-Believe," Letter to the Editor, *The New York Times,* November 19, 1983, sec. 1, p. 24; Edward Planner, "Peel Off, Put Decal of Headline Here," *The New York Times,* December 11, 1983, 11(WC); Edward I. Koch, "Of Decals and Priorities for the South Bronx," Letter to the Editor, *The New York Times,* November 19, 1983, sec. 1, p. 24.
21. Jim Rooney, *Organizing the South Bronx* (Albany: State University of New York Press, 1995); Robert Worth, "Guess Who Saved the South Bronx? Big Government," *Washington Monthly* 31 (April 1999): 26–34; Jill Jonnes, *South Bronx Rising: The Rise, Fall, and Resurrection of an American City* (Bronx: Fordham University Press, 2002); Edward Koch, *Ten Year Housing Plan: Fiscal Years 1989–1998* (New York: Department of Housing Preservation and Development, 1989); Emily Rosenbaum and Paul Schimek, *New Affordable Housing for New Yorkers: An Initial Look at Households Receiving Apartments under New York City's Ten Year Plan* (New York: Department of Housing Preservation and Development, 1989).
22. Neil Smith, "New City, New Frontier: The Lower East as Wild, Wild West," in *Variation on a Theme Park,* 61–62; Michael Wines, "Behind the Park Melee, a New Generation Gap," *The New York Times,* August 8, 1988, 2(B).
23. George James, "Ward is Critical of Police in Clash," *The New York Times,* August 11, 1988, 1(A); Todd S. Purdum, "Ward Releases Report, Calling

Force's Actions 'Not Well Executed,'" *The New York Times*, August 25, 1988, 1(A); David E. Pitt, "PBA Leader Assails Report on Tompkins Square Melee," *The New York Times*, April 21, 1989, 1; Leslie Gevirtz, "Slam Dancer at NYPD," *Village Voice*, September 6, 1988.
24. Karen Schmelzkopf, "Urban Community Gardens as Contested Space," *Geographical Review* 85 (July 1995): 364–381.
25. Malve Von Hassell, *Homesteading in New York City, 1978-1993: The Divided Heart of the Loisada* (Westport, CT: Bergin and Garvey, 1996).
26. Andrew Van Kluenen, "The Squatters: A Chorus of Voices . . . But Is Anyone Listening?" in *From Urban Village to East Village: The Battle for New York's Lower East Side,* ed. Janet L. Abu-Lughod et al. (Cambridge: Blackwell, 1994), 285–312.
27. Christopher Mele, "The Process of Gentrification in Alphabet City," in *From Urban Village to East Village,* 169–184.
28. Sydney H. Schanberg, "Gentrifiers: The Greed," *The New York Times,* May 8, 1982, 23; Community Council of Greater New York, *The Homeless and Single Room Occupants: Three Studies Illuminating the Situation in New York City* (New York: The Council, 1982); Office of the Comptroller, *Soldiers of Misfortune: Homeless Veterans in New York City* (New York: City of New York, 1982); Office of Mental Health, *Who Are the Homeless? A Study of Randomly Selected Men Who Use the New York City Shelters* (Albany: State of New York, 1982); Coalition for the Homeless, *Crowded Out: Homelessness and the Elderly Poor in New York City* (New York: The Coalition, 1984); Sydney H. Schanberg, "Trashing Old People (1)," *The New York Times,* November 28, 1981, 23; Sydney H. Schanberg, "Gentrifiers: The Policy," *The New York Times,* May 22, 1982, 27.
29. *Callahan v. Carey,* Supreme Ct, NY County, Index No. 42582/79, (1979); *Eldredge v. Koch,* 118 Misc. 2d 163; 459 N.Y.S.2d 960; 1983 N.Y. (1983); *McCain v. Koch,* 127 Misc. 2d 23; 484 N.Y.S.2d 985; 1984 N.Y. (1984); Donna Wilson Kirchheimer, "Sheltering the Homeless in New York City: Expansion in an Era of Government Contraction," *Political Science Quarterly* 104 (1989–1990): 607–623.
30. J. Phillip Thompson, "The Failure of Liberal Homeless Policy in the Koch and Dinkins Administration," *Political Science Quarterly* 111 (2001): 639–660; *McCain v. Koch,* 70 N.Y.2d 109; 511 N.E.2d 62; 517 N.Y.S.2d 918; 1987 N.Y. (1987); Taskforce on Housing for Homeless Families, *A Shelter is not a Home* (New York: Manhattan Borough President's Office, 1987); *McCain v. Koch,* 136 A.D.2d 473; 523 N.Y.S.2d 112; 1988 N.Y. App. Div. (1988); Office of the Comptroller, *An Analysis of the Department of Housing Preservation and Development: Renovation of Apartments for the Homeless* (New York: City of New York, 1988).
31. Carolyn A. Eldred and Richard I. Towber, *A One-Day "Snapshot" of Homeless Families at the Forbell Street Shelter and Martinique Hotel* (New York: Human Resources Administration, Office of Program Evaluation, 1986); Dennis Hevesi, "City Traces Origins of Homelessness," *The New York Times,* June 21, 1986, 30; Emanuel Tobier, "The Homeless," in *Setting Municipal Priorities, 1990,* 307–338; Marybeth Shinn and Colleen Gillespie, "The Roles of Housing and Poverty in the Origins of Homelessness," *American Behavioral Scientist* 37 (February 1994): 505–521.
32. Smith, "New City, New Frontier," 81.
33. William Sites, "Public Action: New York City Policy and the Gentrification of the Lower East Side," in *From Urban Village to East Village,* 200.
34. Ronald Lawson, "Tenant Responses to the Urban Housing Crisis, 1970–1984," in *The Tenant Movement in New York City, 1904–1984,* ed. Ronald

Lawson and Mark Naison (New Brunswick: Rutgers University Press, 1986), 241; Sites, "Public Action," 201.
35. Rosalyn Deutsche and Cara Gendel Ryan, "The Fine Art of Gentrification," *October* 13 (Winter 1984): 104; Smith, "New City, New Frontier," 78.
36. James Barron, "Thousands March Against Homelessness," *The New York Times*, December 21, 1987, 3(B); Dorine Greshof and John Dale, "The Residents in Tompkins Square Park," in *From Urban Village to East Village*, 268–270.
37. Jane Gross, "A Fist Look at Homeless is Raw Sight for Tourists," *The New York Times*, November 9, 1987, 1(B).
38. *State of New York v. Clark*, 135 Misc. 2d 22; 515 N.Y.S.2d 382; 1987 N.Y. (1987); Richard Levine, "24 Arrests at Grand Central Criticized," *The New York Times*, March 14, 1987, 31; *State of New York v. Bright; State of New York v. Clark*, 71 N.Y.2d 376; 520 N.E.2d 1355; 526 N.Y.S.2d 66; 1988 N.Y. (1988); Association of the Bar of the City of New York, *Report of the Committee on Legal Problems of the Homeless* (New York: The Association, 1988); Marsha A. Martin, *A Report to the New York City Transit Authority* (Brooklyn: New York City Transit Authority, 1989); Michael Freitag, "For the Homeless, Public Spaces Are Growing Smaller," *The New York Times*, October 1, 1989, 5(E).
39. Newfield and Barrett, *City for Sale*, (1989); Mollenkopf, *A Phoenix in the Ashes*, 1992; J. Phillip Thompson III, *Double Trouble*, 188–198; Wilbur C. Rich, *David Dinkins and New York City Politics: Race, Images, and the Media* (Albany: State University of New York, 2007), 41–51; Roger Biles, "Mayor David Dinkins and the Politics of Race in New York City," in *African American Mayors: Race, Politics, and the American City*, ed. David R. Coburn and Jeffrey S. Adler (Urbana: University of Illinois Press, 2001), 135–136.
40. J. Phillip Thompson, "The Election and Governance of David Dinkins as Mayor of New York," in *Race, Politics, and Governance in the United States*, ed. Huey L. Perry (Gainesville: University Press of Florida, 1996), 68; J. Phillip Thompson, "The Failure of Liberal Homeless Policy in the Koch and Dinkins Administration," 639–660; Anna Lou Dehavenon and Margaret Boone, *Out of Sight! Out of Mind! Or, How New York City and New York State Tried to Abandon the City's Homeless Families in 1993* (New York: Action Research Project on Hunger, Homelessness and Family Health, 1993).
41. Thompson III, *Double Trouble*, 202–203; Rich, *David Dinkins and New York City Politics*, 150–151; Randy Diamond and Adam Nagourney, "Dave Faces New Heat: Act Now, Urge Leaders," *Daily News*, September 11, 1990; "Crime-Ravaged City Cries Out for Help: Dave, Do Something!" *New York Post*, September 7, 1990, 1; Jerry Nachman, "Dave's Style Is Too Measured for a War," *New York Post*, September 7, 1990, 5.
42. Office of the Mayor, *Safe Streets, Safe City: An Omnibus Criminal Justice Program for the City of New York* (New York: The Office, 1990); Citizens Crime Commission, *Restoring a Safe New York* (New York: The Commission, 1990); Lee P. Brown, "Community Policing: A Practical Guide for Police Officials," *Perspectives on Policing* 12 (September 1989): 1–11; Brown, *Policing New York City in the 1990s* (1991); Lee P. Brown, Raymond W. Kelly, and David W. Scott, *Problem-Solving Strategies for Community Policing: A Practical Guide* (New York: New York Police Department, 1992).
43. Brown, *Policing New York City in the 1990s*, 5.
44. David N. Dinkins and Fritz W. Alexander II, *Safe Streets, Safe City II: A Futureprint for Success* (New York: City of New York, 1993).

210 Notes

45. Eli B. Silverman, *NYPD Battles Crime: Innovative Strategies in Policing* (Boston: Northeastern University Press, 1999), 58–60; Police Commissioner's Community Policing Assistant Unit, *Reports* (New York: New York Police Department, 1992 and 1993); Jerome E. McElroy, Colleen A. Cosgrove, and Susan Sadd, *Community Policing: The CPOP in New York* (Newbury Park: Sage Publications, 1993).
46. Claire Jean Kim, *Bitter Fruit: The Politics of Black–Korean Conflict in New York City* (New Haven: Yale University Press, 2003); Pyong Gap Min, *Caught in the Middle: Korean Communities in New York and Los Angeles* (Berkeley: University of California Press, 1996), 73–82; Rich, *David Dinkins and New York City Politics*, 107–115.
47. Rich, *David Dinkins and New York City Politics*, 115–124; Thompson III, *Double Trouble*, 221–227; Richard Girgenti, *A Report to the Governor on the Disturbances in Crown Heights: An Assessment of the City's Preparedness and Response to Civil Disorder* (Albany: New York State Division of Criminal Justice Services, 1993); Richard Girgenti, *A Report to the Governor on the Disturbances of Crown Heights: A Review of the Circumstances Surrounding the Death of Yankel Rosenbaum and the Resulting Prosecution* (Albany: New York State Division of Criminal Justice Services, 1993); "Crown Heights Study Finds Dinkins and Police at Fault in Letting Unrest Escalate," *The New York Times*, July 21, 1993, 1(A).
48. William Murphy, "Police Union Boss Rips 'Lazy' Welfare Takers," *Newsday*, October 24, 1991, 5.
49. James C. McKinley Jr., "Officers Rally and Dinkins Is Their Target," *The New York Times*, September 17, 1992, 1(A); James C. McKinley Jr., "Dinkins Denounces Police Protest as Furthering an Image of Racism," *The New York Times*, September 18, 1992, 1(A); Editorial, "New York's Finest Mob," *The New York Times*, September 18, 1992, 34(A).
50. Sam Roberts, "Dinkins and the Police: A Campaign Issue," *The New York Times*, September 20, 1992, 43.
51. Alison Mitchell, "Giuliani Zeroing in on Crime Issue," *The New York Times*, September 20, 1993, 3(B).
52. George L. Kelling, Michael Julian, and Steven Miller, *Managing "Squeegeeing:" A Problem-Solving Exercise* (New York: New York Police Department, 1994); Bratton, *Turnaround*, 214.
53. Thompson III, *Double Trouble*, 256–263.

NOTES TO CHAPTER 7

1. William J. Bratton, *Monthly Report—August 1994* (New York: NYPD, 1994), 1, in Giuliani Administration Papers, Deputy Mayor Peter Powers, Box 02/01/020, Folder 0466, Municipal Archives of the City of New York (MACNY).
2. John Marzulli and Alice McQuillan, "No-Nonsense Guy Shook Up Gotham," *Daily News*, March 27, 1996.
3. "Notable Quotes on Louima Case," 14 August 1997, Giuliani Administration Papers, Deputy Mayor Anthony Carbonetti, Box 02/06/002, Folder 0067, MACNY.
4. Benjamin Weiser, "City Is to Pay $2.7 Million in Beating Suit," *The New York Times*, April 28, 1999, 1(B).
5. City Council, Committee on Finance Jointly With the Committee on Public Safety, *Oversight: Police Department Deployment/Community Policing* (New York: The City Council, 1994), in Giuliani Administration Papers,

Deputy Mayor Peter Powers, Box 02/01/019, Folder 0460, MACNY; Alison Mitchell, "Giuliani Urges Street Policing Refocused on Crime, *The New York Times,* January 25, 1994, 1(A).
6. Bratton, *Turnaround,* 140–181 and 209–272; *Sunday Edition,* WCBC-TV, January 23, 1994; Michael J. Farrell, *Reengineering and the New Crime Strategies* (New York: New York Police Department, 1994); New York Police Department, *Plan of Action: Report to the Police Commissioner* (New York: The Department, 1994); Seth O. Kaye to Peter J. Powers and Gordon J. Campbell, "Memorandum: Notes from 1/10/94 NYPD Policy Initiatives Meeting with Commissioner William Bratton," 11 January 1994, Giuliani Administration Papers, Deputy Mayor Peter Powers, Box 02/01/019, Folder 0460, MACNY.
7. William J. Bratton, *Monthly Report—August 1994* (New York: NYPD, 1994), 1, in Giuliani Administration Papers, Deputy Mayor Peter Powers, Box 02/01/020, Folder 0466, MACNY.
8. William J. Bratton to Rudolph W. Giuliani, "Executive Summary: Youth Violence Strategies," 15 February 1994, Giuliani Administration Papers, Deputy Mayor Peter Powers, Box 02/01/019, Folder 0460, MACNY.
9. Norimitsu Onishi, "Police Announce Crackdown on Quality-of-Life Offenses," *The New York Times,* March 13, 1994, 33.
10. Rudolph W. Giuliani and William J. Bratton, *Getting Guns Off the Streets of New York* (New York: NYPD, 1994); Rudolph W. Giuliani and William J. Bratton, *Curbing Youth Violence in the Schools and on the Streets* (New York: NYPD, 1994); Rudolph W. Giuliani and William J. Bratton, *Driving Drug Dealers Out of New York* (New York: NYPD, 1994); Rudolph W. Giuliani and William J. Bratton, *Reclaiming the Public Spaces of New York* (New York: NYPD, 1994); William J. Bratton, *New York City Police Department Arrest Processing Innovations, 1994—1995—1996: Financial—Time—Personnel Savings* (New York: NYPD, 1996), in William J. Bratton, *Monthly Report—August 1994* (New York: NYPD, 1994), in Giuliani Administration Papers, Deputy Mayor Peter Powers, Box 02/01/019, Folder 0460, MACNY; William J. Bratton, *Monthly Report—June 1994* (New York: NYPD, 1994), in Giuliani Administration Papers, Deputy Mayor Peter Powers, Box 02/01/019, Folder 0460, MACNY; Onishi, "Police Announce Crackdown on Quality-of-Life Offenses," 33.
11. Farrell, *Reengineering and the New Crime Strategies,* 1994; New York Police Department, *Plan of Action,* 1994; George James, "Police Project on Street Vice Goes Citywide," *The New York Times,* July 6, 1994, 1(B); James Lardner and Thomas Reppetto, *NYPD: A City and Its Police* (New York: Henry Holt and Company, 2000), 323–326.
12. Subcommittee on Public Housing, *New York State Assembly, Public Hearing on the Proposed Merger of the New York City Police and the New York City Housing Police and Transit Police Departments, July 28, 1994, Adam Clayton Powell, Jr., State Office Building* (Albany: The Subcommittee, 1994); Subcommittee on General Oversight, Investigations, and the Resolution of Failed Financial Institutions, Committee on Banking, Finance, and Urban Affairs, United States Congress, House, *Review of Giuliani Plan to Merge Police: Field Hearing Before the Subcommittee on General Oversight, Investigations, and the Resolution of Failed Financial Institutions of the Committee on Banking, Finance, and Urban Affairs, House of Representatives, One Hundred Third Congress, Second session, September 19, 1994* (Washington, DC: General Printing Office, 1995); Peter E. Stangle to Rudolph W. Giuliani, 30 January 1995, Giuliani Administration Papers, Deputy Mayor Peter Powers, Box 02/01/037, Folder 0932, MACNY; City

of New York, *Memorandum of Understanding Between the New York City Housing Authority and the City of New York on Merger of the New York City Housing Authority Police Department and the New York City Police Department* (New York: The City, 1995), in Giuliani Administration Papers, Deputy Mayor Peter Powers, Box 02/01/037, Folder 0932, MACNY; City of New York, *Memorandum of Understanding Among the Metropolitan Transportation Authority, the New York City Transit Authority and the City of New York on Merger of the New York City Transit Authority Police Department and the New York City Police Department* (New York: The City, 1995), in Giuliani Administration Papers, Deputy Mayor Peter Powers, Box 02/01/037, Folder 0932, MACNY; *Nickels v. City of New York*, 85 N.Y.2d 917; 650 N.E.2d 1320; 627 N.Y.S.2d 319; 1995 N.Y. (1995); *Ganley v. Giuliani*, 97–104, 171 Misc. 2d 654; 655 N.Y.S.2d 264; 1997 N.Y. (1997).

13. Paul B. Wice, *Public Defenders and the American Justice System* (Westport: Praeger Publishers, 2005), 34–38; *Legal Aid Society v. City of New York*, 96 Civ. 5141 (SHS), 1997 U.S. Dist. (1997); *Association of Legal Aid Attorneys v. City of New York*, 96 Civ. 8137 (SHS), 1997 U.S. Dist. (1997).
14. Bratton, *Turnaround*, 263–288; Alison Mitchell, "Top Bratton Aide Quits in Anger and Tensions With Mayor Grow," *The New York Times*, February 11, 1995, 1; "NYPD, Inc.: Face Value," *The Economist*, July 29, 1995, 50; Tony Allen-Mills, "Cops & Co Clean Up Mean Street," *The Sunday Times*, September 10, 1995; "Finally We're Winning the War Against Crime: Here's Why," *Time*, January 15, 1996.
15. William J. Bratton and Tom Kelly, "Statement by Police Commissioner William J. Bratton Concerning Travel While in Office," March 28, 1996, Giuliani Administration Papers, Deputy Mayor Peter Powers, Box 02/01/047, Folder 1258, MACNY; Bratton, *Turnaround*, 297–313.
16. Deborah Hart Strober and Gerald S. Srober, *Giuliani: Flawed of Flawless? The Oral Biography* (Hoboken: John Wiley and Sons, 2007), 173.
17. Wayne Barrett, *Rudy! An Investigative Biography of Rudolph Giuliani* (New York: Basic Books, 2000), 346–347 and 315; Strober and Strober, *Giuliani*, 172; Donna Lynne to Howard Safir, "Memorandum: NYPD Redeployment Initiative," April 9, 1996, Giuliani Administration Papers, Deputy Mayor Peter Powers, Box 02/01/047, Folder 1258, MACNY; Yolanda B. Jimenez to Reverend Winston M. Clarke, 23 September 1996, Giuliani Administration Papers, Deputy Mayor Randy Mastro, Box 02/04/006, Folder 0174, MACNY.
18. *United States v. Volpe*, 98 CR 196, 78 F. Supp. 2d 76; 1999 U.S. Dist. (1999).
19. Ibid.; *Nightline*, "The Blue Wall," *ABC News*, August 22, 1997.
20. *United States v. Volpe* (1999).
21. Ibid.
22. Ibid.
23. Sasha Torres, "Giuliani Time: Urban Policing and Brooklyn South," in *Zero Tolerance: Quality of Life and the New Police Brutality in New York City*, eds. Andrea McArdle and Tanya Erzen (New York: New York University Press, 2001), 87.
24. Amnesty International, *United States of America: Police Brutality and Excessive Force in New York City* (Washington, DC: Amnesty International, 1996); *United States v. Livoti*, 98–1608, 196 F.3d 322; 1999 U.S. App. (1999).
25. Amnesty International, *United States of America*, 20, 29–30, 34–35, 47–48, 52–53; *State of New York v. Livoti*, IND. Nos. 2026/95 and 2132/95, 166

Misc. 2d 925; 632 N.Y.S.2d 425; 1995 N.Y. (1995); *United States v. Livoti,* 98 Cr. 25 (SAS), 8 F. Supp. 2d 246; 1998 U.S. Dist. (1998); *United States v. Livoti,* 98 Cr. 25 (SAS), 8 F. Supp. 2d 250; 1998 U.S. Dist. (1998); *United States v. Livoti,* 98 Cr. 25 (SAS), 25 F. Supp. 2d 390; 1998 U.S. Dist. (1998); *United States v. Livoti,* 98 Cr. 25 (SAS), 22 F. Supp. 2d 235; 1998 U.S. Dist. (1998).
26. Barrett, *Rudy!,* 329–330.
27. Melinda Henneberger, "Officers from New York Accused of Drunken Spree in Washington," *The New York Times,* May 19, 1995, 1(A).
28. Norman Siegel to Rudolph Giuliani, March 9, 1994, Giuliani Administration Papers, Deputy Mayor Peter Powers, Box 02/01/037, Folder 0933, MACNY; Sheldon Leffler to Rudolph Giuliani, 10 May 1995, Giuliani Administration Papers, Deputy Mayor Peter Powers, Box 02/01/037, Folder 0933, MACNY; Hector W. Soto to Peter J. Powers, "Memorandum: Monthly Report," 18 January 1995, Giuliani Administration Papers, Deputy Mayor Peter Powers, Box 02/01/037, Folder 0933, MACNY; Allyson Collins, *Shielded from Justice: Police Brutality and Accountability in the United States* (New York: Human Rights Watch, 1998); Carry Pierre-Pierre, "Examining a Jump in Police Brutality Complaints," *The New York Times,* February 22, 1995, 3(B); *Green v. Safir,* Index No. 108239/97, 174 Misc. 2d 400; 664 N.Y.S.2d 232; 1997 N.Y. Misc. (1997); *Green v. Safir,* 1849, 255 A.D.2d 107; 679 N.Y.S.2d 383; 1998 N.Y. App. Div. (1998); *Green v. Safir,* Mo. No. 166, 93 N.Y.2d 882; 711 N.E.2d 639; 689 N.Y.S.2d 425; 1999 N.Y. (1999); Norman Siegel, Robert A. Perry, and Christopher T. Johnson, *NYCLU Report: A Sixth Anniversary Overview of the Civilian Complaint Review Board, July 5, 1993–July 5, 1999* (New York: New York Civil Liberties Union, 1999); Robert A. Perry, *Mission Failure: Civilian Review of Policing in New York City, 1994–2006* (New York: New York Civil Liberties Union, 2006).
29. Michael Meyers, Margaret Fung, and Norman Siegel, *Deflecting Blame: The Dissenting Report of the Mayor's Task Force on Police/Community Relations* (New York: New York Civil Liberties Union, 1998).
30. Sidney L. Harring, "The Diallo Verdict: Another 'Tragic Accident' in New York's War on Crime?" *Social Justice* 27 (2000): 9–11.
31. Beth Roy, *41 Shots . . . And Counting: What Amadou Diallo's Story Teaches Us About Policing, Race, and Justice* (Syracuse: Syracuse University Press, 2009).
32. *Martens v. Giuliani* (2001); *Mandal v. City of New York,* 02 Civ. 1234, 2008 U.S. Dist. (2008); Christopher Dunn, "Balancing the Right to Protest in the Aftermath of September 11," *Harvard Civil Rights—Civil Liberties Law Review* 40 (2005): 335.
33. David M. Herszenhorn, "Giuliani Vows No Concession on Oversight of the Police," *The New York Times,* July 12, 1999, 3(B).
34. Eliot Spitzer, *The New York City Police Department's "Stop & Frisk" Practices: A Report to the People of the State of New York from the Office of the Attorney General* (New York: Civil Rights Bureau, 1999); Civilian Complaint Review Board, *Street Stop Encounter Report: An Analysis of CCRB Complaints Resulting from the New York Police Department's "Stop & Frisk" Practices* (New York: The Board, 2001).
35. Barrett, *Rudy!,* 336–337.
36. United States Commission on Civil Rights, *Police Practices and Civil Rights in New York City* (Washington, DC: The Commission, 2000).
37. Jack Newfield, *The Full Rudy: The Man, the Myth, the Mania* (New York: Thunder's Mouth Press/Nation Books, 2002), 84–86.
38. Barrett, *Rudy!,* 297–305.

39. Neil Smith, "New Globalism, New Urbanism: Gentrification as Global Urban Policy," *Antipode* 34 (July 2002): 427–450.
40. Richard Briffault, "A Government for Our Time? Business Improvement Districts and Urban Governance," *Columbia Law Review* 99 (March 1999): 365–477; *Kessler v. Grand Central District Management Association*, 95 Civ. 10029 (SAS), 960 F. Supp. 760; 1997 U.S. Dist. (1997); *Kessler v. Grand Central District Management Association*, 97–7503, 158 F.3d 92; 1998 U.S. App. (1998).
41. Heather Barr, "More Like Disneyland: State Action, 42 U.S.C. §1983, and Business Improvement Districts in New York," *Columbia Human Rights Law Review* (Winter 1997): 393–429; Douglas Martin, "Districts to Improve Business Proliferate," *The New York Times*, March 25, 1994, 1 and 3(B); Thomas J. Lueck, "Business Districts Grow at Price of Accountability," *The New York Times*, November 20, 1994, 1 and 46.
42. Fred Kaplan, "Pushcarts Face Shove: Vendors Say NYC Wants Them Out," *The Boston Globe*, August 30, 1995, 1; *Bery v. City of New York*, 94 Civ. 4253 (MGC), 94 Civ. 7216 (MGC), 906 F. Supp. 163; 1995 U.S. Dist. (1995); *Bery v. City of New York*, 95–9089 (L), 95–9131, 96–7137, 97 F.3d 689; 1996 U.S. App. (1996); *Lederman v. Giuliani*, 98 Civ. 2024 (LMM), 98 Civ. 2400 (LMM), 2001 U.S. (2001).
43. Barr, "More Like Disneyland," 400–401.
44. Barr, "More Like Disneyland," 399–403; *Archie v. Grand Central Partnership*, 95 Civ. 0694 (SS), 997 F. Supp. 504; 1998 U.S. Dist. (1998); U.S. Department of Housing and Urban Development, *Review of Findings of HUD Investigation of the Grand Central Partnership Social Services Corporation* (Washington, DC: HUD, 1998), Giuliani Administration Papers, Deputy Mayor Rudy Washington, Box 02/08/015, Folder 0423, MACNY; *Grand Central Partnership v. Cuomo*, 98–6027, 166 F.3d 473; 1999 U.S. App. (1999); *Baba v. Grand Central Partnership*, 99 Civ. 5818 (TPG), 2000 U.S. Dist. (2000).
45. Briffault, "A Government for Our Time?," 442–443 and 457–458; New York City Council Report to the Finance Committee, *Cities Within Cities: Business Improvement Districts and the Emergence of the Micropolis* (New York: The City Council, 1995); New York City Council Report to the Finance Committee, *Managing the Micropolis: Proposals to Strengthen BID Performance and Accountability* (New York: The City Council, 1997); Barbara Wolff to Rudy Washington, "Memorandum: City Council's Business Improvement District Report," 18 November 1997, Giuliani Administration Papers, Deputy Mayor Rudy Washington, Box 02/08/006, Folder 0174, MACNY; Rudy Washington to Daniel Biederman, 12 September 1996, Giuliani Administration Papers, Deputy Mayor Rudy Washington, Box 02/08/003, Folder 0071, MACNY; Report of the Legal and Governmental Affairs Division, *Oversight: Business Improvement Districts* (New York: The City Council, 2001).
46. Dan Barry, "Mayor Orders Review of Plan for Substation," *The New York Times*, February 19, 1998, 1(B) and 9(B); Briffault, "A Government for Our Time?" 459–460; Rudy Washington to Joseph Lhota, "Re: Business Improvement Districts," April 3, 1998, Giuliani Administration Papers, Deputy Mayor Rudy Washington, Box 02/08/012, Folder 0362, MACNY; Earl Andrews, Jr., to Dan Biederman, "Re: BID Oversight and Reporting Requirements," April 3, 1998, Giuliani Administration Papers, Deputy Mayor Rudy Washington, Box 02/08/012, Folder 0362, MACNY; Department of Business Services, "BID Program Revisions," Giuliani Administration Papers, Deputy Mayor Rudy Washington, Box 02/08/012, Folder 0362, MACNY.

47. Gretchen Dykstra to Earl Andrews, Jr., April 23, 1998, Giuliani Administration Papers, Deputy Mayor Rudy Washington, Box 02/08/012, Folder 0362, MACNY; City Administration Press Release, "City Will Not Extend Contract with Grand Central Business Improvement District," Giuliani Administration Papers, Deputy Mayor Rudy Washington, Box 02/08/014, Folder 0422, MACNY; Deborah R. Weeks to Bruce Gitlin, 17 September 1998, Giuliani Administration Papers, Deputy Mayor Rudy Washington, Box 02/08/015, Folder 0424, MACNY; Deborah R. Weeks to Norman Sturner, 17 September 1998, Giuliani Administration Papers, Deputy Mayor Rudy Washington, Box 02/08/015, Folder 0424, MACNY; William G. Cohen to Bernard Mendik, 30 November 1998, Giuliani Administration Papers, Deputy Mayor Rudy Washington, Box 02/08/015, Folder 0423, MACNY; C. Virginia Fields to Rudy Washington, 30 December 1998, Giuliani Administration Papers, Deputy Mayor Rudy Washington, Box 02/08/015, Folder 0423, MACNY; Alfred C. Cerullo III, Grand Central Partnership, http://www.grandcentralpartnership.org (accessed November 30, 2009).
48. Deborah Weeks to Rudy Washington, "Memorandum: FY'00 Assessment Increases," 29 June 1999, Giuliani Administration Papers, Deputy Mayor Rudy Washington, Box 02/08/017, Folder 0519, MACNY; George Kaufman and Barbara Randall to Rudolph Giuliani, 15 July 1999, Giuliani Administration Papers, Deputy Mayor Rudy Washington, Box 02/08/017, Folder 0519, MACNY; Brendan Sexton to Rudy Washington, Joe Lhota, Randy Levine, and Joe Rose, "Memorandum: Times Square BID Budget FY2000," 20 July 1999, Giuliani Administration Papers, Deputy Mayor Rudy Washington, Box 02/08/017, Folder 0519, MACNY; Barbara Randall to Rudy Washington, 3 August 1999, Giuliani Administration Papers, Deputy Mayor Rudy Washington, Box 02/08/017, Folder 0519, MACNY.
49. John Tierney, "Clean Up City? Not Unless It's City Hall Way," *The New York Times,* July 29, 1999, 1(B).
50. *Brooklyn Institute of Arts and Sciences v. City of New York,* 99 CV 6071, 64 F. Supp. 2d 184; 1999 U.S. (1999).
51. Blaine Harden, "New York Lore: The Mayor Will Get You for That," *The New York Times,* October 10, 1999, 46.
52. *Brooklyn Institute of Arts and Sciences v. City of New York* (1999); David Barstow, "Mayor Says Judge Rushed Decision in Museum Case," *The New York Times,* November 3, 1999, 3(B).
53. Bob Herbert, "An Insult to Harlem," *The New York Times,* April 7, 1998, 17(A).
54. Themis Chronopoulos, Ethnographic Research (1998); Abby Goodnough, "Youth March Organizer, Celebrating Ruling, Taunts Giuliani," *The New York Times,* August 28, 1998, 1(B); *Million Youth March v. Safir,* 98 Civ. 5946 (LAK), 18 F. Supp. 2d 334; 1998 U.S. Dist. (1998); *Million Youth March v. Safir,* 98–9152, 155 F.3d 124; 1998 U.S. App. (1998).
55. *MacDonald v. Safir,* 98 Civ. 2332 (LBS), 26 F. Supp. 2d 664; 1998 U.S. Dist. (1998).
56. *Million Youth March v. Safir,* 99 Civ. 9261 (JSR), 63 F. Supp. 2d 381; 1999 U.S. Dist. (1999).
57. *MacDonald v. Safir* (1998).
58. *United Yellow Cab Drivers v. Safir,* 98 Civ. 3670 (RPP), 1998 U.S. Dist. (1998); *United Yellow Cab Drivers v. Safir,* 98 Civ. 3670 (WHP), 2002 U.S. Dist. (2002); *Mac Donald v. Safir,* 99–7010, 206 F.3d 183; 2000 U.S. App. (2000).
59. *Housing Works v. Safir,* 98 Civ. 4994 (HB), 101 F. Supp. 2d 163; 2000 U.S. Dist. (2000); *International Action Center v. Safir* (1998); *Universal Church*

of *Practical Knowledge v. Giuliani* (1999); *Bryant v. City of New York*, 04-0199-CV, 404 F.3d 128; 2005 U.S. App. (2005); Jimmy Breslin, "Preface," in *America's Mayor, America's President? The Strange Career of Rudy Giuliani*, ed. Robert Polner (Brooklyn: Soft Skull Press, 2007), xvii.

NOTES TO THE EPILOGUE

1. Charles Murray, "The Shape of Things to Come," *National Review* 43 (July 8, 1991): 29–30; Harvey, *A Brief History of Neoliberalism* (2005).
2. Teresa P. R. Caldeira, *City of Walls: Crime, Segregation, and Citizenship in São Paulo* (Berkeley: University of California Press, 2000).
3. Diane Cardwell, "Mayor Says New York Is Worth the Cost," *The New York Times*, January 8, 2003, 3(B).
4. City Planning Commission, "Hudson Yards," N 040500(A) ZRM, 22 November 2004; City Planning Commission, *Greenpoint-Williamsburg Rezoning: Final Environmental Impact Statement* (New York: City of New York, 2005); City Planning Commission, "West 61st Street Rezoning and Citywide General Large-Scale Development Text Amendment," 05DCP063Y, 29 December 2006; Diane Cardwell and Charles V. Bagli, "Mayor's Big-Thinking Aide Leaves City Hall With Mixed Legacy," *The New York Times*, December 7, 2007, 1(A).
5. New York Civil Liberties Union, *Mission Failure: Civilian Review of Policing in New York City, 1994–2006* (New York: NYCLU, 1997); *Blair v. City of New York*, 08 CIV 4303, 2008 U.S. Dist. (2008); *Lino v. City of New York*, Index No. 10-106579, 2010 N.Y. (2010); Coalition for the Homeless, *Annual Report 2010* (New York: The Coalition, 2010).
6. Jonathan Bowles, Joel Kotkin, and David Giles, *Reviving the City of Aspiration: A Study of Challenges Facing New York City's Middle Class* (New York: Center for an Urban Center, 2009); Joel Kotkin, "The Luxury City vs. The Middle Class," *New Geography*, May 18, 2009, Newgeography.com (accessed August 31, 2010); Marshall Berman and Brian Berger, eds., *New York Calling: From Blackout to Bloomberg* (London: Reaktion Books, 2007). A forthcoming book on the luxury city is Julian Brash, *Bloomberg's New York: Class and Governance in the Luxury City* (Athens: University of Georgia Press, 2011).

Selected Bibliography

Abu-Lughod, Janet L., et al., eds. *From Urban Village to East Village: The Battle for New York's Lower East Side*. Cambridge: Blackwell, 1994.
Allen, Robert C. *Horrible Prettiness: Burlesque and American Culture*. Chapel Hill: University of North Carolina Press, 1991.
Alpern, Andrew. *Apartments for the Affluent: A Historical Survey of Buildings in New York*. New York: McGraw-Hill, 1975.
Auletta, Ken. *The Underclass*. New York: Random House, 1982.
Austin, Joe. *Taking the Train: How Graffiti Art Became an Urban Crisis in New York City*. New York: Columbia University Press, 2001.
Avorn, Jerry L., et al. *Up Against the Ivy Wall: A History of the Columbia Crisis*. New York: Atheneum, 1969.
Axinn, June, and Marc J. Stern. *Dependency and Poverty: Old Problems in a New World*. Lexington, MA: Lexington Books, 1988.
Bacon, Mardges. *Le Corbusier in America: Travels in the Land of the Timid*. Cambridge: MIT Press, 2001.
Banfield, Edward C. *The Unheavenly City Revisited*. New York: Little, Brown & Company, 1974.
Barr, Heather. "More Like Disneyland: State Action, 42 U.S.C. §1983, and Business Improvement Districts in New York." *Columbia Human Rights Law Review* (Winter 1997): 393–429.
Barrett, Wayne. *Rudy! An Investigative Biography of Rudolph Giuliani*. New York: Basic Books, 2000.
Beauregard, Robert A. *Voices of Decline: The Postwar Fate of US Cities*. Oxford: Blackwell, 1993.
Berman, Marshall, and Brian Berger. *New York Calling: From Blackout to Bloomberg*. London: Reaktion Books, 2007.
Biondi, Martha. *To Stand and Fight: The Struggle for Civil Rights in Postwar New York City*. Cambridge: Harvard University Press, 2003.
Bloom, Nicolas Dagen. *Public Housing That Worked: New York in the Twentieth Century*. Philadelphia: University of Pennsylvania Press, 2008.
Bratton, William J., with Peter Knobler. *Turnaround: How America's Top Cop Reversed the Crime Epidemic*. New York: Random House, 1998.
Brecher, Charles, and Raymond D. Horton. "Retrenchment and Recovery: American Cities and the New York Experience. *Public Administration Review* 45 (March–April 1985): 267–274.
——— and Raymond D. Horton, eds. *Setting Municipal Priorities, 1981*. Montclair: Allanheld, Osmun 1980.
Brenner, Neil, and Nik Theodore, eds. *Spaces of Neoliberalism: Urban Restructuring in North America and Western Europe*. Oxford: Wiley-Blackwell, 2003.

Briffault, Richard. "A Government for Our Time? Business Improvement Districts and Urban Governance." *Columbia Law Review* 99 (March 1999): 365–477.
Brown, Wendy. "American Nightmare: Neoliberalism, Neoconservatism, and De-Democratization." *Political Theory* 34 (December 2006): 690–714.
Browne, Arthur, Dan Collins, and Michael Goodwin. *I, Koch: A Decidedly Unauthorized Biography of the Mayor of New York City, Edward I. Koch*. New York: Dodd, 1985.
Cannato, Vincent J. *The Ungovernable City: John Lindsay and His Struggle to Save New York*. New York: Basic Books, 2001.
Caro, Robert. *The Power Broker: Robert Moses and the Fall of New York*. New York: Random House, 1974.
Castleman, Craig. *Getting Up: Subway Graffiti in New York*. Cambridge: MIT Press, 1982.
Chauncey, George. *Gay New York: Gender, Urban Culture, and the Making of the Gay Male World, 1890–1940*. New York: Basic Books, 1994.
Chevigny, Paul. *Gigs: Jazz and Cabaret Laws in New York City*. New York: Routledge, 1991.
Coburn, David R., and Jeffrey S. Adler, eds. *African American Mayors: Race, Politics, and the American City*. Urbana: University of Illinois Press, 2001.
Colomina, Beatriz, ed. *Sexuality and Space*. New York: Princeton Architectural Press, 1992.
Cromley, Elizabeth C. *Alone Together: A History of New York's Early Apartments* (Ithaca: Cornell University Press, 1990).
Davis, Diane E. "El factor Giuliani: delincuencia, la "cero tolerancia" en el trabajo policiaco y la transformación de la esfera pública en el centro de la ciudad de México." *Estudios Sociológicos* XXV (septiembre–diciembre 2007): 639–681.
Deutsche, Rosalyn, and Cara Gendel Ryan. "The Fine Art of Gentrification," *October* 13 (Winter 1984): 91–111.
Dickstein, Morris. *Gates of Eden: American Culture in the Sixties*. New York: Basic Books, 1977.
Dolkart, Andrew S. *Morningside Heights: A History of its Architecture and Development*. New York: Columbia University Press, 1998.
Duménil, Gérard, and Dominique Lévy. *Capital Resurgent: Roots of the Neoliberal Revolution*. Translated by Derek Jeffers. Cambridge: Harvard University Press, 2004.
Evans, Robin. *The Fabrication of Virtue: English Prison Architecture, 1750–1840*. (Cambridge: Cambridge University Press, 1982).
Fahringer, Herald Price. "Zoning Out Free Expression: An Analysis of New York City's Adult Zoning Resolution." *Buffalo Law Review* 46 (Spring 1998): 403–431.
Flamm, Michael W. *Law and Order: Street Crime, Civil Unrest, and the Crisis of Liberalism in the 1960s*. New York: Columbia University Press, 2005.
Floyd, Kevin. "Closing the (Heterosexual) Frontier: Midnight Cowboy as National Allegory." *Science & Society* 65 (Spring 2001): 99–130.
Forty, Adrian. *Words and Buildings: A Vocabulary of Modern Architecture*. New York: Thames & Hudson, 2000.
Frazier, Franklin E. "Negro Harlem: An Ecological Study." *American Journal of Sociology* 43 (July 1937): 72–88.
Freeman, Joshua B. *Working Class New York: Life and Labor since World War II*. New York: The New Press, 2000.
Frieden, Bernard J., and Lynn B. Sagalyn. *Downtown Inc.: How American Rebuilds Cities*. Cambridge: MIT Press, 1989.
Friedman, Milton. *Capitalism and Freedom*. Chicago: University of Chicago Press, 1962.

Selected Bibliography 219

——— and Rose Friedman. *Free to Choose: A Personal Statement*. San Diego: Harcourt Brace Jovanovich, 1979.
George, Nelson. *Buppies, B-Boys, Baps and Bohos: Notes on Post-Soul Black Culture*. New York: Harper Collins, 1992.
——— et al. *Fresh: Hip Hop Don't Stop*. New York: Random House/Sarah Lazin, 1985.
———. *Hip Hop America*. New York: Penguin, 1998.
Gilmartin, Gregory F. *Shaping the City: New York and the Municipal Art Society*. New York: Clarkson Potter, 1995.
Glazer, Nathan. *From a Cause to a Style: Modernist Architecture's Encounter with the American City*. Princeton: Princeton University Press, 2007.
Goffman, Erving. *Behavior in Public Places: Notes on the Social Organization of Gatherings*. New York: Free Press, 1963.
Greenberg, Miriam. *Branding New York: How a City in Crisis Was Sold to the World*. New York: Routledge, 1998.
Gurock, Jeffrey S. *When Harlem Was Jewish, 1870–1930*. New York: Columbia University Press, 1930.
Hackworth, Jason. *The Neoliberal City: Governance, Ideology, and Development in American Urbanism*. Ithaca: Cornell University Press, 2007.
Hager, Steven. *The Illustrated History of Breakdancing, Rap Music, and Graffiti*. New York: St. Martin's Press, 1984.
Harcourt, Bernard. *Illusion of Order: The False Promise of Broken Windows Policing*. Cambridge: Harvard University Press, 2001.
Harring, Sidney L. "The Diallo Verdict: Another 'Tragic Accident' in New York's War on Crime?" *Social Justice* 27 (2000): 9–18.
Harvey, David. *A Brief History of Neoliberalism*. New York: Oxford University Press, 2005.
Hayek, F. A. *The Constitution of Liberty*. Chicago: University of Chicago Press, 1960.
———. *The Road to Serfdom*. Chicago: University of Chicago Press, 1944.
Hearn, Frank. *Moral Order and Social Disorder: The American Search for Civil Society*. New York: Aldyne de Gruyter, 1997.
Henderson, Scott A. *Housing and the Democratic Ideal: The Life and Thought of Charles Abrams*. New York: Columbia University Press, 2000.
Hood, Clifton. *722 Miles: The Building of the Subways and How They Transformed New York*. New York: Simon and Schuster, 1993.
Isenberg, Alison. *Downtown America: A History of the Place and the People Who Made It*. Chicago: University of Chicago Press, 2004.
Jacobs, Jane. *The Death and Life of Great American Cities*. New York: Random House, 1961.
Jeffers, H. Paul. *The Napoleon of New York: Mayor Fiorello La Guardia*. New York: John Wiley & Sons, 2002.
Johnson, Marilynn S. *Street Justice: A History of Police Violence in New York City*. Boston: Beacon Press, 2003.
Jonnes, Jill. *South Bronx Rising: The Rise, Fall, and Resurrection of an American City*. Bronx: Fordham University Press, 2002.
Jordan, David P. *Transforming Paris: The Life and Labors of Baron Haussmann* (Chicago: University of Chicago Press, 1996).
Kahn, Roger. *The Battle for Morningside Heights: Why Students Rebel*. New York: William Morrow and Co., 1970.
Kasson, John F. *Amusing the Million: Coney Island at the Turn of the Century*. New York: Hill & Wang, 1978.
Katznelson, Ira. *City Trenches: Urban Politics and the Patterning of Class in the United States*. Chicago: University of Chicago Press, 1981.

Selected Bibliography

Kelling, George, and Catherine Coles. *Fixing Broken Windows: Restoring Order and Reducing Crime in Our Communities.* New York: Free Press, 1996.

Kessner, Thomas. *Fiorello H. La Guardia and the Making of Modern New York.* New York: McGraw-Hill, 1989.

Kim, Claire Jean. *Bitter Fruit: The Politics of Black–Korean Conflict in New York City.* New Haven: Yale University Press, 2003.

Kohl, Herbert, and James Hinton. *Golden Boy as Anthony Cool: A Photo Essay on Naming and Graffiti.* New York: Dial Press, 1972.

La Vida: A Puerto Rican Family in the Culture of Poverty—San Juan and New York. New York: Secker and Warburg, 1965.

Lankevich, George J. *New York City: A Short History.* New York: New York University Press, 2002.

Lardner, James, and Thomas Reppetto. *NYPD: A City and Its Police.* New York: Henry Holt and Company, 2000.

Le Corbusier. *Essential Le Corbusier: L'Esprit Nouveau Articles.* Oxford: Architectural Press, 1998.

Lemman, Nicholas. "The Origins of the Underclass." *The Atlantic* 258 (July 1986): 54–68.

Levine, Lawrence W. *Highbrow/Lowbrow: The Emergence of Cultural Hierarchy in America.* Cambridge: Harvard University Press, 1988.

Lewis, Oscar. *The Children of Sanchez: Autobiography of a Mexican Family.* New York: Random House, 1961.

———. "The Culture of Poverty." *Scientific American* 215 (October 1966): 19–25.

Ley, David, and Roman Cybriwsky. "Urban Graffiti as Territorial Markers." *Annals of the Association of American Geographers* 64 (December 1974): 491–505.

Lofland, Lyn H. *A World of Strangers: Order and Action in Urban Public Space.* New York: Basic Books, 1973.

Lubove, Roy. *The Professional Altruist: The Emergence of Social Work as a Career, 1880–1930.* Cambridge: Harvard University Press, 1965.

———. *The Progressive and the Slums: Tenement House Reform in New York City, 1890–1917.* Pittsburgh: University of Pittsburgh Press, 1962.

Lurie, Ellen. "Community Action in East Harlem." In *The Urban Condition: People and Policy in the Metropolis,* edited by Leonard J. Duhl, 246–259. New York: Basic Books, 1963.

Mailer, Norman. *The Faith of Graffiti.* New York: Praeger, 1974.

Mannes, Marya. *The New York I Know.* Philadelphia: J. B. Lippincott Company, 1961.

McArdle, Andrea, and Tanya Erzen, eds. *Zero Tolerance: Quality of Life and the New Police Brutality in New York City.* New York: New York University Press, 2001.

McElroy, Jerome E., Colleen A. Cosgrove, and Susan Sadd. *Community Policing: The CPOP in New York.* Newbury Park: Sage Publications, 1993.

McRobbie, Angela, ed. *Zoot Suits and Second-Hand Dressers: An Anthology of Fashion and Music.* Boston: Unwin Hyman, 1988.

Mead, Lawrence M. *Beyond Entitlement: The Social Obligations of Citizenship.* New York: Free Press, 1986.

———. *The New Politics of Poverty: The Nonworking Poor in America.* New York: Basic Books, 1992.

Min, Pyong Gap. *Caught in the Middle: Korean Communities in New York and Los Angeles.* Berkeley: University of California Press, 1996.

Mollenkopf, John H. *A Phoenix in the Ashes: The Rise and Fall of the Koch Coalition in New York City Politics.* Princeton: Princeton University Press, 1994.

——— and Manuel Castells. *Dual City: Restructuring New York*. New York: Russell Sage Foundation, 1991.
Moody, Kim. *From Welfare State to Real Estate: Regime Change in New York City, 1974 to the Present*. New York: The New Press, 2007.
Morris, Charles. *The Cost of Good Intentions*. New York: W. W. Norton, 1980.
Mumford, Eric. *The CIAM Discourse on Urbanism, 1928–1960*. Cambridge: MIT Press, 2000.
Murray, Charles. *Losing Ground: American Social Policy, 1950–1980*. New York: Basic Books, 1981.
Newfield, Jack. *The Full Rudy: The Man, the Myth, the Mania*. New York: Thunder's Mouth Press/Nation Books, 2002.
Newfield, Jack, and Wayne Barrett. *City for Sale: Ed Koch and the Betrayal of New York*. New York: Harper & Row, 1989.
Newman, Oscar. *Defensible Space: Crime Prevention Though Urban Design*. New York: Macmillan, 1972.
Norton, Anne. *Leo Strauss and the Politics of American Empire*. New Haven: Yale University Press, 2004.
Open Space Institute. *Times Square South: Pre-Development Analysis*. New York: KBS Associates, 1981.
Osofsky, Gilbert. *Harlem the Making of a Ghetto: Negro New York, 1890–1930*. New York: Harper & Row, 1966.
Perkins, William Eric. *Droppin' Science: Critical Essays on Rap Music and Hip Hop Culture*. Philadelphia: Temple University Press, 1996.
Perry, Huey L., ed. *Race, Politics, and Governance in the United States*. Gainesville: University Press of Florida, 1996.
Peterson, Paul. *City Limits*. Chicago: University of Chicago Press, 1981.
Plotke, David. *Building a Democratic Political Order: Reshaping American Liberalism in the 1930s and 1940s*. New York: Cambridge University Press, 1996.
Plunz, Richard. *A History of Housing in New York City: Dwelling Type and Social Change in the American Metropolis*. New York: Columbia University Press, 1990.
Portman, John, and Jonathan Barnett. *The Architect As Developer*. New York: McGraw-Hill, 1976.
Portman, John, and Scott Gilchrist. *Marriott Marquis Hotel*. Toronto: Archivision, 1994.
Reichl, Alexander. *Reconstructing Times Square: Politics and Culture in Urban Development*. Lawrence: University Press of Kansas, 1999.
Reinarman, Craig, and Harry G. Levine, eds. *Crack in America: Demon Drugs and Social Justice*. Berkeley: University of California Press, 1997.
Rich, Wilbur C. *David Dinkins and New York City Politics: Race, Images, and the Media*. Albany: State University of New York, 2007.
Rieder, Jonathan. *Canarsie: The Jews and Italians of Brooklyn Against Liberalism*. Cambridge: Harvard University Press, 1985.
Riesenberg, Felix, and Alexander Allard. *Portrait of New York*. New York: MacMillan, 1939.
Riis, Jacob A. *The Children of the Poor*. New York: Charles Scribner's Sons, 1892.
———. *How the Other Half Lives: Studies Among the Tenements of New York*. New York: Charles Scribner's Sons, 1890.
Rooney, Jim. *Organizing the South Bronx*. Albany: State University of New York Press, 1995.
Rose, Tricia. *Black Noise: Rap Music and Black Culture in Contemporary America*. Hanover: University Press of New England, 1994.

Roy, Beth. *41 Shots . . . And Counting: What Amadou Diallo's Story Teaches Us About Policing, Race, and Justice.* Syracuse: Syracuse University Press, 2009.

Ruggie, John Gerard. "International Regimes, Transactions, and Change: Embedded Liberalism in the Postwar Economic Order." *International Organization* 36 (1982): 379–415.

Sagalyn, Lynne B. *Times Square Roulette: Remaking the City Icon.* Cambridge: MIT Press, 2001.

Sampson, Robert, and Stephen Raudenbush. "Systematic Social Observation of Public Spaces: A New Look at Disorder in Urban Neighborhoods." *American Journal of Sociology* 105 (November 1999): 603–651.

Sanjek, Roger. *The Future of Us All: Race and Neighborhood Politics in New York City.* Ithaca: Cornell University Press, 1998.

Schmelzkopf, Karen. "Urban Community Gardens as Contested Space." *Geographical Review* 85 (July 1995): 364–381.

Schneider, Eric C. *Vampires, Dragons, and Egyptian Kings: Youth Gangs in Postwar New York.* Princeton: Princeton University Press 1999.

Schur, Robert. "Manhattan Plaza: Old Style Ripoffs Are Alive and Well." In *Critical Perspectives on Housing*, edited by Rachel G. Bratt, Chester Hartman, and Ann Meyerson, 277–291. Philadelphia: Temple University Press, 1986.

Schwartz, Joel. *The New York Approach: Robert Moses, Urban Liberals, and Redevelopment of the Inner City.* Columbus: Ohio State University Press, 1993.

Scott, James C. *Seeing Like a State: How Certain Schemes to Improve the Human Condition Have Failed.* New Haven: Yale University Press, 1998.

Self, Robert O. *American Babylon: Race and Struggle for Postwar Oakland.* Princeton: Princeton University Press, 2003.

Sexton, Adam, ed. *Rap on Rap: Straight-Up Talk on Hip-Hop Culture.* New York: Delta, 1995.

Shefter, Martin. *Political Crisis/Fiscal Crisis: The Collapse and Revival of New York City.* New York: Columbia University Press, 1992.

———. "Political Incorporation and the Extrusion of the Left: Party Politics and Social Forces in New York City." *Studies in American Political Development* I (1986): 59–79.

Shinn, Marybeth, and Colleen Gillespie. "The Roles of Housing and Poverty in the Origins of Homelessness." *American Behavioral Scientist* 37 (February 1994): 505–521.

Silverman, Eli B. *NYPD Battles Crime: Innovative Strategies in Policing.* Boston: Northeastern University Press, 1999.

Sites, William. *Remaking New York: Primitive Globalization and the Politics of Urban Community.* Minneapolis: University of Minnesota Press, 2003.

Skogan, Wesley. *Disorder and Decline: Crime and the Spiral of Decay in American Neighborhoods.* New York: Free Press, 1990.

Smith, Neil. "New Globalism, New Urbanism: Gentrification As Global Urban Policy." *Antipode* 34 (July 2002): 427–450.

Sontag, Susan. *Illness as Metaphor.* New York: Farrar, Straus and Giroux, 1978.

Sorkin, Michael, ed. *Variations on a Theme Park: The New American City and the End of Public Space.* New York: Hill & Wang, 1992.

Steinberg, Stephen. *Turning Back: The Retreat from Racial Justice in American Thought and Policy.* Boston: Beacon Press, 1995.

Stern, Robert A. M., Thomas Mellins, and David Fishman. *New York 1960: Architecture and Urbanism Between the Second World War and the Bicentennial.* New York: Monacelli Press, 1995.

Stoumen, Lou. *Times Square: 45 Years of Photography.* New York: Aperture, 1985.

Strober, Deborah Hart, and Gerald S. Srober. *Giuliani: Flawed or Flawless? The Oral Biography*. Hoboken: John Wiley and Sons, 2007.
Tabb, William K. *The Long Default: New York City and the Urban Fiscal Crisis*. New York: Monthly Review Press, 1982.
Tanenbaum, Susie J. *Underground Harmonies: Music and Politics in the Subways of New York*. Ithaca: Cornell University Press, 1995.
Taylor, Ralph B. *Breaking Away from Broken Windows: Baltimore Neighborhoods and the Nationwide Fight against Crime, Grime, Fear, and Decline*. Boulder: Westview Press, 2001.
Taylor, William R., ed. *Inventing Times Square: Commerce and Culture at the Crossroads of the World*. New York: Russell Sage Foundation, 1991.
Teaford, Jon C. *The Rough Road to Renaissance: Urban Revitalization in America, 1940–1985*. Baltimore: The Johns Hopkins University Press, 1990.
Thompson III, J. Phillip. *Double Trouble: Black Mayors, Black Communities, and the Call for a Deep Democracy*. New York: Oxford University Press, 2006.
Thompson, J. Phillip. "The Failure of Liberal Homeless Policy in the Koch and Dinkins Administration." *Political Science Quarterly* 111 (2001): 639–660.
Vitale, Alex S. *City of Disorder: How the Quality of Life Campaign Transformed New York Politics*. New York: New York University Press, 2008.
Von Hassell, Malve. *Homesteading in New York City, 1978–1993: The Divided Heart of the Loisada*. Westport: Bergin and Garvey, 1996.
von Hoffman, Alexander. "A Study in Contradictions: The Origins and Legacy of the Housing Act of 1949." *Housing Policy Debate* 11 (2000): 299–326.
Warner, Amos G., Stuart A. Queen, and Ernest B. Harper, *American Charities and Social Work*. New York: Thomas Y. Crowell Co., 1930.
Weber, Nicholas Fox. *Le Corbusier*. London: Weidenfeld & Nicolson, 2006.
Wenocur, Stanley, and Michael Reisch. *From Charity to Enterprise: The Development of American Social Work in a Market Economy*. Urbana: University of Illinois Press, 1989.
White, E. B. *Here is New York*. New York: Little Bookroom, 2000.
Wice, Paul B. *Public Defenders and the American Justice System*. Westport: Praeger Publishers, 2005.
Wilson, James Q. *Thinking about Crime*. New York: Basic Books, 1975.
———. "What Makes a Better Policeman." *The Atlantic* (March 1969): 129–135.
——— and Barbara Boland. "The Effect of the Police on Crime." *Law and Society Review* 12 (1978): 367–390.
——— and Barbara Boland. "The Effect of the Police on Crime: A Response to Jacob and Rich." *Law and Society Review* 16 (1981): 163–169.
——— and George L. Kelling. "The Police and Neighborhood Safety." *The Atlantic* (March 1982): 29–38.
Wilson, William Julius. *The Declining Significance of Race: Blacks and Changing American Institutions*. Chicago: University of Chicago Press, 1978.
———. *The Truly Disadvantaged: The Inner City, the Underclass, and Public Policy*. Chicago: University of Chicago Press, 1987.
Zukin, Sharon. *The Culture of Cities*. Cambridge: Blackwell, 1995.

About the Author

Themis Chronopoulos is an Assistant Professor of History at the State University of New York, Stony Brook. His fields of specialization include Urban History, American Studies, Race and Ethnicity, Popular Culture, Public Policy, and Human Geography. Chronopoulos has previously taught at Miami University, Rhode Island School of Design, Brown University, and the City University of New York, College of Staten Island, and has held a visiting position at the University of Cape Town. His current research projects include social inequality, urban governance, immigration, and spatial fortification in cities located in the Americas, Africa, and Europe.

Index

A

African Americans 8–9, 12, 14, 16, 21, 23–25, 27, 30–32, 42, 44–45, 47–49, 51, 53–55, 62–63, 71, 74–75, 79, 89, 91–92, 95–97, 101–102, 105–106, 108–110, 113–114, 122, 125, 130, 135, 138–139, 142–144, 146–147, 155, 157, 159–160, 162, 165–168, 176, 179, 181–184
Aggressive Policing 1, 3, 4, 60, 88, 93, 109, 119, 149, 168, 181
AIDS 139, 179
Alliance for Downtown 173
Aluminum Company of America (ALCOA) 28
American Labor Party 14
Antoine, Patrick 157–159
Architects' Renewal Committee in Harlem, Inc. (ARCH) 51
Artists 95–96, 98–101, 103–104, 116–117, 134–135, 171, 175
Astor Hotel 69
Auletta, Ken 105

B

Baez, Anthony 160–161
Banfield, Edward C. 86–88
Barker, Elizabeth 14
Baron Haussmann 35
Barr, Heather 172
Barzun, Jacques 48, 49
Beame, Abe 69–70, 82, 104, 112
Beame Administration 69, 81, 103
Biederman, Daniel 171, 174
Bensonhurst 138
Bentham, Jeremy 35
Bernard M. Baruch Houses 34, 36
Bloomberg, Michael 183–184

Brandt Corporation 75–76
Breakdancing 91, 96, 117
Board of Estimate 14, 28, 48, 49, 63, 76
Bratton, William J. 115–116, 145, 147, 149–157, 160, 180
Broadway Association 62–63, 71
Broken windows 1–3, 89–90, 109, 114–116, 127, 140, 147, 150–152, 181
Brown, H. Rap 50
Brown, Lee P. 140–141
Bronx 41, 55, 85, 92–93, 96, 98–99, 101–102, 104, 109–110, 117, 120–129, 133–134, 160, 162–164, 166
Bronxdale 41
Brooklyn Museum 175–176
Bryant Park Business Improvement District 174
Business friendly policies 79, 85, 111, 120, 182
Business Improvement Districts (BIDs) 117, 169–176
Butler, Nicholas Murray 11

C

Canarsie 102
Carey, Hugh 109
Carmichael, Stokely 50
Carter, Zachary W. 165
Caruso, Phil 143, 161
Cathedral of St. John the Divine 8, 19, 44
Central Park 19, 23, 49, 125, 138, 179
Cerullo III, Alfred C. 174
Chamberlain, Lawrence 48
Chicago 42
Christodora 133–134

City Planning Commission 19, 28, 30, 32, 56, 62–63, 126
Civilian Complaint Review Board (CCRB) 128, 144, 161–163, 167, 169
Civil rights 80, 87, 94, 161, 168, 181, 183
Civil Rights Commission 168
Clarke, Una 144
Coalition Against Police Brutality 178
Cocaine 118, 120–121, 123–124, 167
Colomina, Beatriz 91
Columbia University 7, 9–11, 13–20, 33, 43–45, 47–55, 75, 94, 100, 131, 183
Columbia University faculty housing 17–18
Columbus Circle 21, 28–30
Columbus Circle Coliseum 29–30
Commercialized sex 63–70, 75–77, 159, 172, 174
Committee on Slum Clearance 30–31
Community Gardens 129–131
Community policing 140–142, 149–150, 183
Comp Stat 152
Coney Island 62, 104, 159
Congrés Internationaux d'Architecture Moderne (CIAM) 36
Congress of Racial Equality (CORE) 48–49
Conservatives 6, 78–80, 85–86, 88, 105, 112, 145, 175–176
Constitutional rights 59, 180
Cordier, Andrew 50–52
Corpus Christi Church 9
Crack 118, 123–124, 136, 167
Crime 1–4, 18, 21, 40–41, 43–44, 53–54, 58–59, 64–67, 79–80, 85–92, 97, 100–106, 109, 111–112, 116, 119–121, 123, 127, 136, 138–156, 159–160, 163, 166–168, 173, 180–183
Criminal justice system 88–89, 104–105, 121, 140, 153, 161
Cross Bronx Expressway 126
Crown Heights 143–145
Culture of poverty 87
Cuomo, Andrew 169
Cuomo, Mario 84, 139–140, 169–170

D
Davies, Jr., J. Clarence 31–32
Decentralization of the NYPD 152–153

Deli City 69
Demonstrations 145, 177–180
Desk appearance tickets 122, 165–166, 180
Detroit 68
Diallo, Amadou 163–166, 168
Diaz, David 168
Dinkins Administration 84, 138–146
Dinkins, David N. 78–79, 84–85, 90, 115, 119, 132, 138–145, 148, 159, 161, 165, 169, 182–183
Disneyfication 73, 75–76, 159, 171
Disorder
  physical 3–5, 8, 30–31, 33, 56, 86, 124, 180
  social 1, 3–5, 24, 30, 31, 33, 35, 42, 44, 60, 65, 72, 80, 88–89, 91, 97, 105–106, 118–120, 136, 138, 143, 145, 152, 154–155, 159, 180, 182–183
  urban 2–4, 8, 24, 32, 41, 36, 38, 42, 53, 56, 62, 72, 79, 87–88, 90, 99, 111, 118, 120, 124, 127, 135, 180–184
Disorderly conduct 59, 64–65, 145, 150–151, 159, 166–167, 179
Displacement 2, 7–8, 32–33, 42, 45, 53, 59–60, 73, 75, 79, 118, 120, 131, 145, 181, 183–184
DJ-ing 96, 117
Doctoroff, Daniel L. 184
Dorismond, Patrick 167–168
Doyle, Bill 109
Drugs 24, 43, 66, 80, 94, 101, 105, 107, 115, 118, 120–125, 128, 134, 139, 142, 145, 147, 150–152, 154–156, 159, 163–164, 172
Dusenbury, Harold 147–148
Dyson, John S. 109–110, 171

E
East Harlem 38, 40, 85
Emergency Financial Control Board 82
Eminent Domain 51, 60, 76
Empire Theater 69
Europe 6, 25, 81
Exclusionary zoning 4, 63, 181
Exclusion 181, 183–184

F
Farmer, James 48
Federal Housing Administration (FHA) 11, 26

Federal Housing and Home Finance
    Agency 24
Federation of Hellenic Societies of
    Greater New York 177–178
Felonies 119, 122, 158
Felt, James 32
Financial Community Liaison Group 82
Financial Control Board 84
First Amendment 67, 171, 176, 179
Fiscal crisis 2, 54, 69, 73, 78, 82–84,
    86, 93, 103–104, 109–112, 114,
    119–120, 122, 124, 181–183
Flake, Floyd 165, 168
Freeman, Joshua 82
Free Speech 69, 148, 177–179
Fordham University 21, 30
Fordism 36
Frankfurt 6
Frederick Douglass Houses 21
French Revolution 35
Fried, Walter 24
Friedman, Milton 81
Friedmann, Wolfgang G. 53, 100

G

Gangs 43, 93–94, 96–97, 101, 138, 154
Gans, Herbert 5, 75–76
Garelik, Sanford D. 58, 98
General Grant Houses 13–17, 46–47, 54
Gentrification 122, 128–138
Giuliani Administration 1, 77, 85, 90,
    146, 147–180, 183
Giuliani Group 2
Giuliani, Rudolph 1–2, 78–79, 85–86,
    90, 119, 138, 144–145, 148–
    157, 159–177, 183–184
Giuliani Time 157, 159
Glazer, Nathan 92, 106–107
Goffman, Erving 3
Graffiti 48, 84, 91–117, 125, 135, 150,
    152, 154, 171
Grand Central Partnership 171–174
Grand Central Terminal 58, 135–136
Great Britain 6
Great Depression 6, 9, 60, 80, 104
Great Society 79–80, 88
Greenwich Village 124, 147, 151
Griffith, Michael 114
Gross, Elliot 113
Gunn, David L. 91–92, 111, 114–115

H

Harlem 7–16, 18–20, 39, 44, 47–52,
    54–55, 94, 121, 176

Harring, Sidney 163–164
Harrison, Ballard & Allen 63
Harvey, David 81, 182
Hawkins, Yusuf 138
Hebrew Israelites 179
Hip hop 91–93, 96–97, 106, 108–110,
    117
HIV 179
Homelessness 2, 65, 105, 114–116,
    120, 127–128, 131–133,
    135–140, 145, 150–151, 156,
    169–172, 181, 184
Honky tonks 62–63, 68
Housing Act of 1937 6
Housing Act of 1949 6–8, 13, 26
Housing Act of 1954 7
Housing and Urban Development
    (HUD) 169, 172
Housing Works 179
Hoving, P. F. 50
Howard Beach 114, 138,
Hudson River 20
Human rights 4, 48, 137, 148, 161, 180
Hungate, T. L. 43

I

"I Love New York" campaign 110
Institute of Musical Art 9
International Action Center 179
International House 9, 12
International Monetary Fund 81
Isenberg, Steven L. 98–99

J

Jack Dempsey's Restaurant 69
Jacobs, Jane 33–38, 40–41
Jewish Theological Seminary 9
Jews for Racial and Economic Justice
    165
Johnson, Lyndon 88
Juilliard School of Music 9
Juvenile Delinquency 41, 44, 92,
    105–106, 140–141, 167–168

K

Kaskel, C. Clarence 28
Katznelson, Ira 110
Kelling, George L. 1, 89, 115–116, 150
Keynesian economics 81
Kiley, Robert R. 114, 136
Kirk, Grayson 48, 50
Koch Administration 70, 73, 78, 83,
    93, 111–112, 114–115, 118–
    138, 182

Index

Koch, Ed 60, 70, 73, 78, 83–84, 86, 106, 108, 111–115, 118–124, 126- 128, 132, 135–140, 148, 165, 182, 184
Koreans 142–143, 160
Kristol, Irving 86

L

La Guardia, Fiorello 61
La Salle Street "slum" 10, 13–14, 42
Latinos 8, 12, 14, 19, 44, 47, 53, 55, 71, 74–75, 89, 91–92, 101, 106, 108–110, 122, 155, 157, 166–167, 182–184
Le Corbusier 34–38, 40, 56
Legal Aid Society 140, 153
Lewis, Oscar 87
Liberalism 2, 7, 37, 57, 78–82, 88, 181
Lincoln Center area 7, 21, 26, 30–31, 61
Lindsay, John V. 49, 54–55, 59, 80, 98–103, 108, 112, 122
Lindsay Administration 56–57, 66–67, 93, 97, 101
Livoti, Francis 160–161
Loew's State 61
Lofland, Lyn 3
Loitering 1, 58–60, 64–65, 69, 74–75, 119, 122–123, 136, 167
London 6, 28, 29, 109
López Obrador, Andrés Manuel 2
Louima, Abner 147, 157–159, 163
Lower East Side 34, 107, 121–124, 128–137
Low income people 1–4, 6, 8–9, 12–14, 16, 21, 24, 31–33, 37–38, 42–43, 45–46, 51, 53–54, 71–72, 81, 84, 86–90, 104, 112, 116, 123, 131, 133–134, 146, 148, 162, 166–167, 180, 181–182
Lurie Ellen 38, 40
Luxury city 182–184

M

Madison Square Garden 69
Mailer, Norman 99–100
Majestic Theater 69
Manhattan Plaza 70–72
Manhattan Valley 42, 54- 55
Manhattantown 21–24, 26–27, 30, 32, 39
Manhattantown, Inc. 26
Manhattanville 14–15, 17, 20, 51, 52

Manhattanville Houses 14–15, 17
Manhattanville Neighborhood Center 14
Manhattanville Reform Democratic Club 48
Mannes, Marya 25–26
Marches 50, 135, 163, 176–180
Marriot Marquis 73
McGill, William G. 52
Mead, Lawrence 105
Merton, Robert K. 11
Metropolitan Opera House 61, 69
Mexico City 2
Metropolitan Transportation Authority (MTA) 92, 103–104, 112, 114–115, 136, 150, 168, 153
Midnight Cowboy 65
Midtown Project 66
Miller, John 155
Million Marijuana March Organization 179
Million Youth March 176–177
Misdemeanors 119, 122
Model Cities 124
Modernist urban design 2–3, 7–8, 34–38, 40, 42, 51, 56
Morgenthau, Robert M. 68
Morningside Area Alliance 54
Morningside Gardens 13–17, 41, 46, 54–55
Morningside General Neighborhood Renewal Plan 51
Morningside Heights 8–21, 30, 33, 42–55, 59, 94, 100, 131
Morningside Heights, Inc. (MHI) 10, 13–14, 16, 18–20, 42–49, 53–54
Morningside Park 18, 19, 49–51, 54
Morningside Park gymnasium 19, 49–52, 54
Morningside Renewal Council 46, 50
Morningsiders United 47
Moses, Robert 3, 7, 13–14, 17–18, 21–22, 26–27, 29–32, 35, 37, 51, 56–57, 184
Motley, Constance 49
Moyers, Bill 125
Municipal Assistance Corporation 82, 169
Munnecke, Wilbur 12, 13
Murray, Charles 105, 181

N

National Action Network 164
New Deal 5–6, 78–79, 81, 88

New York City Housing Authority (NYCHA) 13–14, 16, 29, 31, 34, 41, 153
New York City Commission on Human Rights 48
New York City Partnership 84–85
New York City Transit Authority (NYCTA) 54, 91, 111, 113–115, 153
New York Civil Liberties Union (NYCLU) 64, 163, 179
New York State Commission Against Discrimination 48
New York State Urban Development Corporation 74
New York Stock Exchange 170
Neoconservatism 2, 78- 81, 84–86, 88–89, 92, 104–109, 148, 169–170, 175, 180–184
Neoliberalism 2, 78–86, 92–93, 104, 109–110, 118–120, 129, 136–137, 148, 169–170, 180–182, 184
Newman, Oscar 40–41
New York Police Department (NYPD) 1–2, 44–47, 50, 53–54, 58–59, 64–70, 73, 79–81, 88, 90, 101, 103–104, 112–115, 118–124, 128–129, 134–136, 138–145, 147–173, 176–180, 182–184
Nixon, Richard 80

O
Office of Midtown Enforcement 70
Ofili, Chris 175
Operation Crossroads 70
Operation Juggernaut 154–157
Operation Pressure Point 122–123, 140
Order Maintenance 1–2, 4, 56, 88, 90, 116, 120–121, 123, 127, 140, 148, 153–154, 156, 176–177, 180–181
Orderly city 1, 182–183
Orton, Lawrence M. 13
Overcrowding 14, 19, 23–24, 31, 35–36, 39, 42–44, 124

P
Panopticon 35
Paramount 61, 69
Paris 6, 35–36, 61
Park West 21, 41
Park West Village 27–28
Pataki, George E. 165, 170

Patrolmen's Benevolent Association (PBA) 66, 80, 119, 128, 143–145, 161
Patterson, Basil 50
Pei, I. M. 52
Pennsylvania Station 135
Penny arcades 62–63
Permits for public gatherings 177–180
Physical solutions 2, 4, 8, 33, 42, 55, 56–57, 59–60, 72, 90, 181–182
Plan for New York City 56
Plan Voisin 36
Police brutality 128, 159–164, 168, 178, 180
Popular disturbances of 1977 104–105
Port Authority 135–136
Portman, John 72–73
Poverty 2, 5–6, 8–9, 24–25, 35, 42, 44–45, 53, 71, 74, 79, 82–84, 87–89, 95, 97–98, 105, 108, 110, 118, 120, 122, 136–137, 142, 145, 153, 159, 181, 184
Progressive Era 5–6
Prostitution 64–71, 120, 142, 152
Protest actions 46, 48, 80, 135, 165, 176–180
Public housing 6–7, 13, 19, 26–27, 38, 40–42, 103, 141, 152–153
Public space 1–4, 8, 24, 44, 53–54, 59, 65, 69, 72–75, 79, 84, 89–93, 95–98, 198–111, 114, 117–121, 123, 127, 129, 132, 135–138, 140, 146, 148, 150–151, 154–157, 167, 176–177, 182–183
Puerto Ricans 8–10, 19, 21, 23–25, 27, 30–32, 39, 42, 45, 47–48, 51, 102, 125, 129–130, 160

R
Radiant City 35
Rangel, Charles 50, 165
Ravitch, Richard 70
Reagan, Ronald 80, 126
Real estate 1, 3, 6, 12–13, 20–21, 28, 63, 69–71, 73, 75, 79, 83–85, 122, 129–131, 133–134, 137, 169, 176, 181–182
Red Cross 21, 30
Redistribution 83, 90, 137, 181
Reno, Janet 166
Riis, Jacob 5
Rikers Island 113, 140
Ripley's Wax Museum 68–69, 77
Riverside Church 9, 48

Index

Riverside Park 17, 44
Rockefeller, David 12–13, 23, 82, 84
Rockefeller Drug Laws 80
Rockefeller, John D. 30
Rockefeller, Nelson 80, 120
Royal Manhattan Hotel 69

S

Safe Corridor 151
Safe Streets, Safe City 140–141, 144
Safir, Howard 156–157, 161–163, 165, 167, 173, 182,
Salmen, Stanley 43, 48
Sampson, John 3
Samuels, Gertrude 13
São Paulo 182
Save Our Homes Committee 14, 16
Schwartz, Joel 43
Scott, James 33, 37
Scratchiti 116
Shelley v. Kramer 12
Shelters for the homeless 118, 132–133, 145, 169, 172
Sleeper, Jim 74
Sharpton, Al 156, 164
Shepard, Matthew 179
Shopping Centers 61, 72
Simon, William 82
Single Room Occupancies (SROs) 9, 23, 32, 42–43, 45–46, 49, 54, 70, 131, 137
Slum clearance 6–7, 13–14, 19, 23–24, 26, 28–31, 42, 45
Smith, Adam 81
Smith, Francis X. 59
Social movement organizations 46, 50, 94, 148, 177, 179–180, 183
Social solutions 4, 59–60, 90, 120, 183
Solomon, Edward V. 47
Sontag, Susan 5
Spatial fortification 17, 19, 45
Spatial ordering 2, 33–35, 37, 56, 89, 181
Spatial regulation 2–3, 59–60, 78, 89–90, 146–148, 151, 156, 169–170, 180–181, 183
Spitzer, Eliot 166
Squatters 128, 130, 135
Squeegee Men 145, 147, 154
Soundview 163–164
St. Luke's Hospital 8, 19
St. Nicholas Houses 47
Stewart, Michael 113–114
Street vendors 121, 152, 154, 171

Stop and frisk 122–123, 164, 166–167, 176, 184
Strong, Frederick L. 58
Students for a Democratic Society (SDS) 50
Stuyvesant Town 41
Sutton, Percy 50

T

TAKI 183 94–95, 101
Task Force on Police Brutality 163
Taxi drivers 154, 178–179
Taylorism 36
Taylor, Zachary 168
Teachers College 9, 43
Thompson, J. Phillip 133, 145
Times Square 58–77, 83, 117, 120, 167, 174, 179, 183
Times Square Business Improvement District 174
Title I 13, 26, 29
Tompkins Square Park 128–130, 133–136, 138
Transit Police 103, 112–115, 136, 140, 149–150, 160
Truman, Harry 6
Tolchin, Martin 125
Tudor City 58, 70–71
Tugwell, Rexford 56

U

Underclass 84, 89, 92, 104–109
Undesirables 1, 3, 12–13, 18, 43–48, 53, 56, 58–60, 63, 67, 70, 72–74, 127, 148, 159, 167, 180
Union Theological Seminary 9
University of Chicago 12, 48
Upper East Side 71
Upper West Side 7–10, 20–22, 24–26, 30, 32, 131, 183
Urban governance 1–2, 78, 84, 139, 148, 169–170, 174–175, 180, 182–184
Urban homesteading 130, 134
Urban renewal 3–8, 16, 20–22, 24, 26, 28, 30–35, 37, 40, 51, 56, 90, 127, 180–181
U.S. Justice Department 165–166, 168

V

Vagrancy 79, 90, 181
Veiller, Lawrence 5

Vienna 6
Vinyl decals for windows 126
Vladeck, William C. 29
Volpe, Justin 157–159
von Hayek, Friedrich 81

W

Wagner, Robert F. 20–21, 29, 45, 62, 64
Walt Disney Co. 111
War on Poverty 88
Washington Consensus 81
Washington Houses 38–39
Washington, Rudy 168–169, 175
Washington Square Park 147, 179
Weinert, Bertram 47, 48
Welfare 56, 79, 84–86, 90, 94, 105, 112, 122, 132, 143–144, 148

West Harlem Community Organization 49
West Harlem renewal area 15
West Side Urban Renewal Area 21
Whyte, William H. 56
Williamsburg Bridge 97
Wilson, James Q. 1, 88–89, 115, 150
World Bank 81
World Fashion Center 61
Woolworth 69
Wright, Frank Lloyd 29
Women's City Club 26
World's Fair 9, 31, 47

Z

Zeckendorf, William 20
Zero tolerance 1, 3–4, 90, 148, 150, 157, 181, 183–184